The Chatto Book of
LOVE
POETRY

Poetry

Fairground Music
The Tree that Walked
Cannibals and Missionaries
Epistles to Several Persons
The Mountain in the Sea
Lies and Secrets
The Illusionists
Waiting for the Music
The Beautiful Inventions
Selected Poems 1954–1982
Partingtime Hall (*with James Fenton*)
The Grey Among The Green

Fiction

Flying to Nowhere
The Adventures of Speedfall
Tell It Me Again
The Burning Boys

Criticism

A Reader's Guide to W. H. Auden
The Sonnet
The Dramatic Works of John Gay (*ed.*)

For Children

Herod Do Your Worst
Squeaking Crust
The Spider Monkey Uncle King
The Last Bid
The Extraordinary Wool Mill and other stories
Come Aboard and Sail Away

The Chatto Book of
LOVE
POETRY

Edited, with an introduction, by
JOHN FULLER

Chatto & Windus
LONDON

Published in 1990 by
Chatto & Windus Ltd
20 Vauxhall Bridge Road
London SW1V 2SA

A CIP catalogue record for this book is available
from the British Library
ISBN 0 7011 3453 4

Introduction and selection © John Fuller 1990

Typography by Humphrey Stone
Photoset by Rowland Phototypesetting Ltd,
Bury St Edmunds, Suffolk
Printed in Great Britain by
Mackays of Chatham plc,
Chatham, Kent

Contents

Yet we reiterate love! love! love!
as if it were coin with a fixed value
instead of a flower that dies, and opens a different bud.

D. H. LAWRENCE 'Lies about Love'

Introduction

What curious objects of love are to be encountered in these pages! There is Bobby Shafto, 'fat and fair,/Combing down his yellow hair.' [45: these numbers in square brackets refer to the poems in the anthology] There is Pam, a 'great big mountainous sports girl.' [194] There are Waller's dwarfs [197]. If you have opened this book in a mood of erotic disarray or erotic speculation, hoping to find in it some confirmation or denial of the strange fit of passion that has seized you, you can surely only wonder at individual taste in the matter of the unique object of desire. There is no reason in love and no more real uniqueness in its beloved human object than may be found in individuals in any of their other guises, as aunts, rulers of African states, chess grandmasters, coal-miners, saints, and so forth. Indeed, an aunt or the ruler of an African state have a recognisable social function, and we all know how to deal with one, when we are required to. There is only one person who knows how to relate to the beloved, and that is the lover. The beloved is unique only within that relation.

As always, there is a way to probe into this locked mystery of the relations of love. It is the way in which all private affairs are made public. It is the way in which human knowledge is transmitted, the means by which the dead talk to us. It is the way in which an aunt or the ruler of an African state may become mysteriously known to us in their private role as beloved. It is through poetry that we understand what it is like to be Helen of Troy or Cleopatra.

Of course, in the precarious world of the feelings, the word can kill. As D. H. Lawrence said, love is a cold egg once named. Say you are happy and that happiness is already past. Say that you love, and immediately you are brought face to face with the likelihood that your love is either completed or incomplete. A poem's notion of love necessarily perceives it from that distance: the great love poems are usually poems of longing or regret. But poetry can never be concerned with the impermanence of the feelings it records; its business is to reassert their permanence in language. And having so celebrated these feelings it leaves us as readers in possession of them in ways which allow us to understand all that is otherwise impossible to understand. The beauty of it is that it is not so much a key to exotic and sensational secrets as to those secrets that are already locked in our own bewildered psyche. It is not Cleopatra we really want to know about. It is ourselves.

The unique human gift of language allows us, like no other animal, to contemplate one thing at a time.

For the dumb creature all experience is a unified whole that cannot be analysed. To describe this unity we would have to be able to reach back through language to an innocence that we have lost, and which we attribute to the animal. This restless quest for understanding the conditions of our life encourages us to isolate what we feel to be life's significant states: religious awe, aesthetic contemplation, rational understanding, love,— everything that seems to distinguish us from the animal kingdom.

Do animals love? Or is this a faculty of the developed fore-brain, an illusion born of language? We are locked out of animals' experience. We can only describe their behaviour. But because we can also describe our own behaviour, we can attribute human feelings to animals where these seem appropriate. We invent the civic bee and the considerate elephant. It is our language, isolating parts of our experience at will, that enables us to do this. It enables us to do the opposite, too: we can identify some parts of our own behaviour which are 'animal' and conclude that our experience of them is unique to us. Although the results of this process bear the marks of sentimentality, its machinery is not sentimental: language codifies animal purposes, distinguishes psychological from biological motives, and separates complex processes into their constituent stages. If procreation itself is teleologically mysterious, it is more so when it comes to be considered (as language can require it to be) as somehow distinct from parturition.

Our myths support the distinction. Eros the blind archer symbolizes the choiceless spermatozoon. The smitten lover (male in a male-dominated world) is attracted to a unique object, often against his will. For the sexual urge may be indiscriminate, but the sexual act is single of purpose, and Eros has nothing on his mind but that goal. The myth allows male vows of fidelity (in social reality necessary for pair-bonding and the rearing of offspring) to be turned into a mere disclaimer of his natural promiscuity. This appears to be sufficient to secure the female's acquiescence. 'Love' is the appropriate emotion of such a disclaimer and such acquiescence. As such it bears some relation to the natural emotions of pair-bonding, but like all myths it is more than the whole story. We become satisfied with this excess of the idea over the reality, and it re-enters our lives as a means of qualifying and valorizing our socio-biological existence. It does so by a number of means, from the slightest expectations and assumptions of interpersonal language to the giant assertions of art.

Poetry has a special place among the arts in this respect, since the form it takes is so frequently that of passionate utterance. Love is a form of address, of one being to another. It concerns complex private emotional states as well as claims of a public or social significance. Poetry shares with erotic obsession a tendency to the lyrical, the speculative, the extravagant, the solipsistic, the philosophical, the bizarre. It takes a lover to dwell on the special attraction of a mole; it takes a poet to conceive the mole to be the shadow of a bee feasting off the sweat running between his beloved's breasts (Carew's 'Upon a Mole in Celia's bosome' [61]). Within the government of idealism to which humanity has gladly given assent, imagination is the legislative, and poetry the executive, arm. We have adopted these ideals to protect us from our sense of lost animal innocence and flawed identity. We have made of them a beautiful distraction from animal guilt and incompleteness; failings of instinct for the most part, though love itself is such a sublimation of instinct that its ready and random visitations can become mythified into something akin to the divine.

To be possessed by feelings as irrational as this, implying a commitment beyond choice or calculation, has always suggested religious parallels: Emily Dickinson's 'Each other's convert . . . though the faith accommodate but two.' [249] But then, religion itself is an illusion that has also made a speciality of language's ability to isolate our broken fears and hopes, our partial understandings. In poetry, the two can blur to suggest little more than the immanence of a longed-for truth: 'Perhaps I always knew what they were saying' wrote W. H. Auden, finding all the sacred objects of his childhood prophetic of his one true love, where the Old Testament metaphor is no accident and the incarnation of the Good Place in the person of the beloved can also be read as the 'proof' of a divine existence ('The Prophets' [22]). The ambiguity must be older than the Song of Solomon.

This idealism in all its manifestations is most familiar to us in Renaissance poetry: Tamburlaine placing Zenocrate at the apex of earthly powers, Chapman's Ovid finding the soul through the senses, Donne proposing that lovers in their bliss are sanctified like saints and have the supernatural powers of saints [169], Shakespeare's loved youth outfacing time with a unique beauty. Writers surely know that such ideas are not true, or can only be made to seem true through language. The wish to believe in them is heroic. The ideas achieve a validity as excessive verbal performances, triumphs of figurative assertion, hyperbole and mock-argument. Idealism is brandished not so much as a torch illuminating the dark recesses of human experience, but as a conjuror's apparatus with which we consciously agree to be deceived. And what immense satisfactions ensue! Human beauty and sexual pleasure are the baits that we swallow in order to believe in their power to transcend age, death and oblivion: little fish to catch bigger fish. Or perhaps the biggest fish we know in order to catch something we have never seen, the Snark of the perfected and eternal.

But poetry is a playful commodity, and its greatest playfulness is to defeat its own playfulness. The poet is delivered, like the Court Fool, into a limbo of licensed mockery in which language may after all reveal truth, simply by not taking itself seriously. In this light it is, after all, a radical truth for Tamburlaine to prefer his wife to the kingdoms of the world or for Donne to sense that the process initiated by wooing is a symbolic miracle greater than the miracles of the saints. Only a world deluded by false ideals could allow poetry this privilege of attacking them. The eighteenth century, for example, is notoriously short of love poetry of this degree of daring, because of the welcome secularization and rationalization of daily life. (The result is love poetry of gusto, innuendo or affection, without much sense of wonder or mystery. I have been happy to include Gay's gift of lampreys [51] and Burns's Jenny, who 'draigl't a' her petticoatie' in the standard manner of compliant girls who allow their dresses to be ruined [272], but I have not included much else.)

The religious revival of the nineteenth century, with its attendant morbidities, proved a fresh seedbed for poetry. Once again the ambiguous or shocking took its force from a playfulness with frightening truths: the madmen of Browning, the goblins of Christina Rossetti, the ghosts of Hardy, though 'symbols', might be real after all, like Donne's saints or Marlowe's power-maniacs. We are, all over again, fascinated. Yes, we agree, a lover *is* a madman, sexuality *is* fatal, we *are* shadowed by our errors of feeling. And why take such risks? It is our way of defining our own importance when we have no god to do it for us.

3

Love is the most commanding absolute of our secular age. It is the classic response to retreating faith; typically, the 'Ah, love, let us be true/To one another!' of Arnold [230]. Only in each other do we find that attentive concern, that intensity of attachment, which we might have liked a god to feel for us. All else is indifference:

> '—The Earth, sayest thou? The Human race?
>   By Me created? Sad its lot?
> Nay: I have no remembrance of such a place:
>   Such world I fashioned not—'

Forgotten by God, then, a poet like Hardy is free to create his own redemptive hauntings. Agnostic love poetry may be cut adrift from the larger certainties, but it clings with greater intensity to bereavement. Hardy and Emma will not meet in Heaven like Tennyson and Hallam, and this gives her spirit a greater poignancy and palpability than Hallam's.

Love relative, the family, links biology with society; love absolute, the romance, links biology with eternity. Literary works from the *chansons cortois* of the twelfth century to the great adulterous novels of the nineteenth century have often been concerned with the difficulty of accommodating the two views. And no wonder, since as organisms we find it so monstrously difficult to step out of our shoes and distinguish between the organism and the organism's idea of itself. When Malcolm Lowry wrote that one cannot live without love, he was not thinking of the perpetuation of the human species. As Auden concluded in a late poem which is a kind of parody of Lowry's statement, in which he is lying awake in a mild love-torment, listening to the rain-tank filling up after a drought: 'Thousands have lived without love, but none without water.' [358] The homosexual normally does not have children, and for Auden love would not issue in children. His ironic priority is both sufficient for one human lifetime, and for a celibate devotion to art.

Love's actual involvement with futurity is notional, itself perhaps a romantic myth. Secular eternity is for the modern lover's purposes entirely rhetorical, as Auden's own riposte shows: '"I will love You for ever," swears the poet. I find this easy to swear too. *I will love You at 4.15 p.m. next Tuesday*: is that still as easy?' ('Dichtung und Wahrheit'). The myth has been long exploited. In 'To His Coy Mistress' [77], Marvell claims that given the control over time that love absolute lays claim to he could love his girl ten years before the Flood and she might refuse him until the conversion of the Jews. This is part of an ingenious argument that they precisely do *not* have time enough, which has the effect of noble defiance. Marvell eagerly proposes to defeat time within the illusory eternity of sexual consummation. It is, of course, not the Poet but the Organism speaking. His poem is a wooing poem, a persuasive device. Auden's 'Dichtung und Wahrheit' is a subtle analysis of motives that can, in truth, accept neither version of romantic eternity. A better-known poem of his, the ballad 'As I walked out one evening', does the job more directly. The immediate inspiration is probably a song by Burns [208]. The poet hears a lover of the Marvellian, *carpe diem* variety sing:

> 'I'll love you dear, I'll love you
>   Till China and Africa meet
> And the river jumps over the mountain
>   And the salmon sings in the street.

[5]

'I'll love you till the ocean
        Is folded and hung up to dry
And the seven stars go squawking
        Like geese about the sky.

The poem then introduces Auden's version of Time's winged chariot:

But all the clocks in the city
        Began to whirr and chime:
'O let not Time deceive you,
        You cannot conquer Time.

'In the burrows of the Nightmare
        Where Justice naked is,
Time watches from the shadow
        And coughs when you would kiss.'

These reserved admonitions of Time, so different from a thundering chariot, introduce a note of social realism characteristic of the 'thirties and yet of course fully prepared for within the period of Arnold. Auden's Nightmare is an extension of Arnold's Darkling Plain, and what Auden insisted upon in the mid-'thirties was that the private good which erotic love represented had nothing to do with Justice. After all, as another poem of his startlingly but reasonably suggests, you might fall in love with Hitler, a possibility that seems to render the Arnoldian gesture of 'Ah, love, let us be true/To one another!' faintly ridiculous.

A better bequest from the Victorians was the notion of the Life Force abetted by scientific understanding. We find this most obviously in Clough: in 'Natura Naturans' [133]; in the Goethean debate between Claude and Eustace about juxtaposition and affinity in *Amours de Voyage* [3]; and in Elspie's response to Philip in *The Bothie of Tober-na-Vuolich*, with its love-symbols of flowing merging water and of the keystone of an arch, imagery which for twentieth-century readers inevitably looks forward to D. H. Lawrence. However much of a prophet Lawrence was, we can never forget the pseudo-scientific validation of his theories in *Fantasia of the Unconscious*, written towards the end of his life. The science that haunted Tennyson with the horrific idea that not only is the individual expendable, but so is the species, becomes a science appealed to by us once more to validate human love. Tennyson's science outraged both love absolute and love relative; Lawrence's science united them. It did so not by backing eternity on a kind of pseudo-scientific emotional hunch, but by asserting it to be prophetically and poetically true in a psychological context that Lawrence as a post-Freudian was able to take for granted. For Lawrence as for Tennyson, death was equally a mystery; but it was also a secular paradigm of rebirth. Psychology explained to Lawrence the predicament of

[6]

a Paul Morel or an Ursula Brangwyn. For them, and for most of his characters, the traditional eternity of love had been converted into a challenging future of crucial choices. His poems, both like the novels and different from them, frequently look like the banner-slogans of a soul warring against family and society for this right to choose a redeeming love. Sometimes the tone even goes beyond that of the crusader, and attains the assertive, peremptory and self-satisfied confidence of the healed patient. It is significant, I think, that the most interesting of his volumes of love poetry is called *Look! We Have Come Through!*

It is Browning, with his much more satisfyingly objective method, who now seems to be the real starting point of modern analytical love-poetry. One paramount theme in Browning is strikingly modern, and that is the illusory nature of the experience of love. Once again, this illusion is connected with our relative experience of time, but it is far from Marvell's classical play with eternity. It acknowledges that because it is the poem which perceives the greatest truths about the paradox that the human lover fails to resolve, it is in the poem alone that they are closest to resolution. The 'moment eternal' of a poem like 'Now' [201] is embodied in the poem itself, which studiously ignores all past and all future:

> The moment eternal . . . just that and no more . . .
> When ecstasy's utmost we clutch at the core
> While cheeks burn, arms open, eyes shut and lips meet!

How beautifully ambiguous that last line is, readable both as sexual climax and as language's frustration at coping with it: an embarrassed blush, a shrug, averted vision and deliberate silence. This poem is, incidentally, far from the passionate perception of youth: it belongs to the maligned later Browning, and to a volume whose proofs he corrected on the morning of the day he died. Browning is a starting-point because he stresses the problematic metaphysical status of love, and also because he is a compulsive ironist. On the one hand, we would not have had the best love poetry of Hardy without him; and on the other, the young Eliot owed him a great deal. Perhaps, indeed, his brilliant 'Love in a Life' is the first really modern love poem [142]. Here I have put it next to variations on the theme by two younger poets of today, Hugo Williams and Christopher Reid. Browning catches our ear and mind no less than our contemporaries because in this he was our pioneer. The sheer existential difficulty of love could now be confronted in a manner which took poets some distance from the complaints, hopes and celebrations of previous eras.

It was precisely in this area, in fact, that I started to look when choosing poems for this anthology. I turned to Browning first, then forwards to Hardy, Lawrence and Graves, simply to establish a starting-point that might also be some kind of core of the modern sensibility.

You might say, why not begin at the beginning? I knew, however, that I did not intend in any case an arrangement by date of birth or publication, since the development of English poetry is perfectly familiar to us and I did not want to exhibit the diachronistic transmission of tradition all over again. Poets are not runners in a relay-race, after all; they wander erratically in the landscape of traditions and discover their favourite haunts. Do we really want W. H. Davies with de la Mare? He is better with Jonson and Campion, and de la Mare himself with Christina Rossetti. Do we really want Auden with MacNeice or Empson? Why shouldn't he link Yeats and Emily Dickinson? MacNeice goes better with Clough, and isn't Empson cousin to Cleveland? Of course, this kind of arrangement is in the end simply another way of exposing traditions, but it is less predictable.

And as for beginnings, I did not know where I might want to begin. I did not simply want range for its own sake, either in breadth of temporal inclusion or thoroughness of period representation: there is inevitably a problem for readers before the sixteenth century, and even some later eras of love poetry are, I suggest, at the moment foreign to our taste. I had early on decided not to include translations, and I did not want to 'translate' any poetry in English, either. The laments of the Anglo-Saxons were out, therefore, and also a good deal of mediaeval poetry, on these grounds alone. And I was determined to be choosy. I did not consider that any poet or poem had an automatic right to be included. There was no democracy of representation. I wanted to deploy my space where it matters. I believe, for example, that once again we are relatively unimpressed by minor Elizabethan sonneteering and wonder with Landor 'why should we/Who draw deep seans along the sea,/Cut them in pieces to beset/The shallows with a cabbage-net?' [16] And we do not read eighteenth-century poetry for its grand passion. My weight is given to the late sixteenth and seventeenth century and to the last 150 years: to the first of these periods we owe the discovery that love, as a creation of the fertile brain, can be creatively expressed in verbal conceit; to the second we owe the discovery of psychology. In the first period the poet says: 'I love, therefore I think.' In the second period the poet says: 'I love, therefore I could become a better person.' Between these two attitudes is to be found most of the worthwhile poetry on this subject, and there is much else (pure Platonism, misogynist satire, self-congratulation, smut) that I am happy to do without. However, I trust that the range is wide enough: from an anonymous lyric of the thirteenth century to work first published in the 1980s and from complex psychological fictions like Browning's 'Dîs Aliter Visum' [129] to the merest squib such as Swift's mock-Latin [48] or Gavin Ewart's one-word poem [13].

I did not at first want to have any but complete poems. Some anthologies have already enshrined fragments or have aggressively 'confirmed' the unreadability of the long poem. I knew that I could not include in my limited space such works as Chaucer's *Troilus and Criseyde*, Keats's *The Eve of St Agnes*, Meredith's *Modern Love* or Clough's *Amours de Voyage*. It is no good pretending that this does not matter. Take the case of Tennyson and the interesting inability of his characters to believe that they really deserve love in the first place: how could I represent this idea without showing to the full the heroic and martyred sacrifices of Julian (in *The Lover's Tale*) or Enoch Arden? Or the fate of the hero of *Maud*, for whom a lost girl is merely the last straw of a whole weight of pain and deprivation? It is impossible. The compromise is to provide somewhat predictable (but absolutely marvellous) lyrics from *Maud*, *Audley Court* and *The Princess*, and one longish but lesser-known poem related to the sacrificial theme: 'Happy: The Leper's Bride' [228]. On this principle I have included one section of the Meredith, two letters from *Amours de Voyage*, a passage of Shelley's *Epipsychidion*, some sonnets of Daniel, Constable, Sidney, Spenser and Shakespeare, and of course I have been unable to resist some extracts from *Don Juan*.

The order of the poems is largely thematic. It is love which writes us into the world in the first place, and it is love which sketches that unique plot within which we act out the secret drama of our own lives. So the anthology underlines its intended dramatic quality by being divided into five acts, moving from speculation and *coup de foudre*, through the troubled enduring of love, its consummations, dangers, joys, perversions and abdications, to loneliness and memory. It should not be too hard to find the sort of poem you want. Crushes, partings, kisses, dreams, jealousy, guilt, and so on, occur in clusters, although there is no absolute compartmentalising, no rigid ordering of the psychological spectrum. Inevitably the notion of period re-enters my dramatic structure: the Elizabethan lyric is concentrated in Act II, Donne comes into his own in Act III, the moderns in Act IV, and Rossetti, Brontë, Housman and Hardy in Act V. This in itself perhaps tells us something about the history of poetic love.

But at this point I have to confront my decision to omit the authors' names in the text itself. I know the arguments against this practice and I have never denied the reader's lawful traffic in bringing to bear on the reading of a poem all sorts of knowledge gleaned outside it. Here, however, most particularly, poets are not to be taken as the subjects of their poems. I wanted to clear the reader of any prejudice about gender, period or reputation. Whatever moods, desires, prejudices, jokes or proposals we find in these pages have long been cut loose from their dry docks and have been trading in strange seas. All that now matters is that the cargo is water-tight.

The poems are continuous in a kind of personal pointillisme, sometimes by association of topic, sometimes for no reason, sometimes for a marginal or purely literary reason, an accident of poetic method, period properties, or unwitting echo. The arrangement allows for all the unlikely but critically suggestive contiguities to which I have already alluded. It is here, I hope, that the reader's pleasure will be freshened. Gershwin's naughty baby rubs shoulders with Marvell's coy lady [76 and 77]. Gay follows Lovelace [320 and 321]. The fervent exclamations of Emily Dickinson's 'Wild nights! Wild nights!' lodges her between Shelley and Keats [98, 99 and 100]. Coleridge's self-pity looks more respectable next to Housman [349 and 350], while Eliot is to be found between Byron and Swinburne, his earliest models [306, 307 and 308]. The sensuality of Heaney and Longley joins that of the Donne of the Elegies [209, 210 and 211]. Shelley and Breton join in hoping that they may be believed after all despite debasement of the wooer's currency [34 and 35]. Lyly's Syrinx nods to Landor's Ianthe [14 and 15]. An anonymous sixteenth-century Kentish maid joins Keats's Devonian dairymaid [32 and 33]. Cole Porter pursuing randy rhymes ('The breeze is chasing the zephyr') sorts metrically with Swinburne ('If love were what the rose is') [103 and 104]. Larkin's imagined glove is followed by Lovelace's 'pretty *Ermin* Cabinet' [36 and 37]. For its conceit about holiness, Hall's 'Epicurean Ode' follows Heaney's 'La Toilette' [170 and 171]. This sort of local detail is what an anthology as such principally has to offer.

It is to be hoped, however, that the whole picture is pleasing and instructive and that it functions in the way I believe an anthology should, not as a fool-proof reference-work or a claimed canon (my choices can never be yours) but as a kind of stage for the heart-injured sensibility to rehearse its readerly roles on. Poems are memorials to feelings that we share. This anthology is, unusually, a kind of prompt-book of emotional understanding, corroboration and provocation. It is meant to be enjoyed, even if we cannot take poetry too seriously. Many of these poems act as magic charms to celebrate reassurance, possibility, heroic erotic acts—all that in reality remains a matter of speculation. The paradox here goes right back to my starting-point, Browning. Browning's search for the eternal moment cannot, finally, be undertaken in the temporal medium of language at all. The corollary to my suggestion that love celebrated is love future or love past is that the erotic is in reality the presiding spirit of the moment's

[10]

urge to completion. The present barely exists for the emotions or the appetites. Possibly the whole purpose of the social myth of romantic love (barely, after all, a thousand years old) can be seen as feeding the circumstantial reflections of literature, which in turn taunt our lives with our own willed delusions.

Textual Note

The authors, and in some cases the sources, of the numbered poems are given in anthology-order in the list on p. 345. There is also an alphabetical index of poets, and an index of titles and first lines.

I have not always used either the earliest or the latest text, sometimes preferring to use an edition of historical interest (e.g. Emily Dickinson as read by W. H. Auden, next to whom on one occasion she appears here). I have not always been able to avoid using a modernised text, but I have not myself modernised or regularised the texts as I have found them, except in the following respects: (a) Since the anthology has numbered items I have felt no need in every case to retain unauthorised titles, titles reluctantly added at a later date, titles that merely repeat the first line of the poem, titles which themselves include a number as part of a series, titles of parts of series which mean little out of series, or unhelpful titles of the 'To—' variety; (b) I have omitted from the titles indications of the composer in cases of songs set to music; (c) I have not retained numbering of stanzas; (d) I have in most cases omitted any appended dates of composition unless these are of particular significance. Extracts are so indicated in the title.

It has obviously been helpful to use such compilations as Ault's *Elizabethan Lyrics* and Saintsbury's three-volume *Minor Poets of the Caroline Period*, though I have avoided anthologies in general, preferring to re-read the collected works of the poets I had in my sights. I have, where possible, used standard editions, though sometimes for convenience I have used selected editions.

Act One

HOLES IN THE HEART

... What a curious way
The whole thing is of clothing souls in clay!
    BYRON *Don Juan*, ix. 75–6

Love's dwelling is in ladies' eyes:
From whence do glance love's piercing darts
That make such holes into our hearts.
   PEELE song from *The Hunting of Cupid*

Wine comes in at the mouth
And love comes in at the eye;
That's all we shall know for truth
Before we grow old and die.
     YEATS 'A Drinking Song'

In truth, o Love, with what a boyish kind
Thou doest proceed in thy most serious wayes.
    SIDNEY *Astrophil and Stella*

1

Love is anterior to life,
 Posterior to death,
Initial of creation, and
 The exponent of breath.

2

A Dialogue between the Head and Heart

Of course, she's only a digestive tube, like all of us.
Yes, but look what it's attached to!

3

from *Amours de Voyage*

VI CLAUDE TO EUSTACE

Juxtaposition, in fine; and what is juxtaposition?
Look you, we travel along in the railway-carriage, or steamer,
And, *pour passer le temps*, till the tedious journey be ended,
Lay aside paper or book, to talk with the girl that is next one;
And, *pour passer le temps*, with the terminus all but in prospect,
Talk of eternal ties and marriages made in heaven.
 Ah, did we really accept with a perfect heart the illusion!
Ah, did we really believe that the Present indeed is the Only!
Or through all transmutation, all shock and convulsion of passion,
Feel we could carry undimmed, unextinguished, the light of our
  knowledge!
 But for his funeral train which the bridegroom sees in the distance,
Would he so joyfully, think you, fall in with the marriage-procession?
But for that final discharge, would he dare to enlist in that service?
But for that certain release, ever sign to that perilous contract?
But for that exit secure, ever bend to that treacherous doorway? –
Ah, but the bride, meantime, – do you think she sees it as he does?
 But for the steady fore-sense of a freer and larger existence,
Think you that man could consent to be circumscribed here into action?
But for assurance within of a limitless ocean divine, o'er
Whose great tranquil depths unconscious the wind-tost surface
Breaks into ripples of trouble that come and change and endure not, –

[15]

But that in this, of a truth, we have our being, and know it,
Think you we men could submit to live and move as we do here?
Ah, but the women, – God bless them! they don't think at all about it.
   Yet we must eat and drink, as you say. And as limited beings
Scarcely can hope to attain upon earth to an Actual Abstract,
Leaving to God contemplation, to His hands knowledge confiding,
Sure that in us if it perish, in Him it abideth and dies not,
Let us in His sight accomplish our petty particular doings, –
Yes, and contented sit down to the victual that He has provided.
Allah is great, no doubt, and Juxtaposition his prophet.
Ah, but the women, alas! they don't look at it in that way.
   Juxtaposition is great; – but, my friend, I fear me, the maiden
Hardly would thank or acknowledge the lover that sought to obtain her,
Not as the thing he would wish, but the thing he must even put up
        with, –
Hardly would tender her hand to the wooer that candidly told her
That she is but for a space, an *ad-interim* solace and pleasure, –
That in the end she shall yield to a perfect and absolute something,
Which I then for myself shall behold, and not another, –
Which, amid fondest endearments, meantime I forget not, forsake not.
Ah, ye feminine souls, so loving and so exacting,
Since we cannot escape, must we even submit to deceive you?
Since so cruel is truth, sincerity shocks and revolts you,
Will you have us your slaves to lie to you, flatter and – leave you?

VII CLAUDE TO EUSTACE

Juxtaposition is great, – but, you tell me, affinity greater.
Ah, my friend, there are many affinities, greater and lesser,
Stronger and weaker; and each, by the favour of juxtaposition,
Potent, efficient, in force, – for a time; but none, let me tell you,
Save by the law of the land and the ruinous force of the will, ah,
None, I fear me, at last quite sure to be final and perfect.
Lo, as I pace in the street, from the peasant-girl to the princess,
Homo sum, nihil humani a me alienum puto, –
Vir sum, nihil fæminei, – and e'en to the uttermost circle,
All that is Nature's is I, and I all things that are Nature's.
Yes, as I walk, I behold, in a luminous, large intuition,
That I can be and become anything that I meet with or look at:
I am the ox in the dray, the ass with the garden-stuff panniers;
I am the dog in the doorway, the kitten that plays in the window,
On sunny slab of the ruin the furtive and fugitive lizard,

[16]

Swallow above me that twitters, and fly that is buzzing about me;
Yea, and detect, as I go, by a faint but a faithful assurance,
E'en from the stones of the street, as from rocks or trees of the forest,
Something of kindred, a common, though latent vitality, greet me;
And, to escape from our strivings, mistakings, misgrowths, and
        perversions,
Fain could demand to return to that perfect and primitive silence,
Fain be enfolded and fixed, as of old, in their rigid embraces.

4

from *Childe Harold's Pilgrimage*

Oh, Love! no habitant of earth thou art –
An unseen seraph, we believe in thee, –
A faith whose martyrs are the broken heart, –
But never yet hath seen, nor e'er shall see
The naked eye, thy form, as it should be;
The mind hath made thee, as it peopled heaven,
Even with its own desiring phantasy,
And to a thought such shape and image given,
As haunts the unquench'd soul – parch'd, wearied, wrung, and riven

Of its own beauty is the mind diseased,
And fevers into false creation: – where,
Where are the forms the sculptor's soul hath seiz'd?
In him alone. Can Nature show so fair?
Where are the charms and virtues which we dare
Conceive in boyhood and pursue as men,
The unreach'd Paradise of our despair,
Which o'er-informs the pencil and the pen,
And overpowers the page where it would bloom again?

Who loves, raves – 'tis youth's frenzy – but the cure
Is bitterer still, as charm by charm unwinds
Which robed our idols, and we see too sure
Nor worth nor beauty dwells from out the mind's
Ideal shape of such; yet still it binds
The fatal spell, and still it draws us on,
Reaping the whirlwind from the oft-sown winds;
The stubborn heart, its alchemy begun,
Seems ever near the prize – wealthiest when most undone.

[17]

5
Search for Love

Those that go searching for love
only make manifest their own lovelessness,

and the loveless never find love,
only the loving find love,
and they never have to seek for it.

6

What thing is love? for, well I wot, love is a thing.
It is a prick, it is a sting,
It is a pretty pretty thing;
It is a fire, it is a coal,
Whose flame creeps in at every hole;
And as my wit doth best devise,
Love's dwelling is in ladies' eyes:
From whence do glance love's piercing darts
That make such holes into our hearts;
And all the world herein accord
Love is a great and mighty lord,
And when he list to mount so high,
With Venus he in heaven doth lie,
And evermore hath been a god
Since Mars and she played even and odd.

7
Love

O Love! what art thou, Love? the ace of hearts,
    Trumping earth's kings and queens, and all its suits;
A player, masquerading many parts
    In life's odd carnival; – a boy that shoots,
From ladies' eyes, such mortal woundy darts;
    A gardener, pulling heart's-ease up by the roots;
The Puck of Passion – partly false – part real –
A marriageable maiden's 'beau-ideal.'

O Love, what art thou, Love? a wicked thing,
    Making green misses spoil their work at school;
A melancholy man, cross-gartering?
    Grave ripe-faced wisdom made an April fool?
A youngster, tilting at a wedding-ring?
    A sinner, sitting on a cuttie stool?
A Ferdinand de Something in a hovel,
Helping Matilda Rose to make a novel?

O Love! what art thou, Love? one that is bad
    With palpitations of the heart – like mine –
A poor bewildered maid, making so sad
    A necklace of her garters – fell design!
A poet, gone unreasonably mad,
    Ending his sonnets with a hempen line?
O Love! – but whither now? forgive me, pray;
I'm not the first that Love hath led astray.

8

In truth, ô Love, with what a boyish kind
    Thou doest proceed in thy most serious wayes.
    That when the heav'n to thee his best displayes,
Yet of that best thou leav'st the best behind.
For like a child that some faire booke doth find,
    With guilded leaves or colour'd Velume playes,
    Or at the most on some fine picture stayes,
But never heeds the fruit of writer's mind:
    So when thou saw'st in Nature's cabinet
Stella, thou straight lookst babies in her eyes,
In her cheeke's pit thou didst thy pitfould set,
And in her breast bopeepe or couching lyes,
    Playing and shining in each outward part:
    But, foole, seekst not to get into her hart.

9

And what is love? It is a doll dressed up
For idleness to cosset, nurse, and dandle.
A thing of soft misnomers, so divine

That silly youth doth think to make itself
Divine by loving, and so goes on
Yawning and doting a whole summer long,
Till Miss's comb is made a pearl tiara,
And common Wellingtons turn Romeo boots;
Then Cleopatra lives at Number Seven,
And Antony resides in Brunswick Square.
Fools! If some passions high have warmed the world,
If queens and soldiers have played high for hearts,
It is no reason why such agonies
Should be more common than the growth of weeds.
Fools! Make me whole again that weighty pearl
The Queen of Egypt melted, and I'll say
That ye may love in spite of beaver hats.

10

Love is Weal, Love is Wo

Love is soft, love is swete, love is good sware;
Love is muchè tene, love is muchel care.
Love is blissenè mest, love is bot yare;
Love is wondred and wo with for to fare.
Love is hap, who it haveth; love is good hele.
Love is lecher and lees, and leef for to tele.
Love is doughty in the world with for to dele.
Love maketh in the land many unlele.

Love is stalwarde and strong to striden on stede.
Love is loveliche a thing to wommanè nede.
Love is hardy and hot as glowindè glede.
Love maketh many may with terès to wede.

Love hath his steward by sty and by strete.
Love maketh many may hire wongès to wete.
Love is hap, who it haveth, on for to hete.
Love is wis, love is war, and wilful ansete.

Love is the softeste thing in hertè may slepe.
Love is craft, love is good with carès to kepe.

Love is lees, love is leef, love is longinge.
Love is fol, love is fast, love is frovringe.
Love is sellich an thing, whoso shal sooth singe.

Love is wele, love is wo, love is gladhede.
Love is lif, love is deth, love may us fede.

Were love al so londdrey as he is first kene,
It were the wordlokstè thing in worlde were, ich wene.

It is y-said in an song, sooth is y-sene,
Love comseth with care and endeth with tene,
Mid lavedy, mid wivè, mid maidè, mid quene.

II

Love

Love is a sickness full of woes,
 All remedies refusing;
A plant that with most cutting grows,
 Most barren with best using.
   Why so?
More we enjoy it, more it dies;
If not enjoyed, it sighing cries,
   Heigh ho!

Love is a torment of the mind,
 A tempest everlasting;
And Jove hath made it of a kind
 Not well, nor full, nor fasting.
   Why so?
More we enjoy it, more it dies;
If not enjoyed, it sighing cries,
   Heigh ho!

Four arms, two necks, one wreathing;
Two pairs of lips, one breathing;
Two hearts that multiply
Sighs interchangeably:

The thought of this confounds me,
And as I speak it wounds me.
It cannot be expressed.
Good help me, whilst I rest.

Bad stomachs have their loathing,
And oh, this all is no thing:
This 'no' with griefs doth prove
Report oft turns to love.

13

The Lover Writes a One-word Poem

You!

14

Proud word you never spoke, but you will speak
   Four not exempt from pride some future day.
Resting on one white hand a warm wet cheek
   Over my open volume you will say,
   'This man loved *me!*' then rise and trip away.

15

Syrinx

Pan's Syrinx was a girl indeed,
Though now she's turned into a reed;
From that dear reed Pan's pipe does come,
A pipe that strikes Apollo dumb;
Nor flute, nor lute, nor gittern can
So chant it as the pipe of Pan:

Cross-gartered swains and dairy girls,
With faces smug and round as pearls,
When Pan's shrill pipe begins to play,
With dancing wear out night and day:
The bagpipe's drone his hum lays by
When Pan sounds up his minstrelsy;
His minstrelsy! oh, base! this quill –
Which at my mouth with wind I fill –
Puts me in mind, though her I miss,
That still my Syrinx' lips I kiss.

16

Does it become a girl so wise,
So exquisite in harmonies,
To ask me when do I intend
To write a sonnet? What? my friend!
A sonnet? Never. Rhyme o'erflows
Italian, which hath scarcely prose;
And I have larded full three-score
With *sorte, morte, cuor, amor.*
But why should we, altho' we have
Enough for all things, gay or grave,
Say, on your conscience, why should we
Who draw deep seans along the sea,
Cut them in pieces to beset
The shallows with a cabbage-net?
Now if you ever ask again
A thing so troublesome and vain,
By all your charms! before the morn,
To show my anger and my scorn,
First I will write your name a-top,
Then from this very ink shall drop
A score of sonnets; every one
Shall call you star, or moon, or sun,
Till, swallowing such warm-water verse,
Even sonnet-sippers sicken worse.

Brown Penny

I whispered, 'I am too young,'
And then, 'I am old enough';
Wherefore I threw a penny
To find out if I might love.
'Go and love, go and love, young man,
If the lady be young and fair.'
Ah, penny, brown penny, brown penny,
I am looped in the loops of her hair.

O love is the crooked thing,
There is nobody wise enough
To find out all that is in it,
For he would be thinking of love
Till the stars had run away
And the shadows eaten the moon
Ah, penny, brown penny, brown penny,
One cannot begin it too soon.

18

Mother, I will have a husband,
And I will have him out of hand.
    Mother, I will sure have one,
    In spite of her that will have none.

John a Dun should have had me long ere this,
He said I had good lips to kiss.
    Mother, I will sure have one,
    In spite of her that will have none.

For I have heard 'tis trim when folks do love,
By good Sir John I swear now I will prove.
    For, mother, I will sure have one,
    In spite of her that will have none.

To the town therefore will I gad,
To get me a husband good or bad.
    Mother, I will have a husband,
And I will have him out of hand.
Mother, I will sure have one,
In spite of her that will have none.

19

The Dreame

Or Scorne, or pittie on me take,
I must the true Relation make,
    I am undone to night;
Love in a subtile Dreame disguis'd,
Hath both my heart and me surpriz'd,
Whom never yet he durst attempt awake;
Nor will he tell me for whose sake
        He did me the Delight,
            Or Spight,
But leaves me to inquire,
In all my wild desire,
    Of sleepe againe, who was his Aid;
    And sleepe so guiltie and afraid,
As since he dares not come within my sight.

20

Aire and Angels

Twice or thrice had I loved thee,
Before I knew thy face or name;
So in a voice, so in a shapelesse flame,
Angells affect us oft, and worship'd bee;
    Still when, to where thou wert, I came,
Some lovely glorious nothing I did see.
    But since my soule, whose child love is,
Takes limmes of flesh, and else could nothing doe,
    More subtile than the parent is,

Love must not be, but take a body too,
    And therefore what thou wert, and who,
        I bid Love aske, and now
That it assume thy body, I allow,
And fixe it selfe in thy lip, eye, and brow.

Whilst thus to ballast love, I thought,
And so more steddily to have gone,
With wares which would sinke admiration,
I saw, I had loves pinnace overfraught,
    Ev'ry thy haire for love to worke upon
Is much too much, some fitter must be sought;
    For, nor in nothing, nor in things
Extreme, and scatt'ring bright, can love inhere;
    Then as an Angell, face, and wings
Of aire, not pure as it, yet pure doth weare,
    So thy love may be my loves spheare;
        Just such disparitie
As is twixt Aire and Angells puritie,
'Twixt womens love, and mens will ever bee.

21

Before the World was Made

If I make the lashes dark
And the eyes more bright
And the lips more scarlet,
Or ask if all be right
From mirror after mirror,
No vanity's displayed:
I'm looking for the face I had
Before the world was made.

What if I look upon a man
As though on my beloved,
And my blood be cold the while
And my heart unmoved?
Why should he think me cruel
Or that he is betrayed?
I'd have him love the thing that was
Before the world was made.

[26]

The Prophets

Perhaps I always knew what they were saying:
Even those earliest messengers who walked
Into my life from books where they were staying,
Those beautiful machines that never talked
But let the small boy worship them and learn
All their long names whose hardness made him proud;
Love was the word they never said aloud
As nothing that a picture can return.

And later when I hunted the Good Place,
Abandoned lead-mines let themselves be caught;
There was no pity in the adit's face,
The rusty winding-engine never taught
One obviously too apt, to say Too Late:
Their lack of shyness was a way of praising
Just what I didn't know, why I was gazing,
While all their lack of answer whispered 'Wait,'
And taught me gradually without coercion,
And all the landscape round them pointed to
The calm with which they took complete desertion
As proof that you existed.

                It was true.
For now I have the answer from the face
That never will go back into a book
But asks for all my life, and is the Place
Where all I touch is moved to an embrace,
And there is no such thing as a vain look.

23

He fumbles at your spirit
   As players at the keys
Before they drop full music on;
   He stuns you by degrees,

Prepares your brittle substance
  For the ethereal blow,
By fainter hammers, further heard,
  Then nearer, then so slow

Your breath has time to straighten,
  Your brain to bubble cool, –
Deals one imperial thunderbolt
  That scalps your naked soul.

24

There is a lady sweet and kind,
Was never face so pleased my mind;
I did but see her passing by,
And yet I love her till I die.

Her gesture, motion, and her smiles,
Her wit, her voice, my heart beguiles,
Beguiles my heart, I know not why,
And yet I love her till I die.

Her free behaviour, winning looks,
Will make a lawyer burn his books;
I touched her not, alas! not I,
And yet I love her till I die.

Had I her fast betwixt mine arms,
Judge you that think such sports were harms,
Were't any harm? no, no, fie, fie,
For I will love her till I die.

Should I remain confinëd there
So long as Phoebus in his sphere,
I to request, she to deny,
Yet would I love her till I die.

Cupid is wingëd and doth range,
Her country so my love doth change:
But change she earth, or change she sky,
Yet will I love her till I die.

Her Triumph

See the Chariot at hand here of Love,
   Wherein my Lady rideth!
Each that drawes, is a Swan, or a Dove,
   And well the Carre Love guideth.
As she goes, all hearts doe duty
          Unto her beauty;
And enamour'd, doe wish, so they might
          But enjoy such a sight,
That they still were to run by her side,
Th(o)rough Swords, th(o)rough Seas, whether she would ride.

Doe but looke on her eyes, they doe light
   All that Loves world compriseth!
Doe but looke on her Haire, it is bright
   As Loves starre when it riseth!
Doe but marke, her forehead's smoother
          Then words that sooth her!
And from her arched browes, such a grace
          Sheds it selfe through the face,
   As alone there triumphs to the life
All the Gaine, all the Good, of the Elements strife.

Have you seene but a bright Lillie grow,
   Before rude hands have touch'd it?
Have you mark'd but the fall o'the Snow
   Before the soyle hath smutch'd it?
Have you felt the wooll o' the Bever?
          Or Swans Downe ever?
Or have smelt o'the bud o'the Brier?
          Or the Nard i' the fire?
   Or have tasted the bag o'the Bee?
O so white! O so soft! O so sweet is she!

Perigot.	It fell vpon a holly eue,
Willye.	hey ho hollidaye,
Per.	When holly fathers wont to shrieue:
Wil.	now gynneth this roundelay.
Per.	Sitting vpon a hill so hye
Wil.	hey ho the high hyll,
Per.	The while my flocke did feede thereby,
Wil.	the while the shepheard selfe did spill:
Per.	I saw the bouncing Bellibone,
Wil.	hey ho Bonibell,
Per.	Tripping ouer the dale alone,
Wil.	she can trippe it very well:
Per.	Well decked in a frocke of gray,
Wil.	hey ho gray is greete,
Per.	And in a Kirtle of greene saye,
Wil.	the greene is for maydens meete:
Per.	A chapelet on her head she wore,
Wil.	hey ho chapelet,
Per.	Of sweete Violets therein was store,
Wil.	she sweeter then the Violet.
Per.	My sheepe did leaue theyr wonted foode,
Wil.	hey ho seely sheepe,
Per.	And gazd on her, as they were wood,
Wil.	woode as he, that did them keepe.
Per.	As the bonilasse passed bye,
Wil.	hey ho bonilasse,
Per.	She roude at me with glauncing eye,
Wil.	as cleare as the christall glasse:
Per.	All as the Sunnye beame so bright,
Wil.	hey ho the Sunnye beame,
Per.	Glaunceth from *Phœbus* face forthright,
Wil.	so loue into thy hart did streame:
Per.	Or as the thonder cleaues the cloudes,
Wil.	hey ho the Thonder,
Per.	Wherein the lightsome leuin shroudes,
Wil.	so cleaues thy soule a sonder:
Per.	Or as Dame *Cynthias* siluer raye
Wil.	hey ho the Moonelight,
Per.	Vpon the glyttering waue doth playe:
Wil.	such play is a pitteous plight.

Per.	The glaunce into my heart did glide,
Wil.	hey ho the glyder,
Per.	Therewith my soule was sharply gryde,
Wil.	such woundes soone wexen wider.
Per.	Hasting to raunch the arrow out,
Wil.	hey ho Perigot.
Per.	I left the head in my hart roote:
Wil.	it was a desperate shot.
Per.	There itranckleth ay more and more,
Wil.	hey ho the arrowe,
Per.	Ne can I find salue for my sore:
Wil.	loue is a curelesse sorrowe.
Per.	And though my bale with death I bought,
Wil.	hey ho heauie cheere,
Per.	Yet should thilk lasse not from my thought:
Wil.	so you may buye gold to deare.
Per.	But whether in paynefull loue I pyne,
Wil.	hey ho pinching payne,
Per.	Or thriue in welth, she shalbe mine.
Wil.	but if thou can her obteine.
Per.	And if for gracelesse greefe I dye,
Wil.	hey ho gracelesse griefe,
Per.	Witnesse, shee slewe me with her eue:
Wil.	let thy follye be the priefe.
Per.	And you, that sawe it, simple shepe,
Wil.	hey ho the fayre flocke,
Per.	For priefe thereof, my death shall weepe,
Wil.	and mone with many a mocke.
Per.	So learnd I loue on a hollye eye,
Wil.	hey ho holidaye,
Per.	That euer since my hart did greue.
Wil.	now endeth our roundelay.

27

In mine one Monument I lye,
    And in my Self am buried;
Sure the quick Lightning of her Eye
    Melted my Soul ith' Scabberd, dead;
And now like some pale ghost I walk,
And with anothers Spirit talk.

Nor can her beams a heat convey
    That may my frozen bosome warm,
Unless her Smiles have pow'r, as they
    That a cross charm can countercharm;
But this is such a pleasing pain,
I'm loth to be alive again.

28

An Apology for Having Loved Before

They that never had the use
Of the grape's surprising juice,
To the first delicious cup
All their reason render up;
Neither do, nor care to know,
Whether it be best or no.

So they that are to love inclined
Swayed by chance, not choice, or art,
To the first that's fair, or kind,
Make a present of their heart;
'Tis not she that first we love,
But whom dying we approve.

To man, that was in the evening made,
Stars gave the first delight,
Admiring, in the gloomy shade,
Those little drops of light;
Then at Aurora, whose fair hand
Removed them from the skies,
He gazing toward the east did stand,
She entertained his eyes.

29

Madrigal

Like the Idalian queen,
Her hair about her eyne,
With neck and breast's ripe apples to be seen,

At first glance of the morn
In Cyprus' gardens gathering those fair flowers
Which of her blood were born,
I saw, but fainting saw, my paramours.
The Graces naked danced about the place,
The winds and trees amazed
With silence on her gazed,
The flowers did smile, like those upon her face;
And as their aspen stalks those fingers band,
That she might read my case,
A hyacinth I wished me in her hand.

30

Of Phyllis

In petticoat of green,
Her hair about her eyne,
Phyllis beneath an oak
Sat milking her fair flock:
Among that strainëd moisture, rare delight!
Her hand seemed milk in milk, it was so white.

31

Cupid and my Campaspe played
At cards for kisses – Cupid paid:
He stakes his quiver, bow and arrows,
His mother's doves, and team of sparrows;
Loses them too; then down he throws
The coral of his lip, the rose
Growing on 's cheek (but none knows how);
With these, the crystal of his brow,
And then the dimple of his chin:
All these did my Campaspe win.
At last he set her both his eyes,
She won, and Cupid blind did rise.
    O Love! has she done this to thee?
    What shall, alas, become of me?

32

Where be ye going, you Devon Maid?
 And what have ye there i' the basket?
Ye tight little fairy, just fresh from the dairy,
 Will ye give me some cream if I ask it?

I love your meads and I love your flowers,
 And I love your junkets mainly,
But 'hind the door I love kissing more,
 Oh, look not so disdainly!

I love your hills and I love your dales,
 And I love your flocks a-bleating –
But oh, on the heather to lie together,
 With both our hearts a-beating!

I'll put your basket all safe in a nook,
 Your shawl I hang up on this willow,
And we will sigh in the daisy's eye
 And kiss on a grass-green pillow.

33

There was a maid came out of Kent,
 Dainty love, dainty love;
There was a maid came out of Kent,
 Dangerous be:
There was a maid came out of Kent,
Fair, proper, small and gent,
As ever upon the ground went,
 For so should it be.

One word is too often profaned
   For me to profane it,
One feeling too falsely disdained
   For thee to disdain it;
One hope is too like despair
   For prudence to smother,
And pity from thee more dear
   Than that from another.

I can give not what men call love,
   But wilt thou accept not
The worship the heart lifts above
   And the Heavens reject not, –
The desire of the moth for the star,
   Of the night for the morrow,
The devotion to something afar
   From the sphere of our sorrow?

35

Say that I should say I love ye,
   Would you say 'tis but a saying?
But if love in prayërs move ye,
   Will you not be moved with praying?

Think I think that love should know ye,
   Will you think 'tis but a thinking?
But if love the thought do show ye,
   Will ye loose your eyes with winking?

Write that I do write you blessëd,
   Will you write 'tis but a writing?
But if truth and love confess it,
   Will ye doubt the true inditing?

No, I say, and think, and write it,
   Write, and think, and say your pleasure;
Love, and truth, and I indite it,
   You are blessëd out of measure.

36
Broadcast

Giant whispering and coughing from
Vast Sunday-full and organ-frowned-on spaces
Precede a sudden scuttle on the drum,
'The Queen', and huge resettling. Then begins
A snivel on the violins:
I think of your face among all those faces,

Beautiful and devout before
Cascades of monumental slithering,
One of your gloves unnoticed on the floor
Beside those new, slightly-outmoded shoes.
Here it goes quickly dark. I lose
All but the outline of the still and withering

Leaves on half-emptied trees. Behind
The glowing wavebands, rabid storms of chording
By being distant overpower my mind
All the more shamelessly, their cut-off shout
Leaving me desperate to pick out
Your hands, tiny in all that air, applauding.

37
Elinda's Glove

SONNET

Thou snowy Farme with thy five Tenements!
    Tell thy white Mistris here was one
    That call'd to pay his dayly Rents:
But she a gathering Flowr's and Hearts is gone,
And thou left voyd to rude Possession.

But grieve not pretty *Ermin* Cabinet,
    Thy Alablaster Lady will come home;
    If not, what Tenant can there fit
The slender turnings of thy narrow Roome,
But must ejected be by his owne dombe?

Then give me leave to leave my Rent with thee;
     Five kisses, one unto a place:
     For though the *Lute's* too high for me;
Yet Servants knowing Minikin nor Base,
Are still allow'd to fiddle with the Case.

38

Stanzas for Music

There be none of Beauty's daughters
     With a magic like thee;
And like music on the waters
     Is thy sweet voice to me:
When, as if its sound were causing
The charmed ocean's pausing,
The waves lie still and gleaming
And the lull'd winds seem dreaming:

And the midnight moon is weaving
     Her bright chain o'er the deep;
Whose breast is gently heaving,
     As an infant's asleep:
So the spirit bows before thee,
To listen and adore thee;
With a full but soft emotion,
Like the swell of Summer's ocean.

39

Behold the brand of beauty tossed!
See how the motion does dilate the flame!
Delighted love his spoils does boast,
And triumph in this game.
Fire, to no place confined,
Is both our wonder and our fear;
Moving the mind,
As lightning hurled through the air.

High heaven the glory does increase
Of all her shining lamps, this artful way;
The sun in figures, such as these,
Joys with the moon to play;
To the sweet strains they advance,
Which do result from their own spheres,
As this nymph's dance
Moves with the numbers which she hears.

40

Fresh Cheese and Cream

Wo'd yee have fresh Cheese and Cream?
Julia's Breast can give you them:
And if more; Each *Nipple* cries,
To your *Cream*, here's *Strawberries*.

41

Was it a dreame, or did I see it playne,
   a goodly table of pure yvory:
   all spred with iuncats, fit to entertayne
   the greatest Prince with pompous roialty.
Mongst which there in a siluer dish did ly
   twoo golden apples of vnualewd price:
   far passing those which Hercules came by,
   or those which Atalanta did entice.
Exceeding sweet, yet voyd of sinfull vice,
   That many sought yet none could euer taste,
   sweet fruit of pleasure brought from paradice
   by loue himselfe, and in his garden plaste.
Her brest that table was so richly spredd,
   my thoughts the guests, which would thereon haue fedd.

O ruddier than the Cherry!
O sweeter than the Berry!
  O Nymph, more bright
  Than Moonshine Night!
Like Kidlings blithe and merry.

Ripe as the melting Cluster,
No Lilly has such Lustre;
  Yet hard to tame,
  As raging Flame,

And fierce as Storms that bluster.
O ruddier, &c.

43

from *The Princess*

'O Swallow, Swallow, flying, flying South,
Fly to her, and fall upon her gilded eaves,
And tell her, tell her, what I tell to thee.

'O tell her, Swallow, thou that knowest each,
That bright and fierce and fickle is the South,
And dark and true and tender is the North.

'O Swallow, Swallow, if I could follow, and light
Upon her lattice, I would pipe and trill,
And cheep and twitter twenty million loves.

'O were I thou that she might take me in,
And lay me on her bosom, and her heart
Would rock the snowy cradle till I died.

'Why lingereth she to clothe her heart with love,
Delaying as the tender ash delays
To clothe herself, when all the woods are green?

'O tell her, Swallow, that thy brood is flown:
Say to her, I do but wanton in the South,
But in the North long since my nest is made.

'O tell her, brief is life but love is long,
And brief the sun of summer in the North,
And brief the moon of beauty in the South.

'O Swallow, flying from the golden woods,
Fly to her, and pipe and woo her, and make her mine,
And tell her, tell her, that I follow thee.'

44

The Complement

O my deerest I shall grieve thee
When I sweare, yet sweete beleeve me,
By thine eyes the tempting booke
On which even crabbed old men looke
I sweare to thee, (though none abhorre them)
Yet I doe not love thee for them.

I doe not love thee for that faire,
Rich fanne of thy most curious haire;
Though the wires thereof be drawne
Finer then the threeds of lawne,
And are softer then the leaves
On which the subtle spinner weaues.

I doe not love thee for those flowers,
Growing on thy cheeks (loves bowers)
Though such cunning them hath spread
None can parte their whit and red:
Loves golden arrowes thence are shot,
Yet for them I loue thee not.

I doe not love thee for those soft,
Red corrall lips I've kist so oft;
Nor teeth of pearle, the double guard
To speech, whence musicke still is heard:
Though from those lips a kisse being taken,
Might tyrants melt and death awaken.

I doe not love thee (O my fairest)
For that richest, for that rarest
Silver pillar which stands vnder
Thy round head, that globe of wonder;
Though that necke be whiter farre,
Then towers of pollisht Ivory are.

I doe not love thee for those mountaines
Hill'd with snow, whence milkey fountaines,
(Suger'd sweete, as sirropt berries)
Must one day run through pipes of cherries;
O how much those breasts doe move me,
Yet for them I doe not love thee:

I doe not love thee for that belly,
Sleeke as satten, soft as jelly,
Though within that Christall round
Heapes of treasure might be found,
So rich that for the least of them,
A King might leave his Diadem.

I doe not love thee for those thighes,
Whose Alablaster rocks doe rise
So high and even that they stand
Like Sea-markes to some happy land.
Happy are those eyes have seene them,
More happy they that saile betweene them.

I love thee not for thy moist palme,
Though the dew thereof be balme:
Nor for thy pretty legge and foote,
Although it be the precious roote,
On which this goodly cedar growes,
(Sweete) I love thee not for those:

Nor for thy wit though pure and quicke,
Whose substance no arithmeticke
Can number downe: nor for those charmes
Mask't in thy embracing armes;
Though in them one night to lie,
Dearest I would gladly die.

I love not for those eyes, nor haire,
Nor cheekes, nor lips, nor teeth so rare;
Nor for thy speech, thy necke, nor breast,
Nor for thy belly, nor the rest:
Nor for thy hand, nor foote so small,
But wouldst thou know (deere sweet) for all.

45

Bobby Shafto's gone to sea,
   Silver buckles at his knee;
He'll come back and marry me,
   Bonny Bobby Shafto!

Bobby Shafto's fat and fair,
   Combing down his yellow hair;
He's my love for evermore,
   Bonny Bobby Shafto!

46

from *Audley Court*

'Sleep, Ellen Aubrey, sleep, and dream of me:
Sleep, Ellen, folded in thy sister's arm,
And sleeping, haply dream her arm is mine.
  'Sleep, Ellen, folded in Emilia's arm;
Emilia, fairer than all else but thou,
For thou art fairer than all else that is.
  'Sleep, breathing health and peace upon her breast:
Sleep, breathing love and trust against her lip:
I go tonight: I come tomorrow morn.
  'I go, but I return: I would I were
The pilot of the darkness and the dream.
Sleep, Ellen Aubrey, love, and dream of me.'

47

*The Author loving these homely meats specially,
viz.: Cream, Pancakes, Buttered Pippin-pies
(laugh, good people) and Tobacco; writ to that
worthy and virtuous gentlewoman, whom he
calleth Mistress, as followeth*

If there were, oh! an Hellespont of cream
Between us, milk-white mistress, I would swim
To you, to show to both my love's extreme,
Leander-like, – yea! dive from brim to brim.
But met I with a buttered pippin-pie
Floating upon 't, that would I make my boat
To waft me to you without jeopardy,
Though sea-sick I might be while it did float.
Yet if a storm should rise, by night or day,
Of sugar-snows and hail of caraways,
Then, if I found a pancake in my way,
It like a plank should bring me to your kays;
   Which having found, if they tobacco kept,
   The smoke should dry me well before I slept.

48

As Sonata in Praes o Molli

Mollis abuti,
Has an acuti
No lasso finis;
Molli dii vinis
O mi de armistris,
Imi na Dis tres;
Cantu disco ver
Meas alo ver.

49

On his Mistress, the Queen of Bohemia

You meaner beauties of the night,
    That poorly satisfy our eyes
More by your number than your light;
    You common people of the skies,
    What are you when the sun shall rise?

You curious chanters of the wood,
    That warble forth Dame Nature's lays,
Thinking your voices understood
    By your weak accents; what's your praise
    When Philomel her voice shall raise?

You violets that first appear,
    By your pure purple mantles known,
Like the proud virgins of the year,
    As if the spring were all your own;
    What are you when the rose is blown?

So, when my Mistress shall be seen
    In form and beauty of her mind,
By virtue first, then choice, a Queen,
    Tell me, if she were not designed
    The eclipse and glory of her kind?

50

To a Fair Lady, Playing with a Snake

Strange! that such horror and such grace
Should dwell together in one place;
A fury's arm, an angel's face!

'Tis innocence, and youth, which makes
In Chloris' fancy such mistakes,
To start at love, and play with snakes.

By this and by her coldness barred,
Her servants have a task too hard;
The tyrant has a double guard!

Thrice happy snake! that in her sleeve
May boldly creep; we dare not give
Our thoughts so unconfined a leave.

Contented in that nest of snow
He lies, as he his bliss did know,
And to the wood no more would go.

Take heed, fair Eve! you do not make
Another tempter of this snake;
A marble one so warmed would speak.

51

To a Young Lady, with some Lampreys

With lovers 'twas of old the fashion
By presents to convey their passion;
No matter what the gift they sent,
The Lady saw that love was meant.
Fair *Atalanta*, as a favour,
Took the boar's head her Hero gave her;
Nor could the bristly thing affront her,
'Twas a fit present from a hunter.
When Squires send woodcocks to the dame,
It serves to show their absent flame:
Some by a snip of woven hair,
In posied lockets bribe the fair;
How many mercenary matches
Have sprung from Di'mond-rings and watches!
But hold – a ring, a watch, a locket,
Would drain at once a Poet's pocket;
He should send songs that cost him nought,
Nor ev'n be prodigal of thought.
   Why then send Lampreys? fye, for shame!
'Twill set a virgin's blood on flame.
This to fifteen a proper gift!
It might lend sixty five a lift.

I know your maiden Aunt will scold,
And think my present somewhat bold.
I see her lift her hands and eyes.
　'What eat it, Niece? eat *Spanish* flies!
'Lamprey's a most immodest diet:
'You'll neither wake nor sleep in quiet.
'Should I to night eat Sago cream,
'Twould make me blush to tell my dream;
'If I eat Lobster, 'tis so warming,
'That ev'ry man I see looks charming;
'Wherefore had not the filthy fellow
'Laid *Rochester* upon your pillow?
'I vow and swear, I think the present
'Had been as modest and as decent.
　'Who has her virtue in her power?
'Each day has its unguarded hour;
'Always in danger of undoing,
'A prawn, a shrimp may prove our ruin!
　'The shepherdess, who lives on sallad,
'To cool her youth, controuls her palate;
'Should *Dian's* maids turn liqu'rish livers,
'And of huge lampreys rob the rivers,
'Then all beside each glade and Visto,
'You'd see Nymphs lying like *Calisto*.
　'The man who meant to heat your blood,
'Needs not himself such vicious food –
　In this, I own, your Aunt is clear,
I sent you what I well might spare:
For when I see you, (without joking)
Your eyes, lips, breasts, are so provoking,
They set my heart more cock-a-hoop,
Than could whole seas of craw-fish soupe.

52

The Snow-ball

Doris, I that could repell
All those darts about thee dwell,
And had wisely learn'd to fear,
Cause I saw a Foe so near;
I that my deaf ear did arm,

'Gainst thy voices powerful charm,
And the lightning of thine eye
Durst (by closing mine) defie,
Cannot this cold snow withstand
From the whiter of thy hand;
Thy deceit hath thus done more
Then thy open force before:
For who could suspect or fear
Treason in a face so clear,
Or the hidden fires descry
Wrapt in this cold out-side lie?
Flames might thus involv'd in ice
The deceiv'd world sacrifice;
Nature, ignorant of this
Strange Antiperistasis,
Would her falling frame admire,
That by snow were set on fire.

53

Upon her feet

Her pretty feet
Like snailes did creep
A little out, and then,
As if they started at Bo-peep,
Did soon draw in agen.

54

Oh, blush not so, oh, blush not so,
Or I shall think ye knowing.
And if ye smile the blushing while,
Then maidenheads are going.

There's a blush for won't, and a blush for shan't –
And a blush for having done it.
There's a blush for thought, and a blush for naught,
And a blush for just begun it.

Oh, sigh not so, oh, sigh not so,
    For it sounds of Eve's sweet pippin.
By those loosened hips you have tasted the pips
    And fought in an amorous nipping.

Will you play once more at nice-cut-core,
    For it only will last our youth out?
And we have the prime of the kissing time,
    We have not one sweet tooth out.

There's a sigh for yes, and a sigh for no,
    And a sigh for I can't bear it!
Oh, what can be done, shall we stay or run?
    Oh, cut the sweet apple and share it!

55

She Walks in Beauty

She walks in beauty, like the night
    Of cloudless climes and starry skies;
And all that's best of dark and bright
    Meet in her aspect and her eyes:
Thus mellow'd to that tender light
    Which heaven to gaudy day denies.

One shade the more, one ray the less,
    Had half impair'd the nameless grace
Which waves in every raven tress,
    Or softly lightens o'er her face;
Where thoughts serenely sweet express
    How pure, how dear their dwelling-place.

And on that cheek, and o'er that brow,
    So soft, so calm, yet eloquent,
The smiles that win, the tints that glow,
    But tell of days in goodness spent,
A mind at peace with all below,
    A heart whose love is innocent!

56

Lines

Lady, there's fragrance in your sighs,
   And sunlight in your glances;
I never saw such lips and eyes
   In pictures or romances;
And Love will readily suppose,
   To make you quite enslaving,
That you have taste for verse and prose,
   Hot pressed, and line engraving.

And then, you waltz so like a Fay,
   That round you envy rankles;
Your partner's head is turned, they say,
   As surely as his ankles;
And I was taught, in days far gone,
   By a most prudent mother,
That in this world of sorrow, one
   Good turn deserves another.

I may not win you! – that's a bore!
   But yet 'tis sweet to woo you;
And for this cause, – and twenty more,
   I send this gay book to you.
If its songs please you, – by this light!
   I will not hold it treason
To bid you dream of me to-night,
   And dance with me next season.

57

Pyrrha! your smiles are gleams of sun
That after one another run
Incessantly, and think it fun.

Pyrrha! your tears are short sweet rain
That glimmering on the flower-lit plain
Zephyrs kiss back to heaven again.

Pyrrha! both anguish me: do please
To shed but (if you wish me ease)
Twenty of those, and two of these.

58

I Saw thee Weep

I saw thee weep – the big bright tear
    Came o'er that eye of blue;
And then methought it did appear
    A violet dropping dew;
I saw thee smile – the sapphire's blaze
    Beside thee ceased to shine;
It could not match the living rays
    That fill'd that glance of thine.

As clouds from yonder sun receive
    A deep and mellow dye,
Which scarce the shade of coming eve
    Can banish from the sky,
Those smiles unto the moodiest mind
    Their own pure joy impart;
Their sunshine leaves a glow behind
    That lightens o'er the heart.

59

Home Travel

What need I travel, since I may
More choicer wonders here survey?
What need I Tyre for purple seek,
When I may find it in a cheek?
Or sack the Eastern shores? there lies
More precious diamonds in her eyes.
What need I dig Peru for ore,
When every hair of her yields more?

Or toil for gums in India,
Since she can breathe more rich than they?
Or ransack Africk? there will be
On either hand more ivory.
But look within: all virtues that
Each nation would appropriate,
And with the glory of them rest,
Are in this map at large exprest;
That who would travel here might know
The little world in folio.

60

A Song

Aske me no more where *Iove* bestowes,
When *Iune* is past, the fading rose:
For in your beauties orient deepe,
These flowers as in their causes, sleepe.

Aske me no more whether doth stray,
The golden Atomes of the day:
For in pure love heaven did prepare
Those powders to inrich your haire.

Aske me no more whether doth hast,
The Nightingale when May is past:
For in your sweet dividing throat,
She winters and keepes warme her note.

Aske me no more where those starres light,
That downewards fall in dead of night:
For in your eyes they sit, and there,
Fixed become as in their sphere.

Aske me no more if East or West,
The Phenix builds her spicy nest:
For vnto you at last shee flies,
And in your fragrant bosome dyes.

61

Vpon a Mole in Celias *bosome*

That lovely spot which thou dost see
In Celias bosome was a Bee,
Who built her amorous spicy nest
I'th Hyblas of her either breast,
But from close Ivery Hyves, she flew
To suck the Arromattick dew,
Which from the neighbour vale distils,
Which parts those two twin-sister hils.
There feasting on Ambrosiall meat,
A rowling file of Balmy sweat,
(As in soft murmurs before death,
Swan-like she sung) chokt up her breath,
So she in water did expire,
More precious then the Phænix fire;
   Yet still her shaddow there remaines
Confind to those Elizian plaines;
With this strict Law, that who shall lay
His bold lips on that milky way,
The sweet, and smart, from thence shall bring
Of the Bees Honey, and her sting.

62

Fuscara, or the Bee Errant

Nature's confectioner, the bee
(Whose suckets are moist alchemy,
The still of his refining mould
Minting the garden into gold),
Having rifled all the fields
Of what dainties Flora yields,
Ambitious now to take excise
Of a more fragrant paradise,
At my Fuscara's sleeve arrived
Where all delicious sweets are hived.
The airy freebooter distrains
First on the violets of her veins,
Whose tincture, could it be more pure,

His ravenous kiss had made it bluer.
Here did he sit and essence quaff
Till her coy pulse had beat him off;
That pulse which he that feels may know
Whether the world's long-lived or no.
The next he preys on is her palm,
That alm'ner of transpiring balm;
So soft, 'tis air but once removed;
Tender as 'twere a jelly gloved.
Here, while his canting drone-pipe scanned
The mystic figures of her hand,
He tipples palmistry and dines
On all her fortune-telling lines.
He bathes in bliss and finds no odds
Betwixt her nectar and the gods',
He perches now upon her wrist,
A proper hawk for such a fist,
Making that flesh his bill of fare
Which hungry cannibals would spare;
Where lilies in a lovely brown
Inoculate carnation.
He *argent* skin with *or* so streamed
As if the milky way were creamed.
From hence he to the woodbine bends
That quivers at her fingers' ends,
That runs division on the tree
Like a thick-branching pedigree.
So' tis not her the bee devours,
It is a pretty maze of flowers;
It is the rose that bleeds, when he
Nibbles his nice phlebotomy.
About her finger he doth cling
I' th' fashion of a wedding-ring,
And bids his comrades of the swarm
Crawl as a bracelet 'bout her arm.
Thus when the hovering publican
Had sucked the toll of all her span,
Tuning his draughts with drowsy hums
As Danes carouse by kettle-drums,
It was decreed, that posie gleaned,
The small familiar should be weaned.
At this the errant's courage quails;

Yet aided by his native sails
The bold Columbus still designs
To find her undiscovered mines.
To th' Indies of her arm he flies,
Fraught both with east and western prize;
Which when he had in vain essayed,
Armed like a dapper lancepresade
With Spanish pike, he broached a pore
And so both made and healed the sore:
For as in gummy trees there's found
A salve to issue at the wound,
Of this her breach the like was true;
Hence trickled out a balsam, too.
But oh, what wasp was 't that could prove
Ravaillac to my Queen of Love!
The King of Bees now's jealous grown
Lest her beams should melt his throne,
And finding that his tribute slacks,
His burgesses and state of wax
Turned to a hospital, the combs
Built rank-and-file like beadsmen's rooms,
And what they bleed but tart and sour
Matched with my Danae's golden shower,
Live-honey all, – the envious elf
Stung her, 'cause sweeter than himself.
    Sweetness and she are so allied
The bee committed parricide.

63

When to my deadlie pleasure,
When to my livelie torment,
Ladie mine eyes remained,
Joyned alas to your beames,

With violence of heav'nly
Beautie tied to vertue,
Reason abasht retyred,
Gladly my senses yeelded.

Gladly my senses yeelding,
Thus to betray my hart's fort,
Left me devoid of all life;

They to the beamie Sunnes went,
Where by the death of all deaths,
Finde to what harme they hastned,

Like to the silly *Sylvan*,
Burn'd by the light he best liked,
When with a fire he first met.

Yet, yet, a life to their death,
Lady you have reserved,
Lady the life of all love;

For though my sense be from me,
And I be dead who want sense,
Yet do we both live in you.

Turned anew by your meanes,
Unto the flowre that ay turnes,
As you, alas, my Sunne bends;

Thus do I fall to rise thus,
Thus do I dye to live thus,
Changed to a change, I change not.

Thus may I not be from you:
Thus be my senses on you:
Thus what I thinke is of you:
Thus what I seeke is in you:
    All what I am, it is you.

64

To Rosemounde

A BALADE

Madame, ye ben of al beaute shryne
As fer as cercled is the mapemounde,
For as the cristal glorious ye shyne,
And lyke ruby ben your chekes rounde.
Therwith ye ben so mery and so jocounde
That at a revel whan that I see you daunce,
It is an oynement unto my wounde,
Thogh ye to me ne do no daliaunce.

For thogh I wepe of teres ful a tyne,
Yet may that wo myn herte nat confounde;
Your semy voys, that ye so smal out twyne,
Maketh my thoght in joy and blis habounde.
So curtaysly I go, with love bounde,
That to myself I sey, in my penaunce,
'Suffyseth me to love you, Rosemounde,
Thogh ye to me ne do no daliaunce.'

Nas never pyk walwed in galauntyne
As I in love am walwed and ywounde,
For which ful ofte I of myself devyne
That I am trewe Tristam the secounde.
My love may not refreyde nor affounde;
I brenne ay in an amorous plesaunce.
Do what you lyst, I wyl your thral be founde,
Thogh ye to me ne do no daliaunce.

65

The Night-piece, to Julia

Her Eyes the Glow-worme lend thee,
The Shooting Starres attend thee;
    And the Elves also,
    Whose little eyes glow,
Like the sparks of fire, befriend thee.

No *Will-o' th'-Wispe* mis-light thee;
Nor Snake, or Slow-worme bite thee:
    But on, on thy way
    Not making a stay,
Since Ghost ther's none to affright thee.

Let not the darke thee cumber;
What though the Moon do's slumber?
    The Starres of the night
    Will lend thee their light,
Like Tapers cleare without number.

Then *Julia* let me wooe thee,
Thus, thus to come unto me:
    And when I shall meet
    Thy silv'ry feet,
My soule Ile poure into thee.

66

Drinke to me, onely, with thine eyes,
    And I will pledge with mine;
Or leaue a kisse but in the cup,
    And Ile not looke for wine.
The thirst, that from the soule doth rise,
    Doth aske a drinke diuine:
But might I of Iove's *Nectar* sup,
    I would not change for thine.
I sent thee, late, a rosie wreath
    Not so much honoring thee,
As giuing it a hope, that there
    It could not withered bee.
But thou thereon did'st onely breath,
    And sent'st it backe to mee:
Since when it growes, and smells, I sweare,
    Not of it selfe, but thee.

Shall I come, sweet love, to thee
    When the evening beams are set?
Shall I not excluded be?
    Will you find no feigned let?
Let me not, for pity, more
Tell the long hours at your door.

Who can tell what thief or foe
    In the covert of the night
For his prey will work my woe,
    Or through wicked foul despite?
So may I die unredressed,
Ere my long love be possessed.

But to let such dangers pass,
    Which a lover's thoughts disdain,
'Tis enough in such a place
    To attend Love's joys in vain.
Do not mock me in thy bed,
While these cold nights freeze me dead.

68

The Ragged Wood

O hurry where by water among the trees
The delicate-stepping stag and his lady sigh,
When they have but looked upon their images –
Would none had ever loved but you and I!

Or have you heard that sliding silver-shoed
Pale silver-proud queen-woman of the sky,
When the sun looked out of his golden hood? –
O that none ever loved but you and I!

O hurry to the ragged wood, for there
I will drive all those lovers out and cry –
O my share of the world, O yellow hair!
No one has ever loved but you and I.

Can you make me a cambric shirt,
   Parsley, sage, rosemary, and thyme,
Without any seam or needlework?
   And you shall be a true lover of mine.

Can you wash it in yonder well,
   Parsley, sage, rosemary, and thyme,
Where never sprung water, nor rain ever fell?
   And you shall be a true lover of mine.

Can you dry it on yonder thorn,
   Parsley, sage, rosemary, and thyme,
Which never bore blossom since Adam was born?
   And you shall be a true lover of mine.

Now you've asked me questions three,
   Parsley, sage, rosemary, and thyme,
I hope you'll answer as many for me,
   And you shall be a true lover of mine.

Can you find me an acre of land,
   Parsley, sage, rosemary, and thyme,
Between the salt water and the sea sand?
   And you shall be a true lover of mine.

Can you plough it with a ram's horn,
   Parsley, sage, rosemary, and thyme,
And sow it all over with one pepper-corn?
   And you shall be a true lover of mine.

Can you reap it with a sickle of leather,
   Parsley, sage, rosemary, and thyme,
And bind it up with a peacock's feather?
   And you shall be a true lover of mine.

When you have done and finished your work,
   Parsley, sage, rosemary, and thyme,
Then come to me for your cambric shirt,
   And you shall be a true lover of mine.

To a Lady that desired I
would love her

Now you have freely given me leave to love,
        What will you doe?
        Shall I your mirth, or passion move
        When I begin to wooe;
Will you torment, or scorne, or love me too?

Each pettie beautie can disdaine, and I
        Spight of your hate
        Without your leave can see, and dye;
        Dispence a nobler Fate,
'Tis easie to destroy, you may create.

Then give me leave to love, and love me too,
        Not with designe
        To rayse, as Loves curst Rebells doe,
        When puling Poets whine,
Fame to their beautie, from their blubbr'd eyne.

Griefe is a puddle, and reflects not cleare
        Your beauties rayes,
        Joyes are pure streames, your eyes appeare
        Sullen in sadder layes,
In chearfull numbers they shine bright with prayse;

Which shall not mention to expresse you fayre
        Wounds, flames, and darts,
        Stormes in your brow, nets in your haire,
        Suborning all your parts,
Or to betray, or torture captive hearts.

I'le make your eyes like morning Suns appeare,
        As milde, and faire;
        Your brow as Crystall smooth, and cleare,
        And your dishevell'd hayre
Shall flow like a calme Region of the Ayre.

Rich Natures store, (which is the Poets Treasure)
        I'le spend, to dresse
    Your beauties, if your mine of Pleasure
        In equall thankfulnesse
You but unlocke, so we each other blesse.

71

The passionate Shepherd to his Love

Come live with me and be my Love,
And we will all the pleasures prove
That valleys, groves, hills, and fields,
Woods, or steepy mountains yields.

And we will sit upon the rocks
Seeing the shepherds feed their flocks,
By shallow rivers, to whose falls
Melodious birds sing madrigals.

And I will make thee beds of roses
And a thousand fragrant posies,
A cap of flowers, and a kirtle
Embroidered all with leaves of myrtle;

A gown made of the finest wool,
Which from our pretty lambs we pull;
Fair linèd slippers for the cold,
With buckles of the purest gold;

A belt of straw and ivy buds
With coral clasps and amber studs:
And if these pleasures may thee move,
Come live with me and be my Love.

The shepherd swains shall dance and sing
For thy delight each May morning:
If these delights thy mind may move,
Then live with me and be my Love.

The Baite

Come live with mee, and bee my love,
And wee will some new pleasures prove
Of golden sands, and christall brookes,
With silken lines, and silver hookes.

There will the river whispering runne
Warm'd by thy eyes, more than the Sunne.
And there the'inamor'd fish will stay,
Begging themselves they may betray.

When thou wilt swimme in that live bath,
Each fish, which every channell hath,
Will amorously to thee swimme,
Gladder to catch thee, than thou him.

If thou, to be so seene, beest loath,
By Sunne, or Moone, thou darknest both,
And if my selfe have leave to see,
I need not their light, having thee.

Let others freeze with angling reeds,
And cut their legges, with shells and weeds,
Qr treacherously poore fish beset,
With strangling snare, or windowie net:

Let coarse bold hands, from slimy nest
The bedded fish in banks out-wrest,
Or curious traitors, sleavesilke flies
Bewitch poore fishes wandring eyes.

For thee, thou needst no such deceit,
For thou thy selfe art thine owne bait;
That fish, that is not catch'd thereby,
Alas, is wiser farre than I.

Love me little, love me long,
Is the burden of my song.
Love that is too hot and strong
    Burneth soon to waste:
Still, I would not have thee cold,
Not too backward, nor too bold;
Love that lasteth till 'tis old
    Fadeth not in haste.
        Love me little, love me long,
        Is the burden of my song.

If thou lovest me too much,
It will not prove as true as touch;
Love me little, more than such,
    For I fear the end:
I am with little well content,
And a little from thee sent
Is enough, with true intent
    To be steadfast friend.
        Love me little, love me long, . . .

Say thou lov'st me while thou live;
I to thee my love will give,
Never dreaming to deceive
    Whiles that life endures:
Nay, and after death, in sooth,
I to thee will keep my truth,
As now, when in my May of youth;
    This my love assures.
        Love me little, love me long, . . .

Constant love is moderate ever,
And it will through life persèver:
Give me that, with true endeavour
    I will it restore.
A suit of durance let it be
For all weathers that for me,
For the land or for the sea,
    Lasting evermore.
        Love me little, love me long, . . .

Winter's cold, or summer's heat,
Autumn's tempests, on it beat,
It can never know defeat,
    Never can rebel:
Such the love that I would gain,
Such the love, I tell thee plain,
Thou must give, or woo in vain:
    So to thee, farewell!
      Love me little, love me long,
      Is the burden of my song.

74

To Julia to expedite her Promise

Since 'tis my doom, Love's undershrieve,
      Why this reprieve?
Why doth my she-advowson fly
      Incumbency?
Panting expectance makes us prove
The antics of benighted love,
And withered mates when wedlock joins,
They're Hymen's monkeys, which he ties by th' loins
To play, alas! but at rebated foins.

To sell thyself dost thou intend
      By candle end,
And hold the contract thus in doubt,
      Life's taper out?
Think but how soon the market fails;
Your sex lives faster than the males;
As if, to measure age's span,
The sober Julian were th' account of man,
Whilst you live by the fleet Gregorian.

Now since you bear a date so short,
                    Live double for 't.
How can thy fortress ever stand
                    If 't be not manned?
The siege so gains upon the place
Thou'lt find the trenches in thy face.
Pity thyself then if not me,
And hold not out, lest like Ostend thou be
Nothing but rubbish at delivery.

The candidates of Peter's chair
                    Must plead grey hair,
And use the simony of a cough
                    To help them off.
But when I woo, thus old and spent,
I'll wed by will and testament.
No, let us love while crisped and curled;
The greatest honours, on the agéd hurled,
Are but gay furloughs for another world.

To-morrow what thou tenderest me
                    Is legacy.
Not one of all those ravenous hours
                    But thee devours.
And though thou still recruited be,
Like Pelops, with soft ivory,
Though thou consume but to renew,
Yet Love as lord doth claim a heriot due;
That's the best quick thing I can find of you.

I feel thou art consenting ripe
                    By that soft gripe,
And those regealing crystal spheres.
                    I hold thy tears
Pledges of more distilling sweets,
The bath that ushers in the sheets.
  Else pious Julia, angel-wise,
  Moves the Bethesda of her trickling eyes
  To cure the spital world of maladies.

[65]

It was a Louer, and his lasse,
   With a hey, and a ho, and a hey nonino,
That o're the greene corne feild did passe,
   In spring time, the onely pretty ring time.
When Birds do sing, hey ding a ding, ding.
Sweet Louers loue the spring.

Betweene the acres of the Rie,
   With a hey, and a ho, & a hey nonino:
These prettie Country folks would lie.
   In spring time, the onely pretty ring time.
When Birds do sing, hey ding a ding, ding.
Sweet Louers love the spring.

This Carroll they began that houre,
   With a hey and a ho, & a hey nonino:
How that a life was but a Flower,
   In spring time, the onely pretty ring time.
When Birds do sing, hey ding a ding, ding.
Sweet Louers loue the spring.

And therefore take the present time.
   With a hey, & a ho, and a hey nonino,
For loue is crowned with the prime.
   In spring time, the onely pretty ring time.
When Birds do sing, hey ding a ding, ding.
Sweet Louers loue the spring.

Embraceable You

DANNY

Dozens of girls would storm up;
   I had to lock my door.
Somehow I couldn't warm up
   To one before.
What was it that controlled me?
   What kept my love-life lean?
My intuition told me
   You'd come on the scene.
Lady, listen to the rhythm of my heart beat,
   And you'll get just what I mean.

REFRAIN

   Embrace me,
My sweet embraceable you.
   Embrace me,
You irreplaceable you.
Just one look at you – my heart grew tipsy in me;
You and you alone bring out the gypsy in me.
   I love all
The many charms about you;
   Above all
I want my arms about you.
Don't be a naughty baby,
Come to papa – come to papa – do!
My sweet embraceable you.

MOLLY

I went about reciting,
   'Here's one who'll never fall!'
But I'm afraid the writing
   Is on the wall.
My nose I used to turn up
   When you'd besiege my heart;
Now I completely burn up
   When you're slow to start.
I'm afraid you'll have to take the consequences;
   You upset the apple cart.

Embrace me,
My sweet embraceable you.
Embrace me,
You irreplaceable you.
In your arms I find love so delectable, dear,
I'm afraid it isn't quite respectable, dear.
But hang it –
Come on, let's glorify love!
Ding dang it!
You'll shout 'Encore!' if I love.
Don't be a naughty papa,
Come to baby – come to baby – do!
My sweet embraceable you.

77

To his Coy Mistress

Had we but World enough, and Time,
This coyness Lady were no crime.
We would sit down, and think which way
To walk, and pass our long Loves Day.
Thou by the *Indian Ganges* side
Should'st Rubies find: I by the Tide
Of *Humber* would complain. I would
Love you ten years before the Flood:
And you should if you please refuse
Till the Conversion of the *Jews*.
My vegetable Love should grow
Vaster then Empires, and more slow.
An hundred years should go to praise
Thine Eyes, and on thy Forehead Gaze.
Two hundred to adore each Breast:
But thirty thousand to the rest.
An Age at least to every part,
And the last Age should show your Heart.
For Lady you deserve this State;
Nor would I love at lower rate.
But at my back I alwaies hear
Times winged Charriot hurrying near:

And yonder all before us lye
Desarts of vast Eternity.
Thy Beauty shall no more be found,
Nor, in thy marble Vault, shall sound
My ecchoing Song: then Worms shall try
That long preserv'd Virginity:
And your quaint Honour turn to dust;
And into ashes all my Lust.
The Grave's a fine and private place,
But none I think do there embrace.
    Now therefore, while the youthful hew
Sits on thy skin like morning glew,
And while thy willing Soul transpires
At every pore with instant Fires,
Now let us sport us while we may;
And now, like am'rous birds of prey,
Rather at once our Time devour,
Than languish in his slow-chapt pow'r.
Let us roll all our Strength, and all
Our sweetness, up into one Ball:
And tear our Pleasures with rough strife,
Thorough the Iron gates of Life.
Thus, though we cannot make our Sun
Stand still, yet we will make him run.

78

If you were coming in the fall,
I'd brush the summer by
With half a smile and half a spurn,
As housewives do a fly.

If I could see you in a year,
I'd wind the months in balls,
And put them each in separate drawers,
Until their time befalls.

If only centuries delayed,
I'd count them on my hand,
Subtracting till my fingers dropped
Into Van Diemen's land.

If certain, when this life was out,
That yours and mine should be,
I'd toss it yonder like a rind,
And taste eternity.

But now, all ignorant of the length
Of time's uncertain wing,
It goads me, like the goblin bee,
That will not state its sting.

79

O Mistris mine where are you roming?
O stay and heare, your true loues coming,
   That can sing both high and low.
Trip no further prettie sweeting.
Iourneys end in louers meeting,
   Euery wise mans sonne doth know.

What is loue, tis not heereafter,
Present mirth, hath present laughter:
   What's to come, is still vnsure.
In delay there lies no plentie,
Then come kisse me sweet and twentie:
   Youths a stuffe will not endure.

80

Come my CELIA, let vs proue,
While we may, the sports of loue;
Time will not be ours, for euer:
He, at length, our good will seuer.
Spend not then his guifts in vaine.
Sunnes, that set, may rise againe:
But if once we loose this light,
'Tis, with vs, perpetuall night.
Why should we deferre our ioyes?
Fame, and rumor are but toyes.
Cannot we delude the eyes
Of a few poore houshold spyes?

Or his easier eares beguile,
So remoued by our wile?
'Tis no sinne, loues fruit to steale,
But the sweet theft to reueale:
To be taken, to be seene,
These haue crimes accounted beene.

81

Delay

UPON ADVICE TO DEFER LOVES CONSUMMATION

Delay, whose parents Phlegm and Slumber are,
Thinkst thou two snails, drawing thy leaden car,
Can keep pace with the fiery wheels of Love's
Chariot, that receives motion from swift doves?
Go visit Fevers, such as conscience rack
With fear of punishment in death; there slack
The pulse, or dwell upon the fatal tongues
Of Judges, shut up their contagious lungs:
Thou mayst a gaol rejoice, but not decree
To Love's glad prisoners a jubilee.
How canst thou think thy frost with icy laws
Can bind my tears, when Love thy cold chain thaws?
He more intense for fighting ice will be,
And raise his heat unto the eighth degree.
Thus through thy coldness I shall fiercer burn,
And by thy winter into cinders turn.
    But since from Ignorance fears oft arise,
And thence are stol'n unequal victories,
Let us describe this foe, muster his force:
A handless thing it is, and chills the source
Of brave attempts. Eyes he pretends too much,
Yet our experience often shows that such
Exactness in surveying opes a gate
To be surpris'd by Semele's sad fate.
'Tis a mere trunk, hath not for progress feet;
Coward that fears his own desires to meet.
His friends are scarce; the Heavens, whose flight debates
The race with thought, are no confederates:

[71]

The world is love in act; suspend this fire,
The globe to its old Chaos will retire:
Infernal souls, but for his loathèd stay,
Might hope their night would open into day.
    How can this cripple then, not with one band,
Aided by Earth, Heaven, Hell, his power withstand,
Who hath of Earth, Heaven, Hell, the forces broke,
Impos'd on Neptune's self his scorching yoke?
But if thou need'st will haunt me, let thy mace
Arrest delight, when I my Love embrace.

82

Macheath.	Were I laid on *Greenland*'s Coast,
	And in my Arms embrac'd my Lass;
	Warm amidst eternal Frost,
	Too soon the Half Year's Night would pass.
Polly.	Were I sold on *Indian* Soil,
	Soon as the burning Day was clos'd,
	I could mock the sultry Toil,
	When on my Charmer's Breast repos'd.
Macheath.	And I would love you all the Day,
Polly.	Every Night would kiss and play,
Macheath.	If with me you'd fondly stray
Polly.	Over the Hills and far away.

Act Two

FOOL – ONLY TOUCH HER!

> . . . I cannot think
> The life and blood of love is ink.
>
> HAMMOND 'On the Infrequency of Celia's Letters'

> Ice may relent to water in a thaw;
> But stone made flesh Loves Chymistry ne're saw.
>
> HENRY KING 'Sonnet: The Double Rock'

> Lost if I steer.
>
> AUDEN 'The earth turns over . . .'

> Kind are her answers,
> But her performance keeps no day;
> Breaks time, as dancers
> From their own music when they stray.
>
> CAMPION

> Touch her! Reach across, just caress her with a finger on her cheek:
> fool, fool – only touch her!
>
> C. K. WILLIAMS 'Love: Shyness'

Importune me no more

When I was fair and young, and favour gracëd me
Of many was I sought, their mistress for to be:
But I did scorn them all, and answered them therefore,
    'Go, go, go, seek some otherwhere!
          Importune me no more!'

How many weeping eyes I made to pine with woe,
How many sighing hearts, I have no skill to show:
Yet I the prouder grew, and answered them therefore,
    'Go, go, go, seek some otherwhere!
          Importune me no more!'

Then spake fair Venus' son, that proud victorious boy
And said, 'Fine Dame, since that you be so coy,
I will so pluck your plumes that you shall say no more,
    "Go, go, go, seek some otherwhere!
          Importune me no more!"'

When he had spake these words, such change grew in my breast
That neither night nor day since that, I could take any rest.
Then, lo! I did repent that I had said before,
    'Go, go, go, seek some otherwhere!
          Importune me no more!'

84

To Cynthia

    Learn'd lapidaries say the diamond
    Bred in the mines and mountains of the East,
    Mixt with heaps of gold-ore is often found,
    In the half-bird's half-beast's, the Griphon's, nest,
    Is first pure water easy to be prest,
        Then ice, then crystal, which great length of time
        Doth to the hardest of all stones sublime.

I think they say the truth, for it may be,
And what they of the diamond have said,
My brightest Cynthia, may be prov'd by thee,
Who having liv'd so long, so chaste a maid,
Thy heart with any diamond being weigh'd,
    Is harder found, and colder than that stone,
    Thy first year's virgin-softness being gone.

For now it is become impenetrable,
And he that will, or form, or cut it, must
(If he to purchase such a gem be able)
Use a proportion of thy precious dust,
Although the valuation be unjust:
    That pains which men to pierce it must bestow,
    Will equal dear in price unto it grow.

But thou, it may be, wilt make this profession,
That diamonds are soft'ned with goats' blood,
And mollified by it will take impression.
This of slain lovers must be understood:
But trust me, dearest Cynthia, 'tis not good,
    Thy beauties so should lovers' minds perplex,
    As make them think thee Angel without sex.

85

Sonnet. The Double Rock

Since thou hast view'd some Gorgon, and art grown
        A solid stone:
To bring again to softness thy hard heart
        Is past my art.
Ice may relent to water in a thaw;
But stone made flesh Loves Chymistry ne're saw.

Therefore by thinking on thy hardness, I
        Will petrify;
And so within our double Quarryes Wombe,
        Dig our Loves Tombe.
Thus strangely will our difference agree;
And, with our selves, amaze the world, to see
How both Revenge and Sympathy consent
To make two Rocks each others Monument.

The Mower's Song

My Mind was once the true survey
Of all these Medows fresh and gay;
And in the greenness of the Grass
Did see its Hopes as in a Glass;
When *Juliana* came, and She
What I do to the Grass, does to my Thoughts and Me.

But these, while I with Sorrow pine,
Grew more luxuriant still and fine;
That none one Blade of Grass you spy'd,
But had a Flower on either side;
When *Juliana* came, and She
What I do to the Grass, does to my Thoughts and Me.

Unthankful Medows, could you so
A fellowship so true forego,
And in your gawdy May-games meet,
While I lay trodden under feet?
When *Juliana* came, and She
What I do to the Grass, does to my Thoughts and Me.

But what you in Compassion ought,
Shall now by my Revenge be wrought:
And Flowr's, and Grass, and I and all,
Will in one common Ruine fall.
For *Juliana* comes, and She
What I do to the Grass, does to my Thoughts and Me.

And thus, ye Meadows, which have been
Companions of my thoughts more green,
Shall now the Heraldry become
With which I shall adorn my Tomb;
For *Juliana* comes, and She
What I do to the Grass, does to my Thoughts and Me.

Thrice toss these oaken ashes in the air.
Thrice sit thou mute in this enchanted chair.
Then thrice three times tie up this true love's knot,
And murmur soft: She will, or she will not.

Go burn these pois'nous weeds in yon blue fire,
These screech-owl's feathers and this prickling briar,
This cypress gathered at a dead man's grave,
That all thy fears and cares an end may have.

Then come, you fairies, dance with me a round;
Melt her hard heart with your melodious sound.
In vain are all the charms I can devise;
She hath an art to break them with her eyes.

88

Lord, when I think
What a paltry thing
Is a glove or a ring,
Or a top of a fan to brag of;
And how much a noddy
Will triumph in a busk-point,
Snatch with the tag off;
    Then I say:
Well fare him that hath ever used close play.

And when I see
What a pitiful grace
Hath a frown in the face,
Or a no in the lips of a lady;
And when I had wist
She would be kissed
When she away did go
    With hey ho;
    I end so:
Never trust any woman more than you know.

Hir face, Hir tong, Hir wit

Hir face,	Hir tong,	Hir wit,
So faire,	So sweete,	So sharpe,
First bent,	Then drew,	Then hit,
Mine eie,	Mine eare,	My hart.
Mine eie,	Mine eare	My hart,
To like,	To learne,	To loue,
Hir face,	Hir tong,	Hir wit,
Doth lead,	doth teach,	Doth moue.
Oh face,	Oh tong,	Oh wit,
With frownes,	With checke,	With smart,
Wrong not,	Vexe not,	Wound not,
Mine eie,	Mine eare,	My hart.
Mine eie,	Mine eare,	My hart,
To learne,	To knowe,	To feare,
Hir face,	Hir tong,	Hir wit,
Doth lead,	Doth teach,	Doth sweare.

90

Disdain me still, that I may ever love,
For who his Love enjoys, can love no more;
The war once past, with peace men cowards prove,
And ships returned do rot upon the shore:
    Then though thou frown, I'll say thou art most fair,
    And still I'll love, though still I must despair.

As heat's to life, so is desire to love,
For these once quenched, both life and love are done:
Let not my sighs, nor tears, thy virtue move;
Like basest metals, do not melt too soon.
    Laugh at my woes, although I ever mourn,
    Love surfeits with rewards, his nurse is scorn.

La Belle Dame Sans Merci

Oh, what can ail thee, knight-at-arms,
   Alone and palely loitering?
The sedge has withered from the lake,
   And no birds sing!

Oh, what can ail thee, knight-at-arms,
   So haggard and so woe-begone?
The squirrel's granary is full,
   And the harvest's done.

I see a lily on thy brow,
   With anguish moist and fever-dew,
And on thy cheek a fading rose
   Fast withereth too.

I met a lady in the meads
   Full beautiful, a fairy's child,
Her hair was long, her foot was light,
   And her eyes were wild.

I made a garland for her head,
   And bracelets too, and fragrant zone;
She looked at me as she did love,
   And made sweet moan.

I set her on my pacing steed,
   And nothing else saw all day long;
For sidelong would she bend, and sing
   A fairy's song.

She found me roots of relish sweet,
   And honey wild, and manna dew;
And sure in language strange she said,
   'I love thee true'.

She took me to her elfin grot,
    And there she wept, and sighed full sore,
And there I shut her wild wild eyes
    With kisses four.

And there she lullèd me asleep,
    And there I dreamed – Ah! woe betide! –
The latest dream I ever dreamed
    On the cold hill side.

I saw pale kings, and princes too,
    Pale warriors, death-pale were they all;
They cried – 'La belle Dame sans merci
    Hath thee in thrall!'

I saw their starved lips in the gloam
    With horrid warning gapèd wide,
And I awoke, and found me here
    On the cold hill side.

And this is why I sojourn here,
    Alone and palely loitering,
Though the sedge is withered from the lake,
    And no birds sing.

92

The Deposition

Though when I lov'd thee thou wert fair,
    Thou art no longer so,
Those glories all the pride they wear
    Unto Opinion ow;
Beauties, like stars, in borrow'd lustre shine,
    And 'twas my Love that gave thee thine.

The flames that dwelt within thine eye,
    Do now, with mine, expire;
Thy brightest Graces fade, and die
    At once with my desire;
Loves fires thus mutual influence return,
    Thine cease to shine, when mine to burn.

Then (proud *Celinda*) hope no more
To bee implor'd or woo'd;
Since by thy scorn thou dost restore
The wealth my love bestow'd;
And thy despis'd Disdain too late shall find
That none are fair but who are kind.

93
Night and Day

VERSE

Like the beat beat beat of the tom-tom
When the jungle shadows fall,
Like the tick tick tock of the stately clock
As it stands against the wall,
Like the drip drip drip of the raindrops
When the sum'r show'r is through,
So a voice within me keeps repeating
You – You – You.

REFRAIN

Night and day you are the one,
Only you beneath the moon and under the sun,
Whether near to me or far
It's no matter, darling, where you are,
I think of you, night and day.
Day and night, why is it so
That this longing for you follows wherever I go?
In the roaring traffic's boom,
In the silence of my lonely room,
I think of you, night and day.
Night and day under the hide of me
There's an, oh, such a hungry yearning burning inside of me,
And its torment won't be through
Till you let me spend my life making love to you
Day and night, night and day.

94
Politics

In our time the destiny of man presents
its meaning in political terms.
THOMAS MANN

How can I, that girl standing there,
My attention fix
On Roman or on Russian
Or on Spanish politics?
Yet here's a travelled man that knows
What he talks about,
And there's a politician
That has read and thought,
And maybe what they say is true
Of war and war's alarms,
But O that I were young again
And held her in my arms!

95

You say you love, but with a voice
    Chaster than a nun's who singeth
The soft Vespers to herself
    While the chime-bell ringeth –
        Oh, love me truly!

You say you love, but then you smile
    Cold as sunrise in September,
As you were Saint Cupid's nun
    And kept his weeks of Ember.
        Oh, love me truly!

You say you love, but then your lips
    Coral-tinted teach no blisses
More than coral in the sea –
    They never pout for kisses.
        Oh, love me truly!

[83]

You say you love, but then your hand
    No soft squeeze for squeeze returneth,
It is like a statue's, dead –
    While mine to passion burneth.
        Oh, love me truly!

Oh, breathe a word or two of fire!
    Smile as if those words should burn me,
Squeeze as lovers should – oh, kiss
    And in thy heart inurn me!
        Oh, love me truly!

96

A Leave-taking

Let us go hence, my songs; she will not hear.
Let us go hence together without fear;
Keep silence now, for singing-time is over,
And over all old things and all things dear.
She loves not you nor me as all we love her.
Yea, though we sang as angels in her ear,
    She would not hear.

Let us rise up and part; she will not know.
Let us go seaward as the great winds go,
Full of blown sand and foam; what help is here?
There is no help, for all these things are so,
And all the world is bitter as a tear.
And how these things are, though ye strove to show,
    She would not know.

Let us go home and hence; she will not weep.
We gave love many dreams and days to keep,
Flowers without scent, and fruits that would not grow,
Saying 'If thou wilt, thrust in thy sickle and reap.'
All is reaped now; no grass is left to mow;
And we that sowed, though all we fell on sleep,
    She would not weep.

Let us go hence and rest; she will not love.
She shall not hear us if we sing hereof,
Nor see love's ways, how sore they are and steep.
Come hence, let be, lie still; it is enough.
Love is a barren sea, bitter and deep;
And though she saw all heaven in flower above,
      She would not love.

Let us give up, go down; she will not care.
Though all the stars made gold of all the air,
And the sea moving saw before it move
One moon-flower making all the foam-flowers fair;
Though all those waves went over us, and drove
Deep down the stifling lips and drowning hair,
      She would not care.

Let us go hence, go hence; she will not see.
Sing all once more together; surely she,
She too, remembering days and words that were,
Will turn a little toward us, sighing; but we,
We are hence, we are gone, as though we had not been there.
Nay, and though all men seeing had pity on me,
      She would not see.

97
Song

O Mary sing thy songs to me
Of love and beautys melody
My sorrows sink beneath distress
My deepest griefs are sorrowless
So used to glooms and cares am I
My tearless troubles seem as joy
O Mary sing thy songs to me
Of love and beautys melody

'To be beloved is all I need
And them I love are loved indeed'
The soul of woman is my shrine
And Mary made my songs divine
O for that time that happy time
To hear thy sweet Piana's chime
In music so divine and clear
That woke my soul in heaven to hear

But heaven itself without thy face
To me would be no resting place
And though the world was one delight
No joy would live but in thy sight
The soul of woman is my shrine
Then Mary make those songs divine
For music love and melody
Breath all of thee and only thee

98

The Indian Serenade

I arise from dreams of thee
In the first sweet sleep of night.
When the winds are breathing low,
And the stars are shining bright:
I arise from dreams of thee,
And a spirit in my feet
Hath led me – who knows how?
To thy chamber window, Sweet!

The wandering airs they faint
On the dark, the silent stream –
The Champak odours fail
Like sweet thoughts in a dream;
The nightingale's complaint,
It dies upon her heart; –
As I must on thine,
Oh, belovèd as thou art!

Oh lift me from the grass!
I die! I faint! I fail!
Let thy love in kisses rain
On my lips and eyelids pale.
My cheek is cold and white, alas!
My heart beats loud and fast; –
Oh! press it to thine own again,
Where it will break at last.

99

Wild nights! Wild nights!
Were I with thee,
Wild nights should be
Our luxury!

Futile the winds
To a heart in port, –
Done with the compass,
Done with the chart.

Rowing in Eden!
Ah! the sea!
Might I but moor
To-night in thee!

100

Bright star! Would I were steadfast as thou art –
    Not in lone splendour hung aloft the night
And watching, with eternal lids apart,
    Like nature's patient, sleepless eremite,
The moving waters at their priestlike task
    Of pure ablution round earth's human shores,
Or gazing on the new soft-fallen mask
    Of snow upon the mountains and the moors;
No – yet still steadfast, still unchangeable,
    Pillowed upon my fair love's ripening breast,
To feel for ever its soft fall and swell,
    Awake for ever in a sweet unrest,
Still, still to hear her tender-taken breath,
And so live ever – or else swoon to death.

101

The Mower to the Glo-Worms

Ye living Lamps, by whose dear light
The Nightingale does sit so late,
And studying all the Summer-night,
Her matchless Songs does meditate;

Ye Country Comets, that portend
No War, nor Prince's funeral,
Shining unto no higher end
Then to presage the Grasses fall;

Ye Glo-worms, whose officious Flame
To wandring Mowers shows the way,
That in the Night have lost their aim,
And after foolish Fires do stray;

Your courteous Lights in vain you wast,
Since *Juliana* here is come,
For She my Mind hath so displac'd
That I shall never find my home.

102

Kind are her answers,
But her performance keeps no day;
Breaks time, as dancers
From their own music when they stray.
All her free favours
And smooth words wing my hopes in vain.
O did ever voice so sweet but only feign?
Can true love yield such delay,
Converting joy to pain?

Lost is our freedom
When we submit to women so.
Why do we need them
When in their best they work our woe?
There is no wisdom
Can alter ends by Fate prefixed.
O why is the good of man with evil mixed?
Never were days yet called two,
But one night went betwixt.

103

Nobody's Chasing Me

REFRAIN 1

The breeze is chasing the zephyr,
The moon is chasing the sea,
The bull is chasing the heifer,
But nobody's chasing me.
The cock is chasing the chicken,
The pewee, some wee pewee,
The cat is taking a lickin',
But nobody's taking me.
Nobody wants to own me,
And I object.
Nobody wants to phone me,
Even collect.
The leopard's chasing the leopard,
The chimp, some champ chimpanzee,
The sheep is chasing the shepherd,
But nobody's chasing me.
Nobody,
Nobody's chasing me.

REFRAIN 2

The flood is chasing the levee,
The wolf is out on a spree,
The Ford is chasing the Chevy,
But nobody's chasing me.
The bee is chasing Hymettus,
The queen is chasing the bee,
The worm is chasing the lettuce,
But nobody's chasing me.
Each night I get the mirror
From off the shelf.
Each night I'm getting queerer,
Chasing myself.
Ravel is chasing Debussy,
The aphis chases the pea,
The gander's chasing the goosey,
But nobody's goosing me.
Nobody,
Nobody's chasing me.

REFRAIN 3

The rain's pursuing the roses,
The snow, the trim Christmas tree,
Big dough pursues Grandma Moses,
But no one's pursuing me.
While Isis chases Osiris,
And Pluto, Proserpine,
My doc is chasing my virus,
But nobody's chasing me.
I'd like to learn canasta
Yet how can I?
What wife without her masta
Can multiply?
The claims are almost a-mixin',
The hams are chasing TV,
The fox is chasing the vixen,
But nobody's vixin' me.
Nobody,
Nobody's chasing me.

The llama's chasing the llama,
Papa is chasing Mama,
Monsieur is chasing Madame,
But nobody's chasing moi.
The dove, each moment, is bolda,
The lark sings, 'Ich liebe dich,'
Tristan is chasing Isolda,
But nobody's chasing mich.
Although I may be Juno,
B'lieve it or not,
I've got a lot of you-know,
And you know what!
The snake with passion is shakin',
The pooch is chasing the flea,
The moose his love call is makin'
[*Sung with head cold*]
But dobody's baki'd be.
Dobody [*sneeze*],
Nobody's chasing me.

104

A Match

If love were what the rose is,
   And I were like the leaf,
Our lives would grow together
In sad or singing weather,
Blown fields or flowerful closes,
   Green pleasure or grey grief;
If love were what the rose is,
   And I were like the leaf.

If I were what the words are,
   And love were like the tune,
With double sound and single
Delight our lips would mingle,
With kisses glad as birds are
   That get sweet rain at noon;
If I were what the words are,
   And love were like the tune.

If you were life, my darling,
　　And I your love were death,
We'd shine and snow together
Ere March made sweet the weather
With daffodil and starling
　　And hours of fruitful breath;
If you were life, my darling,
　　And I your love were death.

If you were thrall to sorrow,
　　And I were page to joy,
We'd play for lives and seasons
With loving looks and treasons
And tears of night and morrow
　　And laughs of maid and boy;
If you were thrall to sorrow,
　　And I were page to joy.

If you were April's lady,
　　And I were lord in May,
We'd throw with leaves for hours
And draw for days with flowers,
Till day like night were shady
　　And night were bright like day;
If you were April's lady,
　　And I were lord in May.

If you were queen of pleasure,
　　And I were king of pain,
We'd hunt down love together,
Pluck out his flying-feather,
And teach his feet a measure,
　　And find his mouth a rein;
If you were queen of pleasure,
　　And I were king of pain.

The way I read a letter's this:
'Tis first I lock the door,
And push it with my fingers next,
For transport it be sure.

And then I go the furthest off
To counteract a knock;
Then draw my little letter forth
And softly pick its lock.

Then, glancing narrow at the wall,
And narrow at the floor,
For firm conviction of a mouse
Not exorcised before,

Peruse how infinite I am
To – no one that you know!
And sigh for lack of heaven, – but not
The heaven the creeds bestow.

On the Infrequency of Celia's Letters

Did not true love disdain to own
His spiritual duration,
From paper fuel, I might guess
Thy love and writing both surcease
Together; but I cannot think
The life and blood of love is ink;
Yet as when Phœbus leaves our coast,
(The surface bound with chains of frost,)
Life is sustain'd by coarse repast,
Such as in spring nauseates the taste;
So in my winter, whilst you shine
In the remotest tropic sign,
Stramineous food, paper and quill,
May fodder hungry love, until

He re-obtain solstitial hours,
To feast upon thy beauty's flowers.
    The wonders then of Nature we
Within ourselves will justify:
Or what monumental boast
The first world made, the latter lost:
Thy pointed flame shall constant 'bide
As an eternal pyramid;
The never-dying lamp of Urns
Revivèd in my bosom burns:
Th' attractive virtue of the North
Resembleth thy magnetic worth;
And from my scorcht heart, through mine eyes
Ætnean flashes shall arise:
We shall make good, when more unite,
The fable of Hermaphrodite:
The spring and harvest of our bliss
The ripe and budding orange is;
We little worlds shall thus rehearse
The wonders of the universe,
As a small watch keeps equal pace
With the vast Sun's impetuous race.

107

Love and Sleep

Lying asleep between the strokes of night
    I saw my love lean over my sad bed,
    Pale as the duskiest lily's leaf or head,
Smooth-skinned and dark, with bare throat made to bite,
Too wan for blushing and too warm for white,
    But perfect-coloured without white or red.
    And her lips opened amorously, and said –
I wist not what, saving one word – Delight.
And all her face was honey to my mouth,
    And all her body pasture to mine eyes;
        The long lithe arms and hotter hands than fire,
The quivering flanks, hair smelling of the south,
    The bright light feet, the splendid supple thighs
        And glittering eyelids of my soul's desire.

The Time Before You

The secret of movement
Is not the secret itself
But the movement
Of there being a secret.

For example, the movement
Of an accordion, which closes
On one side and opens
On the other.

Or your folding one arm
Against your pushing body   .
At the turn towards waking
Which is the full length

Of your dream. When
You look at me as a man
May look, it is like a break
Of real sky where one branch

Crosses its fellow, a brown leaf
Taking September into
A brown stone, or green
Under green, grass below trees.

You ask the difference
Between a green shadow
And a brown one? Here
Is a green answer.

I can only say
I feel that green shadow,
That short, morning shadow,
Through and through me,

With a sense of hair in a coil
Recoiling from the fingers
That held it, smoothing
Its darkness till it would seem

Like whatever it is furthest
From, one of those blonde
Napes velvety as leaves
With the tip pointed towards you.

By now you will have painted
The first of the sea fresh staring
Yellow and changed its name.
So that now I always hear

The sea in the wind, though
I like a wind in which
You hear the rain, however moist
With breath its mask may be.

And after last night's rain
I actually dreamed of you,
Falling asleep for that
Wild purpose, seeing

Your face through the floor
As all the light left
On the flat of a hand.
I wish they could hear

That we lived in one room
And littered a new poetry
Long after both doors, up
And downstairs, shut.

109

So shoots a star as doth my mistress glide
At midnight through my chamber, which she makes
Bright as the sky when moon and stars are spied,
Wherewith my sleeping eyes amazèd wake:
Which ope no sooner than herself she shuts
Out of my sight, away so fast she flies:
Which me in mind of my slack service puts;
For which all night I wake, to plague mine eyes.

Shoot, star, once more! and if I be thy mark
Thou shalt hit me, for thee I'll meet withal.
Let mine eyes once more see thee in the dark,
Else they, with ceaseless waking, out will fall:
   And if again such time and place I lose
   To close with thee, let mine eyes never close.

110

A Dream

   I met her in the leafy woods,
      Early a Summer's night;
   I saw her white teeth in the dark,
      There was no better light.

   Had she not come up close and made
      Those lilies their light spread,
   I had not proved her mouth a rose,
      So round, so fresh, so red.

   Her voice was gentle, soft and sweet,
      In words she was not strong;
   Yet her low twitter had more charm
      Than any full-mouthed song.

   We walked in silence to her cave,
      With but few words to say;
   But ever and anon she stopped
      For kisses on the way.

   And after every burning kiss
      She laughed and danced around;
   Back-bending, with her breasts straight up,
      Her hair it touched the ground.

   When we lay down, she held me fast,
      She held me like a leech;
   Ho, ho! I know what her red tongue
      Is made for, if not speech.

And what is this, how strange, how sweet!
    Her teeth are made to bite
The man she gives her passion to,
    And not to boast their white.

O night of Joy! O morning's grief!
    For when, with passion done,
Rocked on her breast I fell asleep,
    I woke, and lay alone.

III

Eurydice to Orpheus

A PICTURE BY LEIGHTON

But give them me, the mouth, the eyes, the brow!
Let them once more absorb me! One look now
    Will lap me round for ever, not to pass
Out of its light, though darkness lie beyond:
Hold me but safe again within the bond
    Of one immortal look! All woe that was,
Forgotten, and all terror that may be,
Defied, – no past is mine, no future: look at me!

112

Methought I saw my late espoused Saint
    Brought to me like *Alcestis* from the grave,
    Whom *Joves* great Son to her glad Husband gave,
    Rescu'd from death by force though pale and faint.
Mine as whom washt from spot of child-bed taint,
    Purification in the old Law did save,
    And such, as yet once more I trust to have
    Full sight of her in Heaven without restraint,
Came vested all in white, pure as her mind:
    Her face was vail'd, yet to my fancied sight,
    Love, sweetness, goodness, in her person shin'd
So clear, as in no face with more delight.
    But O as to embrace me she enclin'd
    I wak'd, she fled, and day brought back my night.

113

Of youth he singeth

In a herber green asleep whereas I lay,
The birds sang sweet in the middes of the day;
I dreamëd fast of mirth and play:
  In youth is pleasure, in youth is pleasure.

Methought I walked still to and fro,
And from her company I could not go;
But when I waked it was not so:
  In youth is pleasure, in youth is pleasure.

Therefore my heart is surely pight
Of her alone to have a sight,
Which is my joy and heart's delight:
  In youth is pleasure, in youth is pleasure.

114

And is it night? are they thine eyes that shine?
 Are we alone, and here? and here, alone?
May I come near, may I but touch thy shrine?
 Is jealousy asleep, and is he gone?
O Gods, no more! silence my lips with thine!
Lips, kisses, joys, hap, – blessings most divine!

Oh, come, my dear! our griefs are turned to night,
 And night to joys; night blinds pale envy's eyes;
Silence and sleep prepare us our delight;
 Oh, cease we then our woes, our griefs, our cries:
Oh, vanish words! words do but passions move;
O dearest life! joy's sweet! O sweetest love!

The Dreame

Deare love, for nothing lesse than thee
Would I have broke this happy dreame,
      It was a theame
For reason, much too strong for phantasie,
Therefore thou wakd'st me wisely; yet
My Dreame thou brok'st not, but continued'st it,
Thou art so truth, that thoughts of thee suffice,
To make dreames truths; and fables histories;
Enter these armes, for since thou thoughtst it best,
Not to dreame all my dreame, let's act the rest.

As lightning, or a Tapers light,
Thine eyes, and not thy noise wak'd mee;
      Yet I thought thee
(For thou lovest truth) an Angell, at first sight,
But when I saw thou sawest my heart,
And knew'st my thoughts, beyond an Angels art,
When thou knew'st what I dreamt, when thou knew'st when
Excesse of joy would wake me, and cam'st then,
I must confesse, it could not chuse but bee
Prophane, to thinke thee any thing but thee.

Comming and staying show'd thee, thee,
But rising makes me doubt, that now,
      Thou art not thou.
That love is weake, where feare's as strong as hee;
'Tis not all spirit, pure, and brave,
If mixture it of *Feare, Shame, Honor*, have.
Perchance as torches which must ready bee,
Men light and put out, so thou deal'st with mee,
Thou cam'st to kindle, goest to come; Then I
Will dreame that hope againe, but else would die.

The Antiplatonic

For shame, thou everlasting wooer,
Still saying grace and never falling to her!
Love that's in contemplation placed
Is Venus drawn but to the waist.
Unless your flame confess its gender,
And your parley cause surrender,
Y' are salamanders of a cold desire
That live untouched amidst the hottest fire.

What though she be a dame of stone,
The widow of Pygmalion,
As hard and unrelenting she
As the new-crusted Niobe,
Or (what doth more of statue carry)
A nun of the Platonic quarry?
Love melts the rigour which the rocks have bred –
A flint will break upon a feather-bed.

For shame, you pretty female elves,
Cease for to candy up your selves;
No more, you sectarics of the game,
No more of your calcining flame!
Women commence by Cupid's dart
As a king hunting dubs a hart.
Love's votaries enthral each other's soul,
Till both of them live but upon parole.

Virtue's no more in womankind
But the green-sickness of the mind;
Philosophy (their new delight)
A kind of charcoal appetite.
There's no sophistry prevails
Where all-convincing love assails,
But the disputing petticoat will warp,
As skilful gamesters are to seek at sharp.

The soldier, that man of iron,
Whom ribs of horror all environ,
That's strung with wire instead of veins,
In whose embraces you're in chains,
Let a magnetic girl appear,
Straight he turns Cupid's cuirassier.
Love storms his lips, and takes the fortress in,
For all the bristled turnpikes of his chin.

Since love's artillery then checks
The breastworks of the firmest sex,
Come, let us in affections riot;
Th' are sickly pleasures keep a diet.
Give me a lover bold and free,
Not eunuched with formality,
Like an ambassador that beds a queen
With the nice caution of a sword between.

117
The Scales

The proper scale would pat you on the head
But Alice showed her pup Ulysses' bough
Well from behind a thistle, wise with dread;

And though your gulf-sprung mountains I allow
(Snow-puppy curves, rose-solemn dado band)
Charming for nurse, I am not nurse just now.

Why pat or stride them, when the train will land
Me high, through climbing tunnels, at your side,
And careful fingers meet through castle sand.

Claim slyly rather that the tunnels hide
Solomon's gems, white vistas, preserved kings,
By jackal sandhole to your air flung wide.

Say (she suspects) to sea Nile only brings
Delta and indecision, who instead
Far back up country does enormous things.

We met but in one giddy dance,
    Good-night joined hands with greeting;
And twenty thousand things may chance
    Before our second meeting:
For oh! I have been often told
    That all the world grows older,
And hearts and hopes, to-day so cold,
    To-morrow must be colder.

If I have never touched the string
    Beneath your chamber, dear one,
And never said one civil thing
    When you were by to hear one, –
If I have made no rhymes about
    Those looks which conquer Stoics,
And heard those angel tones, without
    One fit of fair heroics, –

Yet do not, though the world's cold school
    Some bitter truths has taught me,
O do not deem me quite the fool
    Which wiser friends have thought me!
There is one charm I still could feel,
    If no one laughed at feeling;
One dream my lute could still reveal, –
    If it were worth revealing.

But Folly little cares what name
    Of friend or foe she handles,
When merriment directs the game,
    And midnight dims the candles;
I know that Folly's breath is weak
    And would not stir a feather;
But yet I would not have her speak
    Your name and mine together.

Oh no! this life is dark and bright,
    Half rapture and half sorrow;
My heart is very full to-night,
    My cup shall be to-morrow:
But they shall never know from me,
    On any one condition,
Whose health made bright my Burgundy,
    Whose beauty was my vision!

119

A little pretty bonny lass was walking
    In midst of May before the sun gan rise.
I took her by the hand and fell to talking
    Of this and that, as best I could devise.
I swore I would, yet still she said I should not
Do what I would, and yet for all I could not.

120

Intimates

Don't you care for my love? she said bitterly.

I handed her the mirror, and said:
Please address these questions to the proper person!
Please make all requests to head-quarters!
In all matters of emotional importance
please approach the supreme authority direct! –
So I handed her the mirror.

And she would have broken it over my head,
but she caught sight of her own reflection
and that held her spellbound for two seconds
while I fled.

First Night

Electrodes attached to a flautist's cheeks:
a measure of nerves, his fear of the performance.

You move the fifty-seven muscles it takes to smile.
It's strange to see you again. A faint tan

is like dust on your memory, a shade or two,
numbers along the spectrum of available paints . . .

A freshness about your eyes suggests you are
newly hatched, like Eve, in an unfamiliar world.

I cross my legs, and watch the twitch of reflex –
Plato's great longing, my foot helplessly kicking space.

Love: Shyness

By tucking her chin in toward her chest, she can look up darkly through
    her lashes at him,
that look of almost anguished vulnerability and sensitivity, a soft,
    near-cry of help,
the implication of a deeply privileged and sole accessibility . . . yours
    alone, yours, yours alone,
but he's so flagrantly uncertain of himself, so clearly frightened, that he
    edges into comedy:
though everybody at the party is aware she's seducing him, he doesn't
    seem to understand;
he diddles with his silly mustache, grins and gawks, gabbles away
    around her about this and that.
Now she's losing interest, you can see it; she starts to glance away, can't
    he see it? Fool!
Touch her! Reach across, just caress her with a finger on her cheek: fool,
    fool – only touch her!

The Farmer's Bride

Three Summers since I chose a maid,
Too young maybe – but more's to do
At harvest-time than bide and woo.
    When us was wed she turned afraid
Of love and me and all things human;
Like the shut of a winter's day.
Her smile went out, and 'twasn't a woman –
    More like a little frightened fay.
        One night, in the Fall, she runned away.

'Out 'mong the sheep, her be,' they said,
'Should properly have been abed;
But sure enough she wasn't there
Lying awake with her wide brown stare.
So over seven-acre field and up-along across the down
We chased her, flying like a hare
Before our lanterns. To Church-Town
    All in a shiver and a scare
We caught her, fetched her home at last
    And turned the key upon her, fast.

She does the work about the house
As well as most, but like a mouse:
    Happy enough to chat and play
    With birds and rabbits and such as they,
    So long as men-folk keep away.
'Not near, not near!' her eyes beseech
When one of us comes within reach.
    The women say that beasts in stall
    Look round like children at her call.
    I've hardly heard her speak at all.
Shy as a leveret, swift as he,
Straight and slight as a young larch tree,
Sweet as the first wild violets, she
To her wild self. But what to me?

The days shorten and the oaks are brown,
    The blue smoke rises to the low gray sky,
One leaf in the still air falls slowly down,
    A magpie's spotted feather lie
On the black earth spread white with rime,
The berries redden up to Christmas-time.
    What's Christmas-time without there be
    Some other in the house than we!

    She sleeps up in the attic there
    Alone, poor maid. 'Tis but a stair
Betwixt us. Oh! my God! the down,
The soft young down of her, the brown,
The brown of her – her eyes, her hair, her hair . . .

124

Inapprehensiveness

We two stood simply friend-like side by side,
Viewing a twilight country far and wide,
Till she at length broke silence. 'How it towers
Yonder, the ruin o'er this vale of ours!
The West's faint flare behind it so relieves
Its rugged outline – sight perhaps deceives,
Or I could almost fancy that I see
A branch wave plain – belike some wind-sown tree
Chance-rooted where a missing turret was.
What would I give for the perspective glass
At home, to make out if 'tis really so!
Has Ruskin noticed here at Asolo
That certain weed-growths on the ravaged wall
Seem' . . . something that I could not say at all,
My thought being rather – as absorbed she sent
Look onward after look from eyes distent
With longing to reach Heaven's gate left ajar –
'Oh fancies that might be, oh, facts that are!
What of a wilding? By you stands, and may
So stand unnoticed till the Judgment Day,
One who, if once aware that your regard
Claimed what his heart holds, – woke, as from its sward

The flower, the dormant passion, so to speak –
Then what a rush of life would startling wreak
Revenge on your inapprehensive stare
While, from the ruin and the West's faint flare,
You let your eyes meet mine, touch what you term
Quietude – that's an universe in germ –
The dormant passion needing but a look
To burst into immense life!'
                              'No, the book
Which noticed how the wall-growths wave' said she
'Was not by Ruskin.'
                    I said 'Vernon Lee?'

125

To a Lady who sent me a copy of verses
at my going to bed

Lady, your art or wit could ne'er devise
To shame me more than in this night's surprise.
Why, I am quite unready, and my eye
Now winking like my candle, doth deny
To guide my hand, if it had aught to write;
Nor can I make my drowsy sense indite
Which by your verses' music (as a spell
Sent from the Sybellean Oracle)
Is charm'd and bound in wonder and delight,
Faster than all the leaden chains of night.

    What pity is it then you should so ill
Employ the bounty of your flowing quill,
As to expend on him your bedward thought,
Who can acknowledge that large love in nought
But this lean wish; that fate soon send you those
Who may requite your rhymes with midnight prose?

    Meantime, may all delights and pleasing themes
Like masquers revel in your maiden dreams,
Whilst dull to write, and to do more unmeet,
I, as the night invites me, fall asleep.

O fond, but fickle and untrue,
Ianthe take my last adieu.
Your heart one day will ask you why
You forced from me this farewell sigh.
Have you not feign'd that friends reprove
The mask of Friendship worn by Love?
Feign'd, that they whisper'd you should be
The same to others as to me?
Ah! little knew they what they said!
How would they blush to be obey'd!
   Too swiftly roll'd the wheels when last
These woods and airy downs we past.
Fain would we trace the winding path,
And hardly wisht for blissful Bath.
At every spring you caught my arm,
And every pebble roll'd alarm.
On me was turn'd that face divine,
The view was on the right so fine:
I smiled . . . those conscious eyes withdrew . . .
The left was now the finer view.
Each trembled for detected wiles,
And blushes tinged our fading smiles.
But Love turns Terror into jest . . .
We laught, we kist, and we confest.
Laugh, kisses, confidence are past,
And Love goes too . . . but goes the last.

127

Respectability

Dear, had the world in its caprice
   Deigned to proclaim 'I know you both,
   'Have recognized your plighted troth,
'Am sponsor for you: live in peace!' –
How many precious months and years
   Of youth had passed, that speed so fast,
   Before we found it out at last,
The world, and what it fears?

How much of priceless life were spent
   With men that every virtue decks,
   And women models of their sex,
Society's true ornament, –
Ere we dared wander, nights like this,
   Thro' wind and rain, and watch the Seine,
   And feel the Boulevart break again
To warmth and light and bliss?

I know! the world proscribes not love;
   Allows my finger to caress
   Your lips' contour and downiness,
Provided it supply a glove.
The world's good word! – the Institute!
   Guizot receives Montalembert!
   Eh? Down the court three lampions flare:
Put forward your best foot!

128

'I say I'll seek her'

I say, 'I'll seek her side
   Ere hindrance interposes;'
   But eve in midnight closes,
And here I still abide.

When darkness wears I see
   Her sad eyes in a vision;
   They ask, 'What indecision
Detains you, Love, from me? –

'The creaking hinge is oiled,
   I have unbarred the backway,
   But you tread not the trackway
And shall the thing be spoiled?

'Far cockcrows echo shrill,
   The shadows are abating,
   And I am waiting, waiting;
But O, you tarry still!'

Dîs Aliter Visum; or, le Byron de nos Jours

Stop, let me have the truth of that!
　Is that all true? I say, the day
Ten years ago when both of us
　Met on a morning, friends – as thus
We meet this evening, friends or what? –

Did you – because I took your arm
　And sillily smiled, 'A mass of brass
'That sea looks, blazing underneath!'
　While up the cliff-road edged with heath,
We took the turns nor came to harm –

Did you consider 'Now makes twice
　'That I have seen her, walked and talked
'With this poor pretty thoughtful thing,
　'Whose worth I weigh: she tries to sing;
'Draws, hopes in time the eye grows nice;

'Reads verse and thinks she understands;
　'Loves all, at any rate, that's great,
'Good, beautiful; but much as we
　'Down at the bath-house love the sea,
'Who breathe its salt and bruise its sands:

'While . . . do but follow the fishing-gull
　'That flaps and floats from wave to cave!
'There's the sea-lover, fair my friend!
　'What then? Be patient, mark and mend!
'Had you the making of your scull?'

And did you, when we faced the church
　With spire and sad slate roof, aloof
From human fellowship so far,
　Where a few graveyard crosses are,
And garlands for the swallows' perch, –

Did you determine, as we stepped
    O'er the lone stone fence, 'Let me get
'Her for myself, and what's the earth
    'With all its art, verse, music, worth –
'Compared with love, found, gained, and kept?

'Schumann's our music-maker now;
    'Has his march-movement youth and mouth?
'Ingres's the modern man that paints;
    'Which will lean on me, of his saints?
'Heine for songs; for kisses, how?'

And did you, when we entered, reached
    The votive frigate, soft aloft
Riding on air this hundred years,
    Safe-smiling at old hopes and fears, –
Did you draw profit while she preached?

Resolving, 'Fools we wise men grow!
    'Yes, I could easily blurt out curt
'Some question that might find reply
    'As prompt in her stopped lips, dropped eye,
'And rush of red to cheek and brow:

'Thus were a match made, sure and fast,
    ''Mid the blue weed-flowers round the mound
'Where, issuing, we shall stand and stay
    'For one more look at baths and bay,
'Sands, sea-gulls, and the old church last –

'A match 'twixt me, bent, wigged and lamed,
    'Famous, however, for verse and worse,
'Sure of the Fortieth spare Arm-chair
    'When gout and glory seat me there,
'So, one whose love-freaks pass unblamed, –

'And this young beauty, round and sound
    'As a mountain-apple, youth and truth
'With loves and doves, at all events
    'With money in the Three per Cents;
'Whose choice of me would seem profound: –

'She might take me as I take her.
    'Perfect the hour would pass, alas!
'Climb high, love high, what matter? Still,
    'Feet, feelings, must descend the hill:
'An hour's perfection can't recur.

'Then follows Paris and full time
    'For both to reason: "Thus with us!"
'She'll sigh, "Thus girls give body and soul
    '"At first word, think they gain the goal,
'"When 'tis the starting-place they climb!

'"My friend makes verse and gets renown;
    '"Have they all fifty years, his peers?
'"He knows the world, firm, quiet and gay;
    '"Boys will become as much one day:
'"They're fools; he cheats, with beard less brown.

'"For boys say, *Love me or I die!*
    '"He did not say, *The truth is, youth*
'"*I want, who am old and know too much;*
    '"*I'd catch youth: lend me sight and touch!*
'"*Drop heart's blood where life's wheels grate dry!*"

'While I should make rejoinder' – (then
    It was, no doubt, you ceased that least
Light pressure of my arm in yours)
    '"I can conceive of cheaper cures
'"For a yawning-fit o'er books and men.

'"What? All I am, was, and might be,
    '"All, books taught, art brought, life's whole strife,
'"Painful results since precious, just
    '"Were fitly exchanged, in wise disgust,
'"For two cheeks freshened by youth and sea?

'"All for a nosegay! – what came first;
    '"With fields on flower, untried each side;
'"I rally, need my books and men,
    '"And find a nosegay'": drop it, then,
'No match yet made for best or worst!'

That ended me. You judged the porch
   We left by, Norman; took our look
At sea and sky; wondered so few
   Find out the place for air and view;
Remarked the sun began to scorch;

Descended, soon regained the baths,
   And then, good-bye! Years ten since then:
Ten years! We meet: you tell me, now,
   By a window-seat for that cliff-brow,
On carpet-stripes for those sand-paths.

Now I may speak: you fool, for all
   Your lore! WHO made things plain in vain?
What was the sea for? What, the grey
   Sad church, that solitary day,
Crosses and graves and swallows' call?

Was there nought better than to enjoy?
   No feat which, done, would make time break,
And let us pent-up creatures through
   Into eternity, our due?
No forcing earth teach heaven's employ?

No wise beginning, here and now,
   What cannot grow complete (earth's feat)
And heaven must finish, there and then?
   No tasting earth's true food for men,
Its sweet in sad, its sad in sweet?

No grasping at love, gaining a share
   O' the sole spark from God's life at strife
With death, so, sure of range above
   The limits here? For us and love,
Failure; but, when God fails, despair.

This you call wisdom? Thus you add
   Good unto good again, in vain?
You loved, with body worn and weak;
   I loved, with faculties to seek:
Were both loves worthless since ill-clad?

Let the mere star-fish in his vault
    Crawl in a wash of weed, indeed,
Rose-jacynth to the finger-tips:
    He, whole in body and soul, outstrips
Man, found with either in default.

But what's whole, can increase no more,
    Is dwarfed and dies, since here's its sphere.
The devil laughed at you in his sleeve!
    You knew not? That I well believe;
Or you had saved two souls: nay, four.

For Stephanie sprained last night her wrist,
    Ankle or something. 'Pooh,' cry you?
At any rate she danced, all say,
    Vilely; her vogue has had its day.
Here comes my husband from his whist.

130
A Thunderstorm in Town

(A REMINISCENCE: 1893)

She wore a new 'terra-cotta' dress,
And we stayed, because of the pelting storm,
Within the hansom's dry recess,
Though the horse had stopped; yea, motionless
        We sat on, snug and warm.

Then the downpour ceased, to my sharp sad pain
And the glass that had screened our forms before
Flew up, and out she sprang to her door:
I should have kissed her if the rain
        Had lasted a minute more.

131

Once at Swanage

The spray sprang up across the cusps of the moon,
    And all its light loomed green
    As a witch-flame's weirdsome sheen
At the minute of an incantation scene;
And it greened our gaze – that night at demilune.

Roaring high and roaring low was the sea
    Behind the headland shores:
    It symboled the slamming of doors,
Or a regiment hurrying over hollow floors . . .
And there we two stood, hands clasped; I and she!

132

Faintheart in a Railway Train

At nine in the morning there passed a church,
At ten there passed me by the sea,
At twelve a town of smoke and smirch,
At two a forest of oak and birch,
    And then, on a platform, she:

A radiant stranger, who saw not me.
I said, 'Get out to her do I dare?'
But I kept my seat in my search for a plea,
And the wheels moved on. O could it but be
    That I had alighted there!

Natura Naturans

Beside me, – in the car, – she sat,
　　She spake not, no, nor·looked to me:
From her to me, from me to her,
　　What passed so subtly stealthily?
As rose to rose that by it blows
　　Its interchanged aroma flings;
Or wake to sound of one sweet note
　　The virtues of disparted strings.

Beside me, nought but this! – but this,
　　That influent as within me dwelt
Her life, mine too within her breast,
　　Her brain, her every limb she felt:
We sat; while o'er and in us, more
　　And more, a power unknown prevailed,
Inhaling, and inhaled, – and still
　　'Twas one, inhaling or inhaled.

Beside me, nought but this; – and passed;
　　I passed; and know not to this day
If gold or jet her girlish hair,
　　If black, or brown, or lucid-grey
Her eye's young glance: the fickle chance
　　That joined us, yet may join again;
But I no face again could greet
　　As hers, whose life was in me then.

As unsuspecting mere a maid
　　As, fresh in maidhood's bloomiest bloom,
In casual second-class did e'er
　　By casual youth her seat assume;
Or vestal, say, of saintliest clay,
　　For once by balmiest airs betrayed
Unto emotions too too sweet
　　To be unlingeringly gainsaid:

Unowning then, confusing soon
    With dreamier dreams that o'er the glass
Of shyly ripening woman-sense
    Reflected, scarce reflected, pass,
A wife may-be, a mother she
    In Hymen's shrine recalls not now,
She first in hour, ah, not profane,
    With me to Hymen learnt to bow.

Ah no! – Yet owned we, fused in one,
    The Power which e'en in stones and earths
By blind elections felt, in forms
    Organic breeds to myriad births;
By lichen small on granite wall
    Approved, its faintest feeblest stir
Slow-spreading, strengthening long, at last
    Vibrated full in me and her.

In me and her – sensation strange!
    The lily grew to pendent head,
To vernal airs the mossy bank
    Its sheeny primrose spangles spread,
In roof o'er roof of shade sun-proof
    Did cedar strong itself outclimb,
And altitude of aloe proud
    Aspire in floreal crown sublime;

Flashed flickering forth fantastic flies,
    Big bees their burly bodies swung,
Rooks roused with civic din the elms,
    And lark its wild reveillez rung;
In Libyan dell the light gazelle,
    The leopard lithe in Indian glade,
And dolphin, brightening tropic seas,
    In us were living, leapt and played:

Their shells did slow crustacea build,
    Their gilded skins did snakes renew,
While mightier spines for loftier kind
    Their types in amplest limbs outgrew;
Yea, close comprest in human breast,
    What moss, and tree, and livelier thing,
What Earth, Sun, Star of force possest,
    Lay budding, burgeoning forth for Spring.

Such sweet preluding sense of old
　　Led on in Eden's sinless place
The hour when bodies human first
　　Combined the primal prime embrace,
Such genial heat the blissful seat
　　In man and woman owned unblamed,
When, naked both, its garden paths
　　They walked unconscious, unashamed:

Ere, clouded yet in mistiest dawn,
　　Above the horizon dusk and dun,
One mountain crest with light had tipped
　　That Orb that is the Spirit's Sun;
Ere dreamed young flowers in vernal showers
　　Of fruit to rise the flower above,
Or ever yet to young Desire
　　Was told the mystic name of Love.

134

Slow Movement

Waking, he found himself in a train, andante,
With wafers of early sunlight blessing the unknown fields
And yesterday cancelled out, except for yesterday's papers
　　Huddling under the seat.

Is still very early, this is a slow movement;
The viola-player's hand like a fish in a glass tank
Rises, remains quivering, darts away
　　To nibble invisible weeds.

Great white nebulae lurch against the window
To deploy across the valley, the children are not yet up
To wave us on – we pass without spectators,
　　Braiding a voiceless creed.

And the girl opposite, name unknown, is still
Asleep and the colour of her eyes unknown
Which might be wells of sun or moons of wish
　　But it is still very early.

The movement ends, the train has come to a stop
In buttercup fields, the fiddles are silent, the whole
Shoal of silver tessellates the aquarium
    Floor, not a bubble rises . . .

And what happens next on the programme we do not know,
If, the red line topped on the gauge, the fish will go mad in the tank
Accelerando con forza, the sleeper open her eyes
    And, so doing, open ours.

135
The Robber Bridegroom

Turn back. Turn, young lady dear
A murderer's house you enter here

I was wooed and won little bird

(I have watched them come bright girls
Out of the rising sun, with curls)
The stair is tall the cellar deep
The wind coughs in the halls

I never wish to sleep

From the ceiling the sky falls
It will press you and press you, dear.

It is my desire to fear

(What a child! she desires her fear)
The house is whirling night, the guests
Grains of dust from the northwest

I do not come for rest

There is no rest for the dead

Ready for the couch of my groom

In a long room beneath the dew
Where the walls embrace and cling.

I wear my wedding ring

He will cut off your finger
And the blood will linger

Little bird!

136

Love and Murder

Strange that in 'crimes of passion' what results
Is women folded into trunks like suits,
Or chopped in handy joints to burn or lose,
Or sallowed with poison, puffed with sea,
Or turned into waistless parcels and bestowed
Under the fuel or the kitchen floor.

Perhaps those ardent murderers so prize
The flesh that it disturbs them not at all
To separate an ankle with an axe,
Or contemplate some leathern lady, long
Of the spare bedroom pungent occupant.
Love, after all, must overcome disgust.

We lesser amorists make do with girls
Prim or unfaithful, loud and ageing wives.
Loving too little to implant them deep
Within our guilty dreams where secretly
They would take off their green and purple clothes
To show the unchanging shamelessness of bone.

Porphyria's Lover

The rain set early in to-night,
　　The sullen wind was soon awake,
It tore the elm-tops down for spite,
　　And did its worst to vex the lake:
　　I listened with heart fit to break.
When glided in Porphyria; straight
　　She shut the cold out and the storm,
And kneeled and made the cheerless grate
　　Blaze up, and all the cottage warm;
　　Which done, she rose, and from her form
Withdrew the dripping cloak and shawl,
　　And laid her soiled gloves by, untied
Her hat and let the damp hair fall,
　　And, last, she sat down by my side
　　And called me. When no voice replied,
She put my arm about her waist,
　　And made her smooth white shoulder bare,
And all her yellow hair displaced,
　　And, stooping, made my cheek lie there,
　　And spread, o'er all, her yellow hair,
Murmuring how she loved me – she
　　Too weak, for all her heart's endeavour,
To set its struggling passion free
　　From pride, and vainer ties dissever,
　　And give herself to me for ever.
But passion sometimes would prevail,
　　Nor could to-night's gay feast restrain
A sudden thought of one so pale
　　For love of her, and all in vain:
　　So, she was come through wind and rain.
Be sure I looked up at her eyes
　　Happy and proud; at last I knew
Porphyria worshipped me; surprise
　　Made my heart swell, and still it grew
　　While I debated what to do.
That moment she was mine, mine, fair,
　　Perfectly pure and good: I found
A thing to do, and all her hair

In one long yellow string I wound
   Three times her little throat around,
And strangled her. No pain felt she;
   I am quite sure she felt no pain.
As a shut bud that holds a bee,
   I warily oped her lids: again
   Laughed the blue eyes without a stain.
And I untightened next the tress
   About her neck; her cheek once more
Blushed bright beneath my burning kiss:
   I propped her head up as before,
   Only, this time my shoulder bore
Her head, which droops upon it still:
   The smiling rosy little head,
So glad it has its utmost will,
   That all it scorned at once is fled,
   And I, its love, am gained instead!
Porphyria's love: she guessed not how
   Her darling one wish would be heard.
And thus we sit together now,
   And all night long we have not stirred,
   And yet God has not said a word!

138

The Mess of Love

We've made a great mess of love
since we made an ideal of it.

The moment I swear to love a woman, a certain woman, all my life
that moment I begin to hate her.

The moment I even say to a woman: I love you! –
my love dies down considerably.

The moment love is an understood thing between us, we are sure of it,
it's a cold egg, it isn't love any more.

Love is like a flower, it must flower and fade;
if it doesn't fade, it is not a flower,
it's either an artificial rag blossom, or an immortelle, for the cemetery.

The moment the mind interferes with love, or the will fixes on it,
or the personality assumes it as an attribute, or the ego takes possession
    of it,
it is not love any more, it's just a mess.
And we've made a great mess of love, mind-perverted, will-perverted,
    ego-perverted love.

139

The Primrose

Aske me why I send you here
This sweet *Infanta* of the yeere?
    Aske me why I send to you
This Primrose, thus bepearl'd with dew?
    I will whisper to your eares,
The sweets of Love are mixt with tears.

    Ask me why this flower do's show
So yellow-green, and sickly too?
    Ask me why the stalk is weak
And bending, (yet it doth not break?)
    I will answer, These discover
What fainting hopes are in a Lover.

140

Sure

Walking upstairs after breakfast
I looked round to see if you were following
And caught sight of you
Turning the corner with a tray
As I closed the bathroom door.

At the Wrong Door

A bank-manager's rapid signature
of hair on the bath enamel, twist
and tail, to confirm that I have missed
you by a minute; mat on the floor,

stamped vigorously with wet; your
absence palpable in the misty,
trickling, inexorcizable ghost
that occupies the whole mirror –

I cannot rub it away – the room
clings to me with such a perfume
of soap and sweat, that I can only

stop to think how somewhere else
you may be standing, naked, lonely,
amid a downfall of dampish towels.

Love in a Life

Room after room,
I hunt the house through
We inhabit together.
Heart, fear nothing, for, heart, thou shalt find her –
Next time, herself! – not the trouble behind her
Left in the curtain, the couch's perfume!
As she brushed it, the cornice-wreath blossomed anew:
Yon looking-glass gleamed at the wave of her feather.

Yet the day wears,
And door succeeds door;
I try the fresh fortune –
Range the wide house from the wing to the centre.
Still the same chance! she goes out as I enter.
Spend my whole day in the quest, – who cares?
But 'tis twilight, you see, – with such suites to explore,
Such closets to search, such alcoves to importune!

143

A Second Attempt

Thirty years after
I began again
An old-time passion:
And it seemed as fresh as when
The first day ventured on:
When mutely I would waft her
In Love's past fashion
Dreams much dwelt upon,
Dreams I wished she knew.

I went the course through,
From Love's fresh-found sensation –
Remembered still so well –
To worn words charged anew,
That left no more to tell:
Thence to hot hopes and fears,
And thence to consummation,
And thence to sober years,
Markless, and mellow-hued.

Firm the whole fabric stood,
Or seemed to stand, and sound
As it had stood before.
But nothing backward climbs,
And when I looked around
As at the former times,
There was Life – pale and hoar;
And slow it said to me,
'Twice-over cannot be!'

144

To One Unequally Matched

Bear it, O matcht unequally, you must,
And in your strength and virtue firmly trust.
The Power that rules our destinies decreed
One heart should harden and another bleed.

145

A Jeat Ring Sent

Thou art not so black, as my heart,
Nor halfe so brittle, as her heart, thou art;
What would'st thou say? shall both our properties by thee bee spoke,
Nothing more endlesse, nothing sooner broke?

Marriage rings are not of this stuffe;
Oh, why should ought lesse precious, or lesse tough
Figure our loves? Except in thy name thou have bid it say,
I'am cheap, and nought but fashion, fling me'away.

Yet stay with mee since thou art come,
Circle this fingers top, which did'st her thombe.
Be justly proud, and gladly safe, that thou dost dwell with me,
She that, Oh, broke her faith, would soon breake thee.

146

My Picture left in Scotland

I now thinke, Love is rather deafe, then blind,
For else it could not be,
That she,
Whom I adore so much, should so slight me,
And cast my love behind:
I'm sure my language to her, was as sweet,
And every close did meet
In sentence, of as subtile feet,
As hath the youngest Hee,
That sits in shadow of *Apollo's* tree.

Oh, but my conscious feares,
That flie my thoughts betweene,
Tell me that she hath seene
My hundred of gray haires,
Told seven and fortie years,
Read so much wast, as she cannot imbrace
My mountaine belly; and my rockie face,
And all these through her eyes, have stopt her eares.

The Definition of Love

My Love is of a birth as rare
As 'tis for object strange and high:
It was begotten by despair
Upon Impossibility.

Magnanimous Despair alone
Could show me so divine a thing,
Where feeble Hope could ne'r have flown
But vainly flapt its Tinsel Wing.

And yet I quickly might arrive
Where my extended Soul is fixt,
But Fate does Iron wedges drive,
And alwaies crouds it self betwixt.

For Fate with jealous Eye does see
Two perfect Loves; nor lets them close:
Their union would her ruine be,
And her Tyrannick pow'r depose.

And therefore her Decrees of Steel
Us as the distant Poles have plac'd,
(Though Loves whole World on us doth wheel)
Not by themselves to be embrac'd.

Unless the giddy Heaven fall,
And Earth some new Convulsion tear;
And, us to joyn, the World should all
Be cramp'd into a *Planisphere*.

As Lines so Loves *oblique* may well
Themselves in every Angle greet:
But ours so truly *Paralel*,
Though infinite can never meet.

Therefore the Love which us doth bind,
But Fate so enviously debarrs,
Is the Conjunction of the Mind,
And Opposition of the Stars.

Last Words to Miriam

Yours is the sullen sorrow,
    The disgrace is also mine;
Your love was intense and thorough,
Mine was the love of a growing flower
    For the sunshine.

You had the power to explore me,
    Blossom me stalk by stalk;
You woke my spirit, and bore me
To consciousness, you gave me the dour
    Awareness – then I suffered a balk.

Body to body I could not
    Love you, although I would.
We kissed, we kissed though we should not.
You yielded, we threw the last cast,
    And it was no good.

You only endured, and it broke
    My craftsman's nerve.
No flesh responded to my stroke;
So I failed to give you the last
    Fine torture you did deserve.

You are shapely, you are adorned
    But opaque and null in the flesh;
Who, had I but pierced with the thorned
Full anguish, perhaps had been cast
    In a lovely illumined mesh

Like a painted window; the best
    Fire passed through your flesh,
Undrossed it, and left it blest
In clean new awareness. But now
    Who shall take you afresh?

Now who will burn you free
    From your body's deadness and dross?
Since the fire has failed in me,
What man will stoop in your flesh to plough
    The shrieking cross?

A mute, nearly beautiful thing
    Is your face, that fills me with shame
As I see it hardening;
I should have been cruel enough to bring
    You through the flame.

149

Who so list to hount, I knowe where is an hynde,
    But as for me, helas, I may no more:
    The vayne travaill hath weried me so sore.
    I ame of theim that farthest commeth behinde;
Yet may I by no meanes my weried mynde
    Drawe from the Diere: but as she fleeth afore,
Faynting I folowe. I leve of therefore,
    Sins in a nett I seke to hold the wynde.
Who list her hount, I put him owte of dowbte,
    As well as I may spend his tyme in vain:
    And, graven with Diamonds, in letters plain
There is written her faier neck rounde abowte:
    Noli me tangere, for Cesars I ame;
    And wylde for to hold, though I seme tame.

150

Your body is stars whose million glitter here:
I am lost amongst the branches of this sky
Here near my breast, here in my nostrils, here
Where our vast arms like streams of fire lie.

How can this end? My healing fills the night
And hangs its flags in world I cannot near.
Our movements range through miles, and when we kiss
The moment widens to enclose long years.

*   *   *   *   *

Beholders of the promised dawn of truth
The explorers of immense and simple lines,
Here is our goal, men cried, but it was lost
Amongst the mountain mists and mountain pines.

So with this face of love, whose breathings are
A mystery shadowed on the desert floor:
The promise hangs, this swarm of stars and flowers,
And then there comes the shutting of a door.

151

The Buried Life

Light flows our war of mocking words, and yet,
Behold, with tears mine eyes are wet!
I feel a nameless sadness o'er me roll.
Yes, yes, we know that we can jest,
We know, we know that we can smile!
But there's a something in this breast,
To which thy light words bring no rest,
And thy gay smiles no anodyne.
Give me thy hand, and hush awhile,
And turn those limpid eyes on mine,
And let me read there, love! thy inmost soul.
Alas! is even love too weak
To unlock the heart, and let it speak?
Are even lovers powerless to reveal
To one another what indeed they feel?
I knew the mass of men concealed
Their thoughts, for fear that if revealed
They would by other men be met
With blank indifference, or with blame reproved;
I knew they lived and moved
Tricked in disguises, alien to the rest
Of men, and alien to themselves – and yet
The same heart beats in every human breast!

But we, my love! – doth a like spell benumb
Our hearts, our voices? must we too be dumb?

Ah! well for us, if even we,
Even for a moment, can get free
Our heart, and have our lips unchained;
For that which seals them hath been deep-ordained!

Fate, which foresaw
How frivolous a baby man would be –
By what distractions he would be possessed,
How he would pour himself in every strife,
And well-nigh change his own identity –
That it might keep from his capricious play
His genuine self, and force him to obey
Even in his own despite his being's law,
Bade through the deep recesses of our breast
The unregarded river of our life
Pursue with indiscernible flow its way;
And that we should not see
The buried stream, and seem to be
Eddying at large in blind uncertainty,
Though driving on with it eternally.

But often, in the world's most crowded streets,
But often, in the din of strife,
There rises an unspeakable desire
After the knowledge of our buried life;
A thirst to spend our fire and restless force
In tracking out our true, original course;
A longing to inquire
Into the mystery of this heart which beats
So wild, so deep in us – to know
Whence our lives come and where they go.
And many a man in his own breast then delves,
But deep enough, alas! none ever mines.
And we have been on many thousand lines,
And we have shown, on each, spirit and power;
But hardly have we, for one little hour,
Been on our own line, have we been ourselves –
Hardly had skill to utter one of all
The nameless feelings that course through our breast,
But they course on for ever unexpressed.
And long we try in vain to speak and act

Our hidden self, and what we say and do
Is eloquent, is well – but 'tis not true!
And then we will no more be racked
With inward striving, and demand
Of all the thousand nothings of the hour
Their stupefying power;
Ah yes, and they benumb us at our call!
Yet still, from time to time, vague and forlorn,
From the soul's subterranean depth upborne
As from an infinitely distant land,
Come airs, and floating echoes, and convey
A melancholy into all our day.
Only – but this is rare –
When a belovèd hand is laid in ours,
When, jaded with the rush and glare
Of the interminable hours,
Our eyes can in another's eyes read clear,
When our world-deafened ear
Is by the tones of a loved voice caressed –
A bolt is shot back somewhere in our breast,
And a lost pulse of feeling stirs again.
The eye sinks inward, and the heart lies plain,
And what we mean, we say, and what we would, we know.
A man becomes aware of his life's flow,
And hears its winding murmur; and he sees
The meadows where it glides, the sun, the breeze.

And there arrives a lull in the hot race
Wherein he doth for ever chase
That flying and elusive shadow, rest.
An air of coolness plays upon his face,
And an unwonted calm pervades his breast.
And then he thinks he knows
The hills where his life rose,
And the sea where it goes.

Coda

Maybe we knew each other better
When the night was young and unrepeated
And the moon stood still over Jericho.

So much for the past; in the present
There are moments caught between heart-beats
When maybe we know each other better.

But what is that clinking in the darkness?
Maybe we shall know each other better
When the tunnels meet beneath the mountain.

Act Three

ASK ME NO MORE

No more, dear love, for at a touch I yield;
Ask me no more.
TENNYSON *The Princess*

To enter in these bonds, is to be free.
DONNE 'To His Mistris Going To Bed'

the lightning and the rainbow appearing in us unbidden, unchecked
like ambassadors.
LAWRENCE 'Manifesto'

Who could ask for anything more?
IRA GERSHWIN 'I Got Rhythm'

Because what if I'm 60 years old and not married,
all alone in a furnished room with pee stains on my underwear
and everyone else is married! All the universe married but me!
GREGORY CORSO 'Marriage'

Rosalind's Madrigal

Love in my bosom like a bee
   Doth suck his sweet;
Now with his wings he plays with me,
   Now with his feet.
Within mine eyes he makes his nest,
His bed amidst my tender breast;
My kisses are his daily feast,
And yet he robs me of my rest:
   Ah, wanton, will ye?

And if I sleep, then percheth he
   With pretty flight,
And makes his pillow of my knee
   The livelong night.
Strike I my lute, he tunes the string;
He music plays if so I sing;
He lends me every lovely thing;
Yet cruel he my heart doth sting:
   Whist, wanton, still ye!

Else I with roses every day
   Will whip you hence,
And bind you, when you long to play,
   For your offence.
I'll shut mine eyes to keep you in,
I'll make you fast it for your sin,
I'll count your power not worth a pin, –
Alas! what hereby shall I win
   If he gainsay me?

What if I beat the wanton boy
   With many a rod?
He will repay me with annoy,
   Because a god.
Then sit thou safely on my knee,
And let thy bower my bosom be;
Lurk in mine eyes, I like of thee.
O Cupid, so thou pity me,
   Spare not, but play thee!

O Cupid! monarch over kings,
Wherefore hast thou feet and wings?
It is to show how swift thou art,
When thou wound'st a tender heart!
Thy wings being clipped, and feet held still,
Thy bow so many could not kill.

It is all one, in Venus' wanton school,
Who highest sits, the wise man or the fool.
  Fools in love's college
  Have far more knowledge
  To read a woman over,
  Than a neat prating lover:
    Nay, 'tis confessed
    That fools please women best.

155

A Forked Radish

Small men make love on stilts, and hold their poise
A step or two; then tumble heavily.
Others dream up frail ladders to the stars:
They teeter at the end in empty sky.

Who strains the laces of his boots will fly
Sprawling to earth, lace broken, balance gone.
All fool themselves who wink at gravity,
And later hit the ground they should have won.

Wise to a body's pull, a few have done
Nothing but stand still, both feet on the ground.
These lovers grew together in the sun,
While a dark root a dark root gripped and bound.

The Author Apologizes to a Lady for His being a Little Man

Natura nusquam magis, quam in minimis tota est.
PLINY

Ολιγον τε φιλον τε.

HOMER

Yes, contumelious fair, you scorn
The amorous dwarf that courts you to his arms,
    But ere you leave him quite forlorn,
    And to some youth gigantic yield your charms,
  Hear him – oh hear him, if you will not try,
And let your judgment check th' ambition of your eye.

    Say, is it carnage makes the man?
  Is to be monstrous really to be great?
    Say, is it wise or just to scan
  Your lover's worth by quantity or weight?
  Ask your mamma and nurse, if it be so;
Nurse and mamma I ween shall jointly answer, no.

    The less the body to the view,
  The soul (like springs in closer durance pent)
    Is all exertion, ever new,
  Unceasing, unextinguish'd, and unspent;
  Still pouring forth executive desire,
As bright, as brisk, and lasting, as the vestal fire.

    Does thy young bosom pant for fame:
  Woud'st thou be of posterity the toast?
    The poets shall ensure thy name,
  Who magnitude of *mind* not *body* boast.
  Laurels on bulky bards as rarely grow,
As on the sturdy oak the virtuous mistletoe.

Look in the glass, survey that cheek –
Where FLORA has with all her roses blush'd;
The shape so tender, – look so meek –
The breasts made to be press'd, not to be crush'd –
Then turn to me, – turn with obliging eyes,
Nor longer nature's works, in miniature, despise.

Young AMMON did the world subdue,
Yet had not more external man than I;
Ah! charmer, should I conquer you,
With him in fame, as well as size, I'll vie.
Then, scornful nymph, come forth to yonder grove,
Where I defy, and challenge, all thy utmost love.

157

Against the Love of Great Ones

Vnhappy youth betrayd by Fate
To such a Love hath *Sainted Hate*,
And *damned* those *Celestiall* bands
Are onely knit with equal hands;
The Love of Great Ones? 'Tis a Love
Gods are incapable to prove;
For where there is a Joy uneven,
There never, never can be Heav'n:
'Tis such a Love as is not sent
To Fiends as yet for punishment;
Ixion willingly doth feele
The Gyre of his eternal wheele,
Nor would he now exchange his paine
For Cloudes and Goddesses againe.

Wouldst thou with tempests lye? Then bow
To th' rougher furrows of her brow;
Or make a Thunder-bolt thy Choyce?
Then catch at her more fatal Voyce;
Or 'gender with the Lightning? trye
The subtler Flashes of her eye:
Poore *Semele* wel knew the same,
Who both imbrac't her God and Flame;
And not alone in Soule did burne,
But in this Love did Ashes turne.

How il doth Majesty injoy
The Bow and Gaity oth' Boy,
As if the *Purple-roabe* should sit,
And sentence give ith' Chayr of *Wit*.

Say ever-dying wretch to whom
Each answer is a certaine dombe,
What is it that you would possesse,
The *Countes,* or the naked *Besse?*
Would you her *Gowne,* or *Title* do?
Her *Box,* or *Gem,* her *Thing* or *show?*
If you meane *Her,* the very *Her*
Abstracted from her caracter;
Unhappy Boy! you may as soone
With fawning wanton with the Moone,
Or with an amorous Complaint
Get prostitute your very Saint;
Not that we are not mortal, or
Fly *Venus* Altars, or abhor
The selfesame Knack for which you pine;
But we (defend us!) are divine,
Female, but Madam borne, and come
From a right-honourable Wombe:
Shal we then mingle with the base,
And bring a silver-tinsell race?
Whilst th' issue Noble wil not passe,
The Gold allayd (almost halfe brasse)
And th' blood in each veine doth appeare,
Part thick *Booreinn,* part *Lady* Cleare:
Like to the sordid Insects sprung
From Father *Sun,* and Mother *Dung;*
Yet lose we not the hold we have,
But faster graspe the trembling slave;
Play at Baloon with's heart, and winde
The strings like scaines, steale into his minde
Ten thousand *Hells,* and *feigned Joyes*
Far worse then they, whilst like whipt Boys,
After his scourge hee's hush with Toys.

This heard Sir, play stil in her eyes,
And be a dying Lives, like Flyes
Caught by their Angle-legs, and whom
The Torch laughs peece-meale to consume.

[141]

Loves Siege

Tis now since I sate down before
　　That foolish Fort, a heart,
(Time strangely spent) a Year, and more,
　　And still I did my part:

Made my approaches, from her hand
　　Unto her lip did rise,
And did already understand
　　The language of her eyes;

Proceeded on with no lesse Art,
　　My Tongue was Engineer:
I thought to undermine the heart
　　By whispering in the ear.

When this did nothing, I brought down
　　Great Canon-oaths, and shot
A thousand thousand to the Town,
　　And still it yeelded not.

I then resolv'd to starve the place
　　By cutting off all kisses,
Praysing and gazing on her face,
　　And all such little blisses.

To draw her out, and from her strength,
　　I drew all batteries in:
And brought my self to lie at length
　　As if no siege had been.

When I had done what man could do,
　　And thought the place mine owne,
The Enemy lay quiet too,
　　And smil'd at all was done.

I sent to know from whence, and where,
 These hopes, and this relief?
A Spie inform'd, Honour was there,
 And did command in chief.

March, march, (quoth I) the word straight give,
 Lets lose no time, but leave her:
That Giant upon ayre will live,
 And hold it out for ever.

To such a place our Camp remove
 As will no siege abide;
I hate a fool that starves her Love
 Onely to feed her pride.

159

Upon Love, by way of question and answer

I bring ye Love, *Quest.* What will love do?
 Ans. Like, and dislike ye:
I bring ye love: *Quest.* What will Love do?
 Ans. Stroake ye to strike ye.
I bring ye love: *Quest.* What will Love do?
 Ans. Love will be-foole ye:
I bring ye love: *Quest.* What will love do?
 Ans. Heate ye to coole ye:
I bring ye love: *Quest.* What will love do?
 Ans. Love gifts will send ye:
I bring ye love: *Quest.* What will love do?
 Ans. Stock ye to spend ye:
I bring ye love: *Quest.* What will love do?
 Ans. Love will fulfill ye:
I bring ye love: *Quest.* What will love do?
 Ans. Kisse ye, to kill ye.

160

To the Tune –
'Once I lov'd a Maiden Fair,' &c.

Fair one! if thus kind you be,
Yet intend a slaughter,
Faith, you'll lose your pains with me,
Elsewhere seek hereafter:
Though your looks be sharp, and quick,
Think not (pray) to drill me;
Love, perchance, may make me sick,
But will never kill me.

Were my mistress ne'er so brown,
Yet, if kind, I'd prize her;
Who's most fair, if she but frown,
I shall soon despise her:
I love kindness, and not face;
Who scorns me, I hate her:
Courtesy gives much more grace,
In my mind, than feature.

Red and white adorn the cheek
Less by far, than smiling;
That's the beauty I most seek,
That charm's most beguiling.
Fair one! now you know my mind
See if th' humour take you;
I shall love you, whilst y' are kind;
When y' are not, forsake you.

161

Listen, mad girl! for giving ear
    May save the eyes hard work:
Tender is he who holds you dear,
    But proud as pope or Turk.

Some have been seen, whom people thought
    Much prettier girls than you . . .
Setting a lover's tears at nought,
    Like any other dew;

And some too have been heard to swear,
    While with wet lids they stood,
No man alive was worth a tear . . .
    They never wept . . . nor would.

162

Natures lay Ideot, I taught thee to love,
And in that sophistrie, Oh, thou dost prove
Too subtile: Foole, thou didst not understand
The mystique language of the eye nor hand:
Nor couldst thou judge the difference of the aire
Of sighes, and say, this lies, this sounds despaire:
Nor by the'eyes water call a maladie
Desperately hot, or changing feaverously.
I had not taught thee then, the Alphabet
Of flowers, how they devisefully being set
And bound up, might with speechless secrecie
Deliver arrands mutely, and mutually.
Remember since all thy words us'd to bee
To every suitor; *I, if my friends agree*;
Since, household charmes, thy husbands name to teach,
Were all the love trickes, that thy wit could reach;
And since, an houres discourse could scarce have made
One answer in thee, and that ill arraid
In broken proverbs, and torne sentences.
Thou art not by so many duties his,
That from the worlds Common having sever'd thee,
Inlaid thee, neither to be seene, nor see,
As mine: who have with amorous delicacies
Refin'd thee'into a blis-full Paradise.
Thy graces and good words my creatures bee;
I planted knowledge and lifes tree in thee,
Which Oh, shall strangers taste? Must I alas
Frame and enamell Plate, and drinke in Glasse?
Chafe waxe for others seales? breake a colts force
And leave him then, beeing made a ready horse?

[145]

163

La Bella Bona Roba

I cannot tell who loves the Skeleton
Of a poor Marmoset, nought but boan, boan.
Give me a nakednesse with her cloath's on.

Such whose white-sattin upper coat of skin,
Cut upon Velvet rich Incarnadin,
Ha's yet a Body (and of Flesh) within.

Sure it is meant good Husbandry in men,
Who do incorporate with Aëry leane,
T' repair their sides, and get their Ribb agen.

Hard hap unto that Huntsman that Decrees
Fat joys for all his swet, when as he sees,
After his 'Say, nought but his Keepers Fees.

Then Love I beg, when next thou tak'st thy Bow,
Thy angry shafts, and dost Heart-chasing go,
Passe *Rascall Deare*, strike me the largest Doe.

164

Invitation to Juno

Lucretius could not credit centaurs;
Such bicycle he deemed asynchronous.
'Man superannuates the horse;
Horse pulses will not gear with ours.'

Johnson could see no bicycle would go;
'You bear yourself, and the machine as well.'
Gennets for germans sprang not from Othello,
And Ixion rides upon a single wheel.

Courage. Weren't strips of heart culture seen
Of late mating two periodicities?
Could not Professor Charles Darwin
Graft annual upon perennial trees?

A Song

Oh doe not wanton with those eyes,
    Lest I be sick with seeing;
Nor cast them downe, but let them rise,
    Lest shame destroy their being.
O, be not angry with those fires,
    For then their threats will kill me;
Nor looke too kind on my desires,
    For then my hopes will spill me.
O, doe not steepe them in thy Teares,
    For so will sorrow slay me;
Nor spread them as distract with feares,
    Mine owne enough betray me.

166

The Change

Love in her Sunny Eyes does basking play;
Love walks the pleasant Mazes of her Hair;
Love does on both her Lips for ever stray;
And *sows* and *reaps* a thousand *kisses* there.
In all her outward parts *Love*'s always seen;
    But, oh, He never went within.

Within *Love*'s foes, his greatest foes abide,
    Malice, Inconstancy, and Pride.
So the Earths face, Trees, Herbs, and Flowers do dress,
    With other beauties numberless:
But at the *Center*, *Darkness* is, and *Hell*;
There wicked *Spirits*, and there the *Damned* dwell.

With me alas, quite contrary it fares;
Darkness and *Death* lies in my weeping eyes,
Despair and Paleness in my face appears,
And Grief, and Fear, *Love*'s greatest Enemies;
But, like the *Persian-Tyrant*, *Love* within
    Keeps his proud *Court*, and ne're is seen.

Oh take *my Heart*, and by that means you'll prove
    Within, too stor'd enough of *Love*:
Give me but Yours, I'll by that change so thrive,
    That *Love* in all my parts shall live.
So powerful is this change, it render can,
My *outside Woman*, and your *inside Man*.

167

My Picture

Here, take my *Likeness* with you, whilst 'tis so;
    For when from hence you go,
    The next Suns rising will behold
    Me pale, and lean, and old.
    The Man who did this *Picture* draw,
Will swear next day my face he never saw.

I really believe, within a while,
    If you upon this *shadow* smile,
    Your *presence* will such vigour give,
    (Your *presence* which makes all things live)
    And *absence* so much alter *Me*,
This will the *substance*, *I* the *shadow* be.

When from your well-wrought *Cabinet* you take it,
    And your bright looks *awake it*;
    Ah be not frighted, if you see,
    The *new-soul'd Picture* gaze on Thee,
    And hear it breath a sigh or two;
For those are the first things that it will do.

My *Rival-Image* will be then thought blest,
    And laugh at me as dispossest;
    But *Thou*, who (if I know thee right)
    I'th' *substance* dost not much delight,
    Wilt rather send again for *Me*,
Who then shall but my *Pictures Picture* be.

168

from *Epipsychidion*

Spouse! Sister! Angel! Pilot of the Fate
Whose course has been so starless! O too late
Belovèd! O too soon adored, by me!
For in the fields of Immortality
My spirit should at first have worshipped thine,
A divine presence in a place divine;
Or should have moved beside it on this earth,
A shadow of that substance, from its birth;
But not as now: – I love thee; yes, I feel
That on the fountain of my heart a seal
Is set, to keep its waters pure and bright
For thee, since in those *tears* thou hast delight.
We – are we not formed, as notes of music are,
For one another, though dissimilar;
Such difference without discord, as can make
Those sweetest sounds, in which all spirits shake
As trembling leaves in a continuous air?

Thy wisdom speaks in me, and bids me dare
Beacon the rocks on which high hearts are wrecked.
I never was attached to that great sect,
Whose doctrine is, that each one should select
Out of the crowd a mistress or a friend,
And all the rest, though fair and wise, commend
To cold oblivion, though it is in the code
Of modern morals, and the beaten road
Which those poor slaves with weary footsteps tread,
Who travel to their home among the dead
By the broad highway of the world, and so
With one chained friend, perhaps a jealous foe,
The dreariest and the longest journey go.

[149]

True Love in this differs from gold and clay,
That to divide is not to take away.
Love is like understanding, that grows bright,
Gazing on many truths; 'tis like thy light,
Imagination! which from earth and sky,
And from the depths of human fantasy,
As from a thousand prisms and mirrors, fills
The Universe with glorious beams, and kills
Error, the worm, with many a sun-like arrow
Of its reverberated lightning. Narrow
The heart that loves, the brain that contemplates,
The life that wears, the spirit that creates
One object, and one form, and builds thereby
A sepulchre for its eternity.

169

The Canonization

For Godsake hold your tongue, and let me love,
   Or chide my palsie, or my gout,
My five gray haires, or ruin'd fortune flout,
     With wealth your state, your minde with Arts improve,
      Take you a course, get you a place,
      Observe his honour, or his grace,
Or the Kings reall, or his stamped face
   Contemplate, what you will, approve,
   So you will let me love.

Alas, alas, who's injur'd by my love?
   What merchants ships have my sighs drown'd?
Who saies my teares have overflow'd his ground?
     When did my colds a forward spring remove?
      When did the heats which my veines fill
      Adde one more to the plaguie Bill?
Soldiers finde warres, and Lawyers finde out still
   Litigious men, which quarrels move,
   Though she and I do love.

Call us what you will, wee are made such by love;
    Call her one, mee another flye,
We'are Tapers too, and at our owne cost die,
    And wee in us finde the'Eagle and the Dove.
        The Phœnix ridle hath more wit
        By us, we two being one, are it.
So to one neutrall thing both sexes fit,
    Wee dye and rise the same, and prove
    Mysterious by this love.

Wee can dye by it, if not live by love,
    And if unfit for tombes and hearse
Our legend bee, it will be fit for verse;
    And if no peece of Chronicle wee prove
        We'll build in sonnets pretty roomes;
        As well a well wrought urne becomes
The greatest ashes, as halfe-acre tombes,
    And by these hymnes, all shall approve
    Us *Canoniz'd* for Love:

And thus invoke us; You whom reverend love
    Made one anothers hermitage;
You, to whom love was peace, that now is rage;
    Who did the whole worlds soule contract, and drove
        Into the glasses of your eyes
        (So made such mirrors, and such spies,
That they did all to you epitomize,)
    Countries, Townes, Courts: Beg from above
    A patterne of your love!

170

La Toilette

The white towelling bathrobe
ungirdled, the hair still wet,
first coldness of the underbreast
like a ciborium in the palm.

Our bodies are the temples
of the Holy Ghost. Remember?
And the little, fitted, deep-slit drapes
on and off the holy vessels

regularly? And the chasuble
so deftly hoisted? But vest yourself
in the word you taught me
and the stuff I love: slub silk.

171

An Epicurean Ode

Since that this thing we call the world,
By chance on atoms is begot,
Which though in daily motions hurl'd,
     Yet weary not;
     How doth it prove,
Thou art so fair, and I in love?

Since that the soul doth only lie
Immers'd in matter, chain'd in sense,
How can, Romira, thou and I
     With both dispense?
     And thus ascend
In higher flights than wings can lend.

Since man's but pasted up of earth,
And ne'er was cradled in the skies,
What *terra lemnia* gave thee birth?
     What diamond, eyes?
     Or thou alone,
To tell what others were, came down?

A Last Confession

What lively lad most pleasured me
Of all that with me lay?
I answer that I gave my soul
And loved in misery,
But had great pleasure with a lad
That I loved bodily.

Flinging from his arms I laughed
To think his passion such
He fancied that I gave a soul
Did but our bodies touch,
And laughed upon his breast to think
Beast gave beast as much.

I gave what other women gave
That stepped out of their clothes,
But when this soul, its body off,
Naked to naked goes,
He it has found shall find therein
What none other knows,

And give his own and take his own
And rule in his own right:
And though it loved in misery
Close and cling so tight,
There's not a bird of day that dare
Extinguish that delight.

To his Scornful Mistress

Love in's first infant days had's wardrobe full;
Sometimes we found him courting in a Bull:
Then, drest in snowy plumes, his long neck is
Made pliable and fit to reach a kiss:
When aptest for embraces, he became
Either a winding snake, or curling flame:
And cunningly a pressing kiss to gain,
The Virgin's honour in a grape would stain:
When he consulted lawns for privacies,
The Shepherd, or his ram, was his disguise:
But the blood raging to a rape, put on
A Satyr, or a wilder stallion;
And for variety, in Thetis' court
Did like a dolphin with the Sea-nymph sport:
But since the sad barbarian yoke hath bow'd
The Grecian neck, Love hath less change allow'd:
Contracted lives in eyes; no flaming robes
Wears, but are lent him in your crystal globes:
Not worth a water'd garment, when he wears
That element he steals it from my tears.
A snake he is, alas! when folded in
Your frowns, where too much sting guards the fair skin:
A Shepherd unto cares, and only sips
The blushing grape of your Nectarean lips:
The Ram, Bull, Stallion, Satyrs only fight
Love's battles now in my wild appetite.
He in his Swan too suffers a restraint,
Cygnæan only in my dying plaint.
    Since all his actions Love to morals turns,
And faintly now in things less real burns,
In such a weakness contraries destroy,
And she his murd'ress is, who now is coy.

174

Hear, ye ladies that despise,
  What the mighty Love has done;
Fear examples, and be wise:
  Fair Calisto was a nun;
Leda, sailing on the stream,
  To deceive the hopes of man,
Love accounting but a dream,
  Doted on a silver swan;
    Danaë, in a brazen tower,
    Where no love was, loved a shower.

Hear, ye ladies that are coy,
  What the mighty Love can do;
Fear the fierceness of the boy:
  The chaste moon he makes to woo;
Vesta, kindling holy fires,
  Circled round about with spies,
Never dreaming loose desires,
  Doting at the altar dies;
    Ilion, in a short hour, higher
    He can build, and once more fire.

175

O whistle, and I'll come to ye, my lad,
O whistle, and I'll come to ye, my lad;
Tho' father, and mother, and a' should gae mad,
  Thy JEANIE will venture wi' ye, my lad.

But warily tent, when ye come to court me,
And come nae unless the back-yett be a-jee;
Syne up the back-style and let naebody see,
  And come as ye were na coming to me –
  And come as ye were na comin to me. –
    O whistle &c.

At kirk, or at market whene'er ye meet me,
Gang by me as tho' that ye car'd nae a flie;
But steal me a blink o' your bonie black e'e,
    Yet look as ye were na looking at me –
    Yet look as ye were na looking at me. –
      O whistle &c.

Ay vow and protest that ye care na for me,
And whyles ye may lightly my beauty a wee;
But court nae anither, tho' jokin ye be,
    For fear that she wyle your fancy frae me –
    For fear that she wyle your fancy frae me. –

176

In Three Days

So, I shall see her in three days
And just one night, but nights are short,
Then two long hours, and that is morn.
See how I come, unchanged, unworn!
Feel, where my life broke off from thine,
How fresh the splinters keep and fine, –
Only a touch and we combine!

Too long, this time of year, the days!
But nights, at least the nights are short.
As night shows where her one moon is,
A hand's-breadth of pure light and bliss,
So life's night gives my lady birth
And my eyes hold her! What is worth
The rest of heaven, the rest of earth?

O loaded curls, release your store
Of warmth and scent, as once before
The tingling hair did, lights and darks
Outbreaking into fairy sparks,
When under curl and curl I pried
After the warmth and scent inside,
Thro' lights and darks how manifold –
The dark inspired, the light controlled!
As early Art embrowns the gold.

What great fear, should one say, 'Three days
'That change the world might change as well
'Your fortune; and if joy delays,
'Be happy that no worse befell!'
What small fear, if another says,
'Three days and one short night beside
'May throw no shadow on your ways;
'But years must teem with change untried,
'With chance not easily defied,
'With an end somewhere undescried.'
No fear! – or if a fear be born
This minute, it dies out in scorn.
Fear? I shall see her in three days
And one night, now the nights are short,
Then just two hours, and that is morn.

177

Gallop apace, you fierie footed steedes,
Towards *Phœbus* lodging, such a wagoner
As *Phaetan* would whip you to the west,
And bring in clowdie night immediately.
Spread thy close curtaine loue-performing night,
That runnawayes eyes may wincke, and *Romeo*
Leape to these armes, vntalkt of and vnseene.
Louers can see to do their amorous rights,
By their owne bewties, or if loue be blind,
It best agrees with night, come ciuill night,
Thou sober suted matron all in blacke,
And learne me how to loose a winning match,
Plaide for a paire of stainlesse maydenhoods.
Hood my vnmand bloud bayting in my cheekes,
With thy blacke mantle, till strange loue grown bold,
Thinke true loue acted simple modestie:
Come night, come *Romeo*, come thou day in night,
For thou wilt lie vpon the winges of night,
Whiter then new snow on a Rauens backe:
Come gentle night, come louing black browd night,
Giue me my *Romeo*, and when I shall die,
Take him and cut him out in little starres,
And he will make the face of heauen so fine,

That all the world will be in loue with night,
And pay no worship to the garish Sun.
O I haue bought the mansion of a loue,
But not possest it, and though I am sold,
Not yet enioyd, so tedious is this day,
As is the night before some festiuall,
To an impatient child that hath new robes
And may not weare them.

178

Calypso

Dríver drive fáster and máke a good rún
Down the Springfield Line únder the shíning sún.

Flý like an aéroplane, dón't pull up shórt
Till you bráke for Grand Céntral Státion, New Yórk.

For thére in the míddle of thát waiting-háll
Should be stánding the óne that I love best of áll.

If he's nót there to méet me when Í get to tówn,
I'll stánd on the síde-walk with téars rolling dówn.

For hé is the óne that I lóve to look ón,
The ácme of kíndness and pérfectión.

He présses my hánd and he sáys he loves mé,
Which I fínd an admiráble pecúliaritý.

The wóods are bright gréen on both sídes of the líne;
The trées have their lóves though they're dífferent from míne.

But the póor fat old bánker in the sún-parlor cár
Has nó one to lóve him excépt his cigár.

If Í were the Héad of the Chúrch or the Státe,
I'd pówder my nóse and just téll them to wáit.

For lóve's more impórtant and pówerful thán
Éven a príest or a pólitición.

179

Meeting at Night

The grey sea and the long black land,
And the yellow half-moon large and low;
And the startled little waves that leap
In fiery ringlets from their sleep,
As I gain the cove with pushing prow,
And quench its speed i' the slushy sand.

Then a mile of warm sea-scented beach;
Three fields to cross till a farm appears;
A tap at the pane, the quick sharp scratch
And blue spurt of a lighted match,
And a voice less loud, thro' its joys and fears,
Than the two hearts beating each to each!

180

The Cold Kiss

Such icy kisses, anchorites that live
Secluded from the world, to dead skulls give;
And those cold maids on whom Love never spent
His flame, nor know what by desire is meant,
To their expiring fathers such bequeath,
Snatching their fleeting spirits in that breath:
The timorous priest doth with such fear and nice
Devotion touch the Holy Sacrifice.

Fie, Chariessa! whence so chang'd of late,
As to become in love a reprobate?
Quit, quit this dullness, Fairest, and make known
A flame unto me equal with mine own.
Shake off this frost, for shame, that dwells upon
Thy lips; or if it will not so be gone,
Let's once more join our lips, and thou shalt see
That by the flame of mine 'twill melted be.

For *Loves*-sake, kisse me once againe,
   I long, and should not beg in vaine,
Here's none to spie, or see;
     Why doe you doubt, or stay?
I'le taste as lightly as the Bee,
That doth but touch his flower, and flies away.
   Once more, and (faith) I will be gone,
   Can he that loves, aske lesse then one?
    Nay, you may erre in this,
     And all your bountie wrong:
This could be call'd but halfe a kisse.
What w'are but once to doe, we should doe long.
   I will but mend the last, and tell
   Where, how it would have relish'd well;
    Joyne lip to lip, and try:
     Each suck (the) others breath.
And whilst our tongues perplexed lie,
Let who will thinke us dead, or wish our death.

Come, let me take thee to my breast,
   And pledge we ne'er shall sunder;
And I shall spurn, as vilest dust,
   The warld's wealth and grandeur:
And do I hear my Jeanie own,
   That equal transports move her?
I ask for dearest life alone
   That I may live to love her.

Thus in my arms, wi' a' thy charms,
   I clasp my countless treasure;
I seek nae mair o' Heaven to share,
   Than sic a moment's pleasure:
And by thy een, sae bonie blue,
   I swear I'm thine for ever!
And on thy lips I seal my vow,
   And break it shall I never!

183
Her Mouth and Mine

As I lay dreaming, open-eyed,
With some one sitting at my side,
I saw a thing about to fly
Into my face, where it would lie;
For just above my head there stood
A smiling hawk as red as blood.
On which the bird, whose quiet nest
Has always been in my left breast,
Seeing that red hawk hovering there,
And smiling with such deadly care –
Flew fascinated to my throat,
And there it moaned a feeble note.
I saw that hawk, so red, and still,
And closed my eyes – it had its will:
For, uttering one triumphant croon,
It pounced with sudden impulse down;
And there I lay, no power to move,
To let it kiss or bite its love.
But in those birds – Ah, it was strange –
There came at last this other change:
That fascinated bird of mine
Worried the hawk and made it whine;
The hawk cried feebly – 'Oh dear, oh!
Greedy-in-love, leave go! Leave go!'

184
Kissing and bussing

Kissing and bussing differ both in this;
We busse our Wantons, but our Wives we kisse.

To the State of Love
Or the Senses' Festival

I saw a vision yesternight,
Enough to sate a Seeker's sight;
I wished myself a Shaker there,
And her quick pants my trembling sphere.
It was a she so glittering bright,
You'd think her soul an Adamite;
A person of so rare a frame,
Her body might be lined with' same.
Beauty's chiefest maid of honour,
You may break Lent with looking on her.
   Not the fair Abbess of the skies,
   With all her nunnery of eyes,
   Can show me such a glorious prize!

And yet, because 'tis more renown
To make a shadow shine, she's brown;
A brown for which Heaven would disband
The galaxy, and stars be tanned;
Brown by reflection as her eye
Deals out the summer's livery.
Old dormant windows must confess
Her beams; their glimmering spectacles,
Struck with the splendour of her face,
Do th' office of a burning-glass.
   Now where such radiant lights have shown,
   No wonder if her cheeks be grown
   Sunburned, with lustre of her own.

My sight took pay, but (thank my charms!)
I now impale her in mine arms;
(Love's compasses confining you,
Good angels, to a circle too.)
Is not the universe strait-laced
When I can clasp it in the waist?
My amorous folds about thee hurled,
With Drake I girdle in the world;
I hoop the firmament, and make
This, my embrace, the zodiac.
    How would thy centre take my sense
    When admiration doth commence
    At the extreme circumference?

Now to the melting kiss that sips
The jellied philtre of her lips;
So sweet there is no tongue can praise't
Till transubstantiate with a taste.
Inspired like Mahomet from above
By th' billing of my heavenly dove,
Love prints his signets in her smacks,
Those ruddy drops of squeezing wax,
Which, wheresoever she imparts,
They're privy seals to take up hearts.
    Our mouths encountering at the sport,
    My slippery soul had quit the fort,
    But that she stopped the sally-port.

Next to these sweets, her lips dispense
(As twin conserves of eloquence)
The sweet perfume her breath affords,
Incorporating with her words.
No rosary this vot'ress needs –
Her very syllables are beads;
No sooner 'twixt those rubies born,
But jewels are in ear-rings worn.
With what delight her speech doth enter;
It is a kiss o' th' second venter.
    And I dissolve at what I hear,
    As if another Rosamond were
    Couched in the labyrinth of my ear.

Yet that's but a preludious bliss,
Two souls pickeering in a kiss.
Embraces do but draw the line,
'Tis storming that must take her in.
When bodies join and victory hovers
'Twixt the equal fluttering lovers,
This is the game; make stakes, my dear!
Hark, how the sprightly chanticleer
(That Baron Tell-clock of the night)
Sounds boutesel to Cupid's knight.
    Then have at all, the pass is got,
    For coming off, oh, name it not!
    Who would not die upon the spot?

186

Darling Shell, where hast thou been,
What far regions hast thou seen;
From what pastimes art thou come:
Can we make amends at home?

Whether thou hast tuned the dance
    To the maids of ocean,
Know I not – but Ignorance
    Never hurts Devotion –

This I know, my darling Shell,
I shall ever love thee well,
Though too little to resound
While the Nereids dance around;

For, of all the shells that are,
    Thou art sure the brightest:
Thou, Ianthe's infant care,
    Most these eyes delightest –

Earlier to whose aid she owes
Teeth like budding snowdrop rows;
Teeth, whose love-incited pow'rs,
I have felt in happier hours.

On my shoulder, on my neck,
   Still the cherisht mark remains,
Well pourtray'd in many a speck
   Round thy smooth and quiet veins.

Who can wonder then, if thou
Hearest breathe my tender vow;
If thy lips, so pure, so bright,
Are dim with kisses, day and night?

187

To Mrs K. T.
(Who asked him why he was dumb)

Stay, should I answer, Lady, then
In vain would be your question:
Should I be dumb, why then again
Your asking me would be in vain.
Silence nor speech, on neither hand,
Can satisfy this strange demand.
Yet, since your will throws me upon
This wished contradiction,
I'll tell you how I did become
So strangely, as you hear me, dumb.
   Ask but the chap-fallen Puritan;
'Tis zeal that tongue-ties that good man.
(For heat of conscience all men hold
Is th' only way to catch their cold.)
How should Love's zealot then forbear
To be your silenced minister?
Nay, your Religion which doth grant
A worship due to you, my Saint,
Yet counts it that devotion wrong
That does it in the Vulgar Tongue.
My ruder words would give offence
To such an hallowed excellence,
As th' English dialect would vary
The goodness of an Ave Mary.
   How can I speak that twice am checked
By this and that religious sect?

Still dumb, and in your face I spy
Still cause and still divinity.
As soon as blest with your salute,
My manners taught me to be mute.
For, lest they cancel all the bliss
You signed with so divine a kiss,
The lips you seal must needs consent
Unto the tongue's imprisonment.
My tongue in hold, my voice doth rise
With a strange E-la to my eyes,
Where it gets bail, and in that sense
Begins a new-found eloquence.

O listen with attentive sight
To what my pratling eyes indite!
Or, lady, since 'tis in your choice
To give or to suspend my voice,
With the same key set ope the door
Wherewith you locked it fast before.
Kiss once again, and when you thus
Have doubly been miraculous,
My Muse shall write with handmaid's duty
The Golden Legend of your beauty.

He whom his dumbness now confines
But means to speak the rest by signs.

I.C.

188

Alas! madame, for stelyng of a kysse,
    Have I so much your mynd then offended?
Have I then done so greuously amysse,
    That by no meanes it may be amended?
Then revenge you, and the next way is this:
    An othr kysse shall have my lyffe endid.
For to my mowth the first my hert did suck,
The next shall clene oute of my brest it pluck.

Jenny kiss'd me when we met,
   Jumping from the chair she sat in;
Time, you thief, who love to get
   Sweets into your list, put that in!
Say I'm weary, say I'm sad,
   Say that health and wealth have miss'd me,
Say I'm growing old, but add,
    Jenny kiss'd me.

190

In the Vaulted Way

In the vaulted way, where the passage turned
To the shadowy corner that none could see,
You paused for our parting, – plaintively;
Though overnight had come words that burned
My fond frail happiness out of me.

And then I kissed you, – despite my thought
That our spell must end when reflection came
On what you had deemed me, whose one long aim
Had been to serve you; that what I sought
Lay not in a heart that could breathe such blame.

But yet I kissed you; whereon you again
As of old kissed me. Why, why was it so?
Do you cleave to me after that light-tongued blow?
If you scorned me at eventide, how love then?
The thing is dark, Dear. I do not know.

191

Kisses Loathsome

I abhor the slimie kisse,
(Which to me most loathsome is.)
Those lips please me which are plac't
Close, but not too strictly lac't:
Yeilding I wo'd have them; yet
Not a wimbling Tongue admit:
What sho'd poking-sticks make there,
When the ruffe is set elsewhere?

192

I mun be married a Sunday;
I mun be married a Sunday;
Whosoever shall come that way,
I mun be married a Sunday.

Roister Doister is my name;
Roister Doister is my name;
A lusty brute I am the same;
I mun be married a Sunday.

Christian Custance have I found;
Christian Custance have I found;
A widow worth a thousand pound;
I mun be married a Sunday.

Custance is as sweet as honey;
Custance is as sweet as honey;
I her lamb, and she my coney;
I mun be married a Sunday.

When we shall make our wedding feast,
When we shall make our wedding feast,
There shall be cheer for man and beast,
I mun be married a Sunday.
      I mun be married a Sunday, &c.

Whan'll we be marry'd,
My ain dear Nicol o'Cod?
We'll be marry'd o' Monday,
An' is na the reason gude?
Will we be marry'd nae sooner,
My own dear Nicol o'Cod?
Wad ye be marry'd o' Sunday?
I think the auld runt be gane mad.

Whae'll we hae at the wadding,
My own dear Nicol o'Cod?
We'll hae father and mother,
An' is na the reason gude?
Will we na hae nae mae,
My ain dear Nicol o' Cod?
Wad ye hae a' the hail warld?
I think the auld runt be gane mad.

What'll we hae to the wadding,
My ain dear Nicol o'Cod?
We'll hae cheese and bread,
An' is na the reason gude?
Will we na hae nae mae,
My ain dear Nicol o'Cod?
Wad ye hae sack and canary?
I think the auld runt be gane mad.

Whan'll we gang to our bed,
My ain dear Nicol o'Cod?
We'll gang whan other folk gang,
An' is nae the reason gude?
Will we na gang nae sooner,
My ain dear Nicol o'Cod?
Wad ye gang at the sunsetting?
I think the auld runt be gane mad.

What will we do i' our bed,
My ain dear Nicol o'Cod?
We will kiss and clap,
An' is nae the reason gude?
Will we na do nae mae,
My ain dear Nicol o'Cod?
Wad ye do 't a' the night o'er?
I think the auld runt be gane mad.

194

Pot-Pourri from a Surrey Garden

Miles of pram in the wind and Pam in the gorse track,
   Coco-nut smell of the broom, and a packet of Weights
Press'd in the sand. The thud of a hoof on a horse-track –
    A horse-riding horse for a horse-track –
    Conifer county of Surrey approached
Through remarkable wrought-iron gates.

Over your boundary now, I wash my face in a bird-bath,
   Then which path shall I take? that over there by the pram?
Down by the pond! or – yes, I will take the slippery third path,
    Trodden away with gym shoes,
    Beautiful fir-dry alley that leads
To the bountiful body of Pam.

Pam, I adore you, Pam, you great big mountainous sports girl,
   Whizzing them over the net, full of the strength of five:
That old Malvernian brother, you zephyr and khaki shorts girl,
    Although he's playing for Woking,
    Can't stand up
To your wonderful backhand drive.

See the strength of her arm, as firm and hairy as Hendren's;
   See the size of her thighs, the pout of her lips as, cross,
And full of a pent-up strength, she swipes at the rhododendrons,
    Lucky the rhododendrons,
    And flings her arrogant love-lock
Back with a petulant toss.

Over the redolent pinewoods, in at the bathroom casement,
    One fine Saturday, Windlesham bells shall call:
Up the Butterfield aisle rich with Gothic enlacement,
        Licensed now for embracement,
        Pam and I, as the organ
Thunders over you all.

195

Hail Matrimony, made of Love!
To thy wide gates how great a drove
On purpose to be yok'd do come;
Widows and Maids and Youths also,
That lightly trip on beauty's toe,
Or sit on beauty's bum.

Hail fingerfooted lovely Creatures!
The females of our human natures,
Formèd to suckle all Mankind.
'Tis you that come in time of need,
Without you we should never breed,
Or any comfort find.

For if a Damsel's blind or lame,
Or Nature's hand has crook'd her frame,
Or if she's deaf, or is wall-eyed;
Yet, if her heart is well inclin'd,
Some tender lover she shall find
That panteth for a Bride.

The universal Poultice this,
To cure whatever is amiss
In Damsel or in Widow gay!
It makes them smile, it makes them skip;
Like birds, just curèd of the pip,
They chirp and hop away.

Then come, ye maidens! come, ye swains!
Come and be cur'd of all your pains
In Matrimony's Golden Cage –

Love from the North

I had a love in soft south land,
    Beloved through April far in May;
He waited on my lightest breath,
    And never dared to say me nay.

He saddened if my cheer was sad,
    But gay he grew if I was gay;
We never differed on a hair,
    My yes his yes, my nay his nay.

The wedding hour was come, the aisles
    Were flushed with sun and flowers that day;
I pacing balanced in my thoughts:
    'It's quite too late to think of nay.' –

My bridegroom answered in his turn,
    Myself had almost answered 'yea:'
When through the flashing nave I heard
    A struggle and resounding 'nay.'

Bridemaids and bridegroom shrank in fear,
    But I stood high who stood at bay:
'And if I answer yea, fair Sir,
    What man art thou to bar with nay?'

He was a strong man from the north,
    Light-locked, with eyes of dangerous grey:
'Put yea by for another time
    In which I will not say thee nay.'

He took me in his strong white arms,
    He bore me on his horse away
O'er crag, morass, and hairbreadth pass,
    But never asked me yea or nay.

He made me fast with book and bell,
    With links of love he makes me stay;
Till now I've neither heart nor power
    Nor will nor wish to say him nay.

Of the Marriage of the Dwarfs

Design, or chance, makes others wive:
But Nature did this match contrive;
Eve might as well have Adam fled,
As she denied her little bed
To him, for whom Heaven seemed to frame,
And measure out, this only dame.
　　Thrice happy is that humble pair,
Beneath the level of all care!
Over whose heads those arrows fly
Of sad distrust and jealousy;
Secured in as high extreme,
As if the world held none but them.
　　To him the fairest nymphs do show
Like moving mountains, topped with snow;
And every man a Polypheme
Does to his Galatea seem;
None may presume her faith to prove;
He proffers death that proffers love.
　　Ah, Chloris, that kind Nature thus
From all the world had severed us;
Creating for ourselves us two,
As love has me for only you!

A Nuptiall Song, or Epithalamie, on Sir Clipseby Crew *and his Lady*

What's that we see from far? the spring of Day
Bloom'd from the East, or faire Injewel'd May
　　Blowne out of April; or some New-
　　Star fill'd with glory to our view,
　　　　　　Reaching at heaven,
To adde a nobler Planet to the seven?
　　Say, or doe we not descrie
Some Goddesse, in a cloud of Tiffanie
　　　　To move, or rather the
　　Emergent *Venus* from the Sea?

'Tis she! 'tis she! or else some more Divine
Enlightned substance; mark how from the Shrine
    Of holy Saints she paces on,
    Treading upon *Vermilion*
                And *Amber*; Spice-
ing the Chaste Aire with fumes of Paradise.
    Then come on, come on, and yeeld
A savour like unto a blessed field,
           When the bedabled Morne
    Washes the golden eares of corne.

See where she comes; and smell how all the street
Breathes Vine-yards and Pomgranats: O how sweet!
    As a fir'd Altar, is each stone,
    Perspiring pounded Cynamon.
            The Phenix nest,
Built up of odours, burneth in her breast.
    Who therein wo'd not consume
His soule to Ash-heaps in that rich perfume?
           Bestroaking Fate the while
    He burnes to Embers on the Pile.

Himen, O Himen! Tread the sacred ground;
Shew thy white feet, and head with Marjoram crown'd:
    Mount up thy flames, and let thy Torch
    Display the Bridegroom in the porch,
            In his desires
More towring, more disparkling then thy fires:
    Shew her how his eyes do turne
And roule about, and in their motions burne
           Their balls to Cindars: haste,
    Or else to ashes he will waste.

Glide by the banks of Virgins then, and passe
The Shewers of Roses, lucky-foure-leav'd grasse:
    The while the cloud of younglings sing,
    And drown yee with a flowrie Spring:
           While some repeat
Your praise, and bless you, sprinkling you with Wheat:
    While that others doe divine;
Blest is the Bride, on whom the Sun doth shine;
           And thousands gladly wish
    You multiply, as doth a Fish.

And beautious Bride we do confess y'are wise,
In dealing forth these bashfull jealousies:
    In Lov's name do so; and a price
    Set on your selfe, by being nice:
          . But yet take heed;
What now you seem, be not the same indeed,
    And turne *Apostate*: Love will
Part of the way be met; or sit stone-still.
         On then, and though you slow-
    ly go, yet, howsoever, go.

And now y'are enter'd; see the Codled Cook
Runs from his *Torrid Zone*, to prie, and look,
    And blesse his dainty Mistresse: see,
    The Aged point out, This is she,
         Who now must sway
The House (Love shield her) with her Yea and Nay:
    And the smirk Butler thinks it
Sin, in's Nap'rie, not to express his wit;
        Each striving to devise
    Some gin, wherewith to catch your eyes.

To bed, to bed, kind Turtles, now, and write
This the short'st day, and this the longest night;
    But yet too short for you: 'tis we,
    Who count this night as long as three,
        Lying alone,
Telling the Clock strike Ten, Eleven, Twelve, One.
    Quickly, quickly then prepare;
And let the Young-men and the Bride-maids share
        Your Garters; and their joynts
    Encircle with the Bride-grooms Points.

By the Brides eyes, and by the teeming life
Of her green hopes, we charge ye, that no strife,
    (Farther then Gentlenes tends) gets place
    Among ye, striving for her lace:
        O doe not fall
Foule in these noble pastimes, lest ye call
    Discord in, and so divide
The youthfull Bride-groom, and the fragrant Bride:
        Which Love fore-fend; but spoken
    Be't to your praise, no peace was broken.

Strip her of Spring-time, tender-whimpring-maids,
Now *Autumne*'s come, when all those flowrie aids
  Of her Delayes must end; Dispose
  That *Lady-smock*, that *Pansie*, and that *Rose*
    Neatly apart;
But for *Prick-madam*, and for *Gentle-heart*;
  And soft-*Maidens-blush*, the Bride
Makes holy these, all others lay aside:
    Then strip her, or unto her
  Let him come, who dares undo her.

And to enchant yee more, see every where
About the Roofe a *Syren* in a Sphere;
  (As we think) singing to the dinne
  Of many a warbling *Cherubim*:
    O marke yee how
The soule of Nature melts in numbers: now
  See, a thousand *Cupids* flye,
To light their Tapers at the Brides bright eye.
    To Bed; or her they'l tire,
  Were she an Element of fire.

And to your more bewitching, see, the proud
Plumpe Bed beare up, and swelling like a cloud,
  Tempting the two too modest; can
  Yee see it brusle like a Swan,
    And you be cold
To meet it, when it woo's and seemes to fold
  The Armes to hugge it? throw, throw
Your selves into the mighty over-flow
    Of that white Pride, and Drowne
  The night, with you, in floods of Downe.

The bed is ready, and the maze of Love
Lookes for the treaders; every where is wove
  Wit and new misterie; read, and
  Put in practise, to understand
    And know each wile,
Each hieroglyphick of a kisse or smile;
  And do it to the full; reach
High in your own conceipt, and some way teach
    Nature and Art, one more
  Play then they ever knew before.

If needs we must for Ceremonies-sake,
Blesse a *Sack-posset*; Luck go with it; take
    The Night-Charme quickly; you have spells,
    And magicks for to end, and hells,
           To passe; but such
And of such Torture as no one would grutch
    To live therein for ever: Frie
And consume, and grow again to die,
        And live, and in that case,
    Love the confusion of the place.

But since It must be done, dispatch, and sowe
Up in a sheet your Bride, and what if so
    It be with Rock, or walles of Brasse,
    Ye Towre her up, as *Danae* was;
          Thinke you that this,
Or hell it selfe a powerfull Bulwarke is?
    I tell yee no; but like a
Bold bolt of thunder he will make his way,
        And rend the cloud, and throw
    The sheet about, like flakes of snow.

All now is husht in silence; *Midwife-moone*,
With all her *Owle-ey'd* issue begs a boon
    Which you must grant; that's entrance; with
    Which extract, all we can call pith
          And quintiscence
Of Planetary bodies; so commence
    All faire *Constellations*
Looking upon yee, That two Nations
        Springing from two such Fires,
    May blaze the vertue of their Sires.

Marriage

Should I get married? Should I be good?
Astound the girl next door with my velvet suit and faustus hood?
Don't take her to movies but to cemeteries
tell all about werewolf bathtubs and forked clarinets
then desire her and kiss her and all the preliminaries
and she going just so far and I understanding why
not getting angry saying You must feel! It's beautiful to feel!
Instead take her in my arms lean against an old crooked tombstone
and woo her the entire night the constellations in the sky –

When she introduces me to her parents
back straightened, hair finally combed, strangled by a tie,
should I sit knees together on their 3rd degree sofa
and not ask Where's the bathroom?
How else to feel other than I am,
often thinking Flash Gordon soap –
O how terrible it must be for a young man
seated before a family and the family thinking
We never saw him before! He wants our Mary Lou!
After tea and homemade cookies they ask What do you do for a living?

Should I tell them? Would they like me then?
Say All right get married, we're losing a daughter
but we're gaining a son –
And should I then ask Where's the bathroom?

O God, and the wedding! All her family and her friends
and only a handful of mine all scroungy and bearded
just wait to get at the drinks and food –
And the priest! he looking at me as if I masturbated
asking me Do you take this woman for your lawful wedded wife?
And I trembling what to say say Pie Glue!
I kiss the bride all those corny men slapping me on the back

She's all yours, boy! Ha-ha-ha!
And in their eyes you could see some obscene honeymoon going on –
Then all that absurd rice and clanky cans and shoes
Niagara Falls! Hordes of us! Husbands! Wives! Flowers! Chocolates!

All streaming into cozy hotels
All going to do the same thing tonight
The indifferent clerk he knowing what was going to happen
The lobby zombies they knowing what
The whistling elevator man he knowing
The winking bellboy knowing
Everybody knowing! I'd be almost inclined not to do anything!
Stay up all night! Stare that hotel clerk in the eye!
Screaming: I deny honeymoon! I deny honeymoon!
running rampant into those almost climactic suites
yelling Radio belly! Cat shovel!
O I'd live in Niagara forever! in a dark cave beneath the Falls
I'd sit there the Mad Honeymooner
devising ways to break marriages, a scourge of bigamy
a saint of divorce –

But I should get married I should be good
How nice it'd be to come home to her
and sit by the fireplace and she in the kitchen
aproned young and lovely wanting my baby
and so happy about me she burns the roast beef
and comes crying to me and I get up from my big papa chair
saying Christmas teeth! Radiant brains! Apple deaf!
God what a husband I'd make! Yes, I should get married!
So much to do! like sneaking into Mr Jones' house late at night
and cover his golf clubs with 1920 Norwegian books
Like hanging a picture of Rimbaud on the lawnmower
like pasting Tannu Tuva postage stamps all over the picket fence
like when Mrs Kindhead comes to collect for the Community Chest
grab her and tell her There are unfavorable omens in the sky!
And when the mayor comes to get my vote tell him
When are you going to stop people killing whales!
And when the milkman comes leave him a note in the bottle
Penguin dust, bring me penguin dust, I want penguin dust –

Yet if I should get married and it's Connecticut and snow
and she gives birth to a child and I am sleepless, worn,
up for nights, head bowed against a quiet window, the past behind me,
finding myself in the most common of situations a trembling man
knowledged with responsibility not twig-smear nor Roman coin soup –
O what would that be like!
Surely I'd give it for a nipple a rubber Tacitus

For a rattle a bag of broken Bach records
Tack Della Francesca all over its crib
Sew the Greek alphabet on its bib
And build for its playpen a roofless Parthenon

No, I doubt I'd be that kind of father
not rural not snow no quiet window
but hot smelly tight New York City
seven flights up, roaches and rats in the walls
a fat Reichian wife screeching over potatoes Get a job!
And five nose running brats in love with Batman
And the neighbors all toothless and dry haired
like those hag masses of the 18th century
all wanting to come in and watch TV
The landlord wants his rent
Grocery store Blue Cross Gas & Electric Knights of Columbus
Impossible to lie back and dream Telephone snow, ghost parking –
No! I should not get married I should never get married!
But – imagine If I were married to a beautiful sophisticated woman
tall and pale wearing an elegant black dress and long black gloves
holding a cigarette holder in one hand and a highball in the other
and we lived high up in a penthouse with a huge window
from which we could see all of New York and ever farther on clearer
    days
No, can't imagine myself married to that pleasant prison dream –

O but what about love? I forget love
not that I am incapable of love
it's just that I see love as odd as wearing shoes –
I never wanted to marry a girl who was like my mother
And Ingrid Bergman was always impossible
And there's maybe a girl now but she's already married
And I don't like men and –
but there's got to be somebody!
Because what if I'm 60 years old and not married,
all alone in a furnished room with pee stains on my underwear
and everybody else is married! All the universe married but me!

Ah, yet well I know that were a woman possible as I am possible
then marriage would be possible –
Like SHE in her lonely alien gaud waiting her Egyptian lover
so I wait – bereft of 2,000 years and the bath of life.

Whenas the rye reach to the chin,
And chopcherry, chopcherry ripe within,
Strawberries swimming in the cream,
And schoolboys playing in the stream;
Then oh, then oh, then oh, my true Love said,
Till that time come again
She could not live a maid.

201

Now

Out of your whole life give but a moment!
All of your life that has gone before,
All to come after it, – so you ignore,
So you make perfect the present, – condense,
In a rapture of rage, for perfection's endowment,
Thought and feeling and soul and sense –
Merged in a moment which gives me at last
You around me for once, you beneath me, above me –
Me – sure that despite of time future, time past,
This tick of our life-time's one moment you love me!
How long such suspension may linger? Ah, Sweet –
The moment eternal – just that and no more –
When ecstasy's utmost we clutch at the core
While cheeks burn, arms open, eyes shut and lips meet!

202

from *Maud*

I have led her home, my love, my only friend.
There is none like her, none.
And never yet so warmly ran my blood
And sweetly, on and on
Calming itself to the long-wished-for end,
Full to the banks, close on the promised good.

None like her, none.
Just now the dry-tongued laurels' pattering talk
Seemed her light foot along the garden walk,
And shook my heart to think she comes once more;
But even then I heard her close the door,
The gates of Heaven are closed, and she is gone.

There is none like her, none.
Nor will be when our summers have deceased.
O, art thou sighing for Lebanon
In the long breeze that streams to thy delicious East,
Sighing for Lebanon,
Dark cedar, though thy limbs have here increased,
Upon a pastoral slope as fair,
And looking to the South, and fed
With honeyed rain and delicate air,
And haunted by the starry head
Of her whose gentle will has changed my fate,
And made my life a perfumed altar-flame;
And over whom thy darkness must have spread
With such delight as theirs of old, thy great
Forefathers of the thornless garden, there
Shadowing the snow-limbed Eve from whom she came.

203

from *The Princess*

Ask me no more: the moon may draw the sea;
    The cloud may stoop from heaven and take the shape
    With fold to fold, of mountain or of cape;
But O too fond, when have I answered thee?
        Ask me no more.

Ask me no more: what answer should I give?
    I love not hollow cheek or faded eye:
    Yet, O my friend, I will not have thee die!
Ask me no more, lest I should bid thee live;
        Ask me no more.

Ask me no more: thy fate and mine are sealed:
  I strove against the stream and all in vain:
  Let the great river take me to the main:
No more, dear love, for at a touch I yield;
           Ask me no more.

204

from *The Princess*

'Now sleeps the crimson petal, now the white;
Nor waves the cypress in the palace walk;
Nor winks the gold fin in the porphyry font:
The fire-fly wakens: waken thou with me.

  Now droops the milkwhite peacock like a ghost,
And like a ghost she glimmers on to me.

  Now lies the Earth all Danaë to the stars,
And all thy heart lies open unto me.

  Now slides the silent meteor on, and leaves
A shining furrow, as thy thoughts in me.

  Now folds the lily all her sweetness up,
And slips into the bosom of the lake:
So fold thyself, my dearest, thou, and slip
Into my bosom and be lost in me.'

205

O sweet delight, O more than human bliss,
With her to live that ever loving is!
To hear her speak whose words so well are placed,
That she by them, as they in her, are graced;
Those looks to view that feast the viewer's eye,
How blest is he that may so live and die!

Such love as this the golden times did know,
When all did reap, yet none took care to sow.
Such love as this an endless summer makes,
And all distaste from frail affection takes.
So loved, so blest in my beloved am I,
Which till their eyes ache, let iron men envy.

206

Alysoun

Betwene March and Averil,
   When spray biginneth to springe,
The litel fowl hath hire wil
   On hire lud to singe.
   Ich libbe in love-longinge
   For semlokest of alle thinge;
   Heo may me blisse bringe –
     Ich am in hire baundòun.
     An hendy hap ich habbe y-hent;
     Ich'ot from hevene it is me sent;
     From alle wimmen my love is lent,
      And light on Alysoun.

On hew hire her is fair ynough,
   Hire browe browne, hire eye blake;
With lofsom chere heo on me lough,
   With middel smal and wel y-make.
   Bute heo me wille to hire take
   For to been hire owen make,
   Longe to liven ich'ille forsake,
     And feye fallen adown.
     An hendy hap, *etc.*

Nightes when I wende and wake –
   Forthy myn wonges waxeth won –
Levedy, al for thine sake
Longing is y-lent me on.
   In world n'is non so witer mon
   That al hire bounté telle con:
   Hire swire is whitere than the swon,
     And fairest may in town.
     An hendy hap, *etc.*

Ich am for wowing al forwake,
  Wery so water in wore,
Lest any reve me my make
  Ich habbe y-yirned yore.
Betere is tholien while sore
Than mournen evermore.
Gainest under gore,
  Herkne to my roun.
    An hendy hap, *etc.*

207

'S Wonderful

PETER

Life has just begun:
Jack has found his Jill.
Don't know what you've done,
But I'm all a-thrill.
How can words express
Your divine appeal?
You could never guess
All the love I feel.
From now on, lady, I insist,
For me no other girls exist.

REFRAIN

'S wonderful! 'S marvelous –
  You should care for me!
'S awful nice! 'S Paradise –
  'S what I love to see!
You've made my life so glamorous,
You can't blame me for feeling amorous.
  Oh, 's wonderful! 'S marvelous –
  That you should care for me!

Don't mind telling you,
In my humble fash,
That you thrill me through
With a tender pash.
When you said you care,
'Magine my emosh;
I swore, then and there,
Permanent devosh.
You made all other boys seem blah;
Just you alone filled me with AAH!

REFRAIN

'S wonderful! 'S marvelous –
   You should care for me!
'S awful nice! 'S Paradise –
   'S what I love to see!
My dear, it's four leaf clover time;
From now on my heart's working overtime.
   Oh, 's wonderful! 'S marvelous –
   That you should care for me!

208

A red red Rose

O my Luve's like a red, red rose,
   That's newly sprung in June;
O my Luve's like the melodie
   That's sweetly play'd in tune. –

As fair art thou, my bonie lass,
   So deep in luve am I;
And I will love thee still, my Dear,
   Till a' the seas gang dry. –

Till a' the seas gang dry, my Dear,
   And the rocks melt wi' the sun:
I will love thee still, my Dear,
   While the sands o' life shall run. –

And fare thee weel, my only Luve!
    And fare thee weel, a while!
And I will come again, my Luve,
    Tho' it were ten thousand mile! –

209
Field Work

I

Where the sally tree went pale in every breeze,
where the perfect eye of the nesting blackbird watched,
where one fern was always green

I was standing watching you
take the pad from the gatehouse at the crossing
and reach to lift a white wash off the whins.

I could see the vaccination mark
stretched on your upper arm, and smell the coal smell
of the train that comes between us, a slow goods,

waggon after waggon full of big-eyed cattle.

II

But your vaccination mark is on your thigh,
an O that's healed into the bark.

Except a dryad's not a woman
you are my wounded dryad

in a mothering smell of wet
and ring-wormed chestnuts.

Our moon was small and far,
was a coin long gazed at

brilliant on the *Pequod*'s mast
across Atlantic and Pacific waters.

[187]

Not the mud slick,
not the black weedy water
full of alder cones and pock-marked leaves.

Not the cow parsley in winter
with its old whitened shins and wrists,
its sibilance, its shaking.

Not even the tart green shade of summer
thick with butterflies
and fungus plump as a leather saddle.

No. But in a still corner,
braced to its pebble-dashed wall,
heavy, earth-drawn, all mouth and eye,

the sunflower, dreaming umber.

Catspiss smell,
the pink bloom open:
I press a leaf
of the flowering currant
on the back of your hand
for the tight slow burn
of its sticky juice
to prime your skin,
and your veins to be crossed
criss-cross with leaf-veins.
I lick my thumb
and dip it in mould,
I anoint the anointed
leaf-shape. Mould
blooms and pigments
the back of your hand
like a birthmark –
my umber one,
you are stained, stained
to perfection.

Light Behind the Rain

I

Come hugging your breasts
As if to comfort them,
Ripening in your armpit
Fingertip, knuckle-bone
And then, like a branch,
Canopy the windfalls.

II

You will reduce me to an eel
That drenches the stubble, inhales
The dew, a thorn in a puddle
Dimpling the water's membrane.

III

My shadow covers you,
The foxglove or harebell
Where insects go to sleep,
Or the pimpernel
That closes for a cloud.

IV

Implicate in your hair
Timorous featherbrains,
Headaches in the hedge,
Eggs warming and cooling
On cobwebs, thistledown,
White ones you pluck out.

To his Mistris Going to Bed

Come, Madam, come, all rest my powers defie,
Until I labour, I in labour lie.
The foe oft-times having the foe in sight,
Is tir'd with standing though he never fight.
Off with that girdle, like heavens Zone glistering,
But a far fairer world incompassing.
Unpin that spangled breastplate which you wear,
That th'eyes of busie fooles may be stopt there.
Unlace your self, for that harmonious chyme,
Tells me from you, that now it is bed time.
Off with that happy busk, which I envie,
That still can be, and still can stand so nigh.
Your gown going off, such beautious state reveals,
As when from flowry meads th'hills shadow steales.
Off with that wyerie Coronet and shew
The haiery Diademe which on you doth grow:
Now off with those shooes, and then safely tread
In this loves hallow'd temple, this soft bed.
In such white robes, heaven's Angels us'd to be
Receavd by men; Thou Angel bringst with thee
A heaven like Mahomets Paradice; and though
Ill spirits walk in white, we easly know,
By this these Angels from an evil sprite,
Those set our hairs, but these our flesh upright.
    Licence my roaving hands, and let them go,
Before, behind, between, above, below.
O my America! my new-found-land,
My kingdome, safeliest when with one man man'd,
My Myne of precious stones, My Emperie,
How blest am I in this discovering thee!
To enter in these bonds, is to be free;
Then where my hand is set, my seal shall be.
    Full nakedness! All joyes are due to thee,
As souls unbodied, bodies uncloth'd must be,
To taste whole joyes. Gems which you women use
Are like Atlanta's balls, cast in mens views,
That when a fools eye lighteth on a Gem,
His earthly soul may covet theirs, not them.

Like pictures, or like books gay coverings made
For lay-men, are all women thus array'd;
Themselves are mystick books, which only wee
(Whom their imputed grace will dignifie)
Must see reveal'd. Then since that I may know;
As liberally, as to a Midwife, shew
Thy self: cast all, yea, this white lynnen hence,
There is no pennance due to innocence.
    To teach thee, I am naked first; why then
What needst thou have more covering than a man.

212

The Source

*'The dead living in their memories are, I am persuaded,
the source of all that we call instinct.'*
                W. B. YEATS

Taking me into your body
you take me out of my own,
releasing an energy,
a spirit, not mine alone

but theirs locked in my cells.
One generation after
another, the blood rose and fell
that lifts us together.

Such ancient, undiminished
longings – my longing! Such
tenderness, such famished
desires! My fathers in search

of fulfilment storm through
my body, releasing now
loved women locked in you
and hungering to be found.

Love on the Farm

What large, dark hands are those at the window
Grasping in the golden light
Which weaves its way thorugh the evening wind
  At my heart's delight?

Ah, only the leaves! But in the west
I see a redness suddenly come
Into the evening's anxious breast –
  'Tis the wound of love goes home!

The woodbine creeps abroad
Calling low to her lover:
  The sun-lit flirt who all the day
  Has poised above her lips in play
  And stolen kisses, shallow and gay
  Of pollen, now has gone away –
  She woos the moth with her sweet, low word;
And when above her his moth-wings hover
Then her bright breast she will uncover
And yield her honey-drop to her lover.

Into the yellow, evening glow
Saunters a man from the farm below;
Leans, and looks in at the low-built shed
Where the swallow has hung her marriage bed.
  The bird lies warm against the wall.
  She glances quick her startled eyes
  Towards him, then she turns away
  Her small head, making warm display
  Of red upon the throat. Her terrors sway
  Her out of the nest's warm, busy ball,
  Whose plaintive cry is heard as she flies
  In one blue stoop from out the sties
  Into the twilight's empty hall.
Oh, water-hen, beside the rushes
Hide your quaintly scarlet blushes,
Still your quick tail, lie still as dead,
Till the distance folds over his ominous tread!

The rabbit presses back her ears,
Turns back her liquid, anguished eyes
And crouches low; then with wild spring
Spurts from the terror of *his* oncoming;
To be choked back, the wire ring
Her frantic effort throttling:
   Piteous brown ball of quivering fears!
Ah, soon in his large, hard hands she dies,
And swings all loose from the swing of his walk!
Yet calm and kindly are his eyes
And ready to open in brown surprise
Should I not answer to his talk
Or should he my tears surmise.

I hear his hand on the latch, and rise from my chair
Watching the door open; he flashes bare
His strong teeth in a smile, and flashes his eyes
In a smile like triumph upon me; then careless-wise
He flings the rabbit soft on the table board
And comes towards me: ah! the uplifted sword
Of his hand against my bosom! and oh, the broad
Blade of his glance that asks me to applaud
His coming! With his hand he turns my face to him
And caresses me with his fingers that still smell grim
Of the rabbit's fur! God, I am caught in a snare!
I know not what fine wire is round my throat;
I only know I let him finger there
My pulse of life, and let him nose like a stoat
Who sniffs with joy before he drinks the blood.

And down his mouth comes to my mouth! and down
His bright dark eyes come over me, like a hood
Upon my mind! his lips meet mine, and a flood
Of sweet fire sweeps across me, so I drown
Against him, die, and find death good.

Mark Antony

When as the nightingale chanted her vespers,
   And the wild forester couched on the ground,
Venus invited me in th' evening whispers
   Unto a fragrant field with roses crowned,
      Where she before had sent
      My wishes' compliment;
      Unto my heart's content
      Played with me on the green.
        Never Mark Antony
        Dallied more wantonly
        With the fair Egyptian Queen.

First on her cherry cheeks I mine eyes feasted,
   Thence fear of surfeiting made me retire;
Next on her warmer lips, which, when I tasted,
   My duller spirits made active as fire.
      Then we began to dart,
      Each at another's heart,
      Arrows that knew no smart,
      Sweet lips and smiles between.
        Never Mark, &c.

Wanting a glass to plait her amber tresses
   Which like a bracelet rich deckéd mine arm,
Gaudier than Juno wears when as she graces
   Jove with embraces more stately than warm,
      Then did she peep in mine
      Eyes' humour crystalline;
      I in her eyes was seen
      As if we one had been.
        Never Mark, &c.

Mystical grammar of amorous glances;
   Feeling of pulses, the physic of love;
Rhetorical courtings and musical dances;
   Numbering of kisses arithmetic prove;
     Eyes like astronomy;
     Straight-limbed geometry;
     In her art's ingeny
     Our wits were sharp and keen.
       Never Mark Antony
       Dallied more wantonly
       With the fair Egyptian Queen.

215

Kitty and I

The gentle wind that waves
   The green boughs here and there,
Is showing how my hand
   Waved Kitty's finer hair.

The Bee, when all his joints
   Are clinging to a Blossom,
Is showing how I clung
   To Kitty's softer bosom.

The Rill, when his sweet voice
   Is hushed by water-creases,
Is Kitty's sweeter voice
   Subdued by my long losses.

Those little stars that shine
   So happy in the skies,
Are those sweet babes I saw,
   Whose heaven was Kitty's eyes.

The Moon, that casts her beam
   Upon the hill's dark crest,
Is Kitty's whiter arm
   Across my hairy breast.

The hazel nuts, when paired
    Unseen beneath the boughs,
Are Kitty and myself,
    Whenever Chance allows.

216

The Good-morrow

I wonder by my troth, what thou, and I
Did, till we lov'd? were we not wean'd till then?
But suck'd on countrey pleasures, childishly?
Or snorted we in the seaven sleepers den?
T'was so; But this, all pleasures fancies bee.
If ever any beauty I did see,
Which I desir'd, and got, t'was but a dreame of thee.

And now good morrow to our waking soules,
Which watch not one another out of feare;
For love, all love of other sights controules,
And makes one little roome, an every where.
Let sea-discoverers to new worlds have gone,
Let Maps to other, worlds on worlds have showne,
Let us possesse one world, each hath one, and is one.

My face in thine eye, thine in mine appeares,
And true plaine hearts doe in the faces rest,
Where can we finde two better hemispheares
Without sharpe North, without declining West?
What ever dyes, was not mixt equally;
If our two loves be one, or, thou and I
Love so alike, that none doe slacken, none can die.

217
Manifesto

I

A woman has given me strength and affluence.
Admitted!
All the rocking wheat of Canada, ripening now,
has not so much of strength as the body of one woman
sweet in ear, nor so much to give
though it feed nations.

Hunger is the very Satan.
The fear of hunger is Moloch, Belial, the horrible God.
It is a fearful thing to be dominated by the fear of hunger.

Not bread alone, not the belly nor the thirsty throat.
I have never yet been smitten through the belly, with the lack of bread,
no, nor even milk and honey.

The fear of the want of these things seems to be quite left out of me.
For so much, I thank the good generations of mankind.

II

And the sweet, constant, balanced heat
of the suave sensitive body, the hunger for this
has never seized me and terrified me.
Here again, man has been good in his legacy to us, in these two primary
    instances.

Then the dumb, aching, bitter, helpless need,
the pining to be initiated,
to have access to the knowledge that the great dead
have opened up for us, to know, to satisfy
the great and dominant hunger of the mind;
man's sweetest harvest of the centuries, sweet, printed books,
bright, glancing, exquisite corn of many a stubborn
glebe in the upturned darkness;
I thank mankind with passionate heart
that I just escaped the hunger for these,
that they were given when I needed them,
because I am the son of man.

I have eaten, and drunk, and warmed and clothed my body,
I have been taught the language of understanding,
I have chosen among the bright and marvellous books,
like any prince, such stores of the world's supply
were open to me, in the wisdom and goodness of man.
So far, so good.
Wise, good provision that makes the heart swell with love!

But then came another hunger
very deep, and ravening;
the very body's body crying out
with a hunger more frightening, more profound
than stomach or throat or even the mind;
redder than death, more clamorous.

The hunger for the woman. Alas,
it is so deep a Moloch, ruthless and strong,
'tis like the unutterable name of the dread Lord,
not to be spoken aloud.
Yet there it is, the hunger which comes upon us,
which we must learn to satisfy with pure, real satisfaction;
or perish, there is no alternative.

I thought it was woman, indiscriminate woman,
mere female adjunct of what I was.
Ah, that was torment hard enough
and a thing to be afraid of,
a threatening, torturing, phallic Moloch.
A woman fed that hunger in me at last.
What many women cannot give, one woman can;
so I have known it.

She stood before me like riches that were mine.
Even then, in the dark, I was tortured, ravening, unfree,
Ashamed, and shameful, and vicious.
A man is so terrified of strong hunger;
and this terror is the root of all cruelty.
She loved me, and stood before me, looking to me.
How could I look, when I was mad? I looked sideways, furtively,
being mad with voracious desire.

V

This comes right at last.
When a man is rich, he loses at last the hunger fear.
I lost at last the fierceness that fears it will starve.
I could put my face at last between her breasts
and know that they were given for ever
that I should never starve,
never perish;
I had eaten of the bread that satisfies
and my body's body was appeased,
there was peace and richness,
fulfilment.

Let them praise desire who will,
but only fulfilment will do,
real fulfilment, nothing short.
It is our ratification,
our heaven, as a matter of fact.
Immortality, the heaven, is only a projection of this strange but actual
     fulfilment,
here in the flesh.

So, another hunger was supplied,
and for this I have to thank one woman,
not mankind, for mankind would have prevented me;
but one woman,
and these are my red-letter thanksgivings.

VI

To be, or not to be, is still the question.
This ache for being is the ultimate hunger.
And for myself, I can say 'almost, almost, oh, very nearly.'
Yet something remains.
Something shall not always remain.
For the main already is fulfilment.

What remains in me, is to be known even as I know.
I know her now: or perhaps, I know my own limitation against her.
Plunging as I have done, over, over the brink
I have dropped at last headlong into nought, plunging upon sheer hard
    extinction;
I have come, as it were, not to know,
died, as it were; ceased from knowing; surpassed myself.
What can I say more, except that I know what it is to surpass myself?

It is a kind of death which is not death.
It is going a little beyond the bounds.
How can one speak, where there is a dumbness on one's mouth?
I suppose, ultimately she is all beyond me,
she is all not-me, ultimately.

It is that that one comes to.
A curious agony, and a relief, when I touch that which is not me in any
    sense,
it wounds me to death with my own not-being; definite, inviolable
    limitation,
and something beyond, quite beyond, if you understand what that
    means.
It is the major part of being, this having surpassed oneself,
this having touched the edge of the beyond, and perished, yet not
    perished.

I want her though, to take the same from me.
She touches me as if I were herself, her own.
She has not realised yet, that fearful thing, that I am the other,
she thinks we are all of one piece.
It is painfully untrue.

I want her to touch me at last, ah, on the root and quick of my darkness
and perish on me as I have perished on her.

Then, we shall be two and distinct, we shall have each our separate
    being.
And that will be pure existence, real liberty.
Till then, we are confused, a mixture, unresolved, unextricated one from
    the other.
It is in pure, unutterable resolvedness, distinction of being, that one is
    free,
not in mixing, merging, not in similarity.
When she has put her hand on my secret, darkest sources, the darkest
    outgoings,
when it has struck home to her, like a death, 'this is *him*!'
she has no part in it, no part whatever,
it is the terrible *other*,
when she knows the fearful *other flesh*, ah, darkness unfathomable and
    fearful, contiguous and concrete,
when she is slain against me, and lies in a heap like one outside the
    house,
when she passes away as I have passed away,
being pressed up against the *other*,
then I shall be glad, I shall not be confused with her,
I shall be cleared, distinct, single as if burnished in silver,
having no adherence, no adhesion anywhere,
one clear, burnished, isolated being, unique,
and she also, pure, isolated, complete,
two of us, unutterably distinguished, and in unutterable conjunction.

    Then we shall be free, freer than angels, ah, perfect.

After that, there will only remain that all men detach themselves and
    become unique,
that we are all detached, moving in freedom more than the angels,
conditioned only by our own pure single being,
having no laws but the laws of our own being.

Every human being will then be like a flower, untrammelled.
Every movement will be direct.
Only to be will be such delight, we cover our faces when we think of it
lest our faces betray us to some untimely fiend.
Every man himself, and therefore, a surpassing singleness of mankind.
The blazing tiger will spring upon the deer, undimmed,
the hen will nestle over her chickens,
we shall love, we shall hate,
but it will be like music, sheer utterance,
issuing straight out of the unknown,
the lightning and the rainbow appearing in us unbidden, unchecked,
like ambassadors.

We shall not look before and after.
We shall *be, now.*
We shall know in full.
We, the mystic NOW.

218

I Got Rhythm

Days can be sunny,
    With never a sigh;
Don't need what money
    Can buy.

Birds in the tree sing
    Their dayful of song.
Why shouldn't we sing
    Along?

I'm chipper all the day,
    Happy with my lot.
How do I get that way?
    Look at what I've got:

I got rhythm,
I got music,
I got my man –
Who could ask for anything more?

I got daisies
In green pastures,
I got my man—
Who could ask for anything more?

Old Man Trouble,
I don't mind him –
You won't find him
    'Round my door.

I got starlight,
I got sweet dreams,
I got my man –
Who could ask for anything more –
Who could ask for anything more?

219

The Sunne Rising

Busie old foole, unruly Sunne,
    Why dost thou thus,
Through windowes, and through curtaines call on us?
Must to thy motions lovers seasons run?
    Sawcy pedantique wretch, goe chide
    Late school boyes, and sowre prentices,
  Goe tell Court-huntsmen, that the King will ride,
  Call countrey ants to harvest offices;
Love, all alike, no season knowes, nor clyme,
Nor houres, dayes, moneths, which are the rags of time.

Thy beames, so reverend, and strong
　　Why shouldst thou thinke?
I could eclipse and cloud them with a winke,
But that I would not lose her sight so long:
　　If her eyes have not blinded thine,
　　Looke, and to morrow late, tell mee,
　Whether both the'India's of spice and Myne
　Be where thou leftst them, or lie here with mee.
Aske for those Kings whom thou saw'st yesterday,
And thou shalt heare, All here in one bed lay.

　　She'is all States, and all Princes, I,
　　Nothing else is.
Princes doe but play us; compar'd to this,
All honor's mimique; All wealth alchimie.
　　Thou sunne art halfe as happy'as wee,
　　In that the world's contracted thus;
　Thine age askes ease, and since thy duties bee
　To warme the world, that's done in warming us.
Shine here to us, and thou art every where;
This bed thy center is, these walls, thy spheare.

220

Fish in the unruffled lakes
The swarming colours wear,
Swans in the winter air
A white perfection have,
And the great lion walks
Through his innocent grove;
Lion, fish, and swan
Act, and are gone
Upon Time's toppling wave.

We till shadowed days are done,
We must weep and sing
Duty's conscious wrong,
The devil in the clock,
The Goodness carefully worn
For atonement or for luck;
We must lose our loves,
On each beast and bird that moves
Turn an envious look.

Sighs for folly said and done
Twist our narrow days;
But I must bless, I must praise
That you, my swan, who have
All gifts that to the swan
Impulsive Nature gave,
The majesty and pride,
Last night should add
Your voluntary love.

221

Mine by the right of the white election!
Mine by the royal seal!
Mine by the sign in the scarlet prison
Bars cannot conceal!

Mine, here in vision and in veto!
Mine, by the grave's repeal
Titled, confirmed, – delirious charter!
Mine, while the ages steal!

The Extasie

Where, like a pillow on a bed,
   A Pregnant banke swel'd up, to rest
The violets reclining head,
   Sat we two, one anothers best.
Our hands were firmely cimented
   With a fast balme, which thence did spring,
Our eye-beames twisted, and did thred
   Our eyes, upon one double string;
So to'entergraft our hands, as yet
   Was all the meanes to make us one,
And pictures in our eyes to get
   Was all our propagation.
As 'twixt two equall Armies, Fate
   Suspends uncertaine victorie,
Our soules, (which to advance their state,
   Were gone out,) hung 'twixt her, and mee.
And whil'st our soules negotiate there,
   Wee like sepulchrall statues lay;
All day, the same our postures were,
   And wee said nothing, all the day.
If any, so by love refin'd,
   That he soules language understood,
And by good love were growen all minde,
   Within convenient distance stood,
He (though he knew not which soul spake,
   Because both meant, both spake the same)
Might thence a new concoction take,
   And part farre purer than he came.
This Extasie doth unperplex
   (We said) and tell us what we love,
Wee see by this, it was not sexe,
   Wee see, we saw not what did move:
But as all severall soules containe
   Mixture of things, they know not what,
Love, these mixt soules, doth mixe againe,
   And makes both one, each this and that.

A single violet transplant,
    The strength, the colour, and the size,
(All which before was poore, and scant,)
    Redoubles still, and multiplies.
When love, with one another so
    Interinanimates two soules,
That abler soule, which thence doth flow,
    Defects of loneliness controules.
Wee then, who are this new soule, know,
    Of what we are compos'd, and made,
For, th'Atomies of which we grow,
    Are soules, whom no change can invade.
But O alas, so long, so farre
    Our bodies why doe wee forbeare?
They are ours, though they are not wee, Wee are
    The intelligences, they the spheares.
We owe them thankes, because they thus,
    Did us, to us, at first convay,
Yeelded their forces, sense, to us,
    Nor are drosse to us, but allay.
On man heavens influence workes not so,
    But that it first imprints the ayre,
Soe soule into the soule may flow,
    Though it to body first repaire.
As our blood labours to beget
    Spirits, as like soules as it can,
Because such fingers need to knit
    That subtile knot, which makes us man:
So must pure lovers soules descend
    T'affections, and to faculties,
Which sense may reach and apprehend,
    Else a great Prince in prison lies.
To'our bodies turne wee then, that so
    Weake men on love reveal'd may looke;
Loves mysteries in soules doe grow,
    But yet the body is his booke.
And if some lover, such as wee,
    Have heard this dialogue of one,
Let him still marke us, he shall see
    Small change, when we'are to bodies gone.

Meeting point

Time was away and somewhere else,
There were two glasses and two chairs
And two people with the one pulse
(Somebody stopped the moving stairs):
Time was away and somewhere else.

And they were neither up nor down;
The stream's music did not stop
Flowing through heather, limpid brown,
Although they sat in a coffee shop
And they were neither up nor down.

The bell was silent in the air
Holding its inverted poise –
Between the clang and clang a flower,
A brazen calyx of no noise:
The bell was silent in the air.

The camels crossed the miles of sand
That stretched around the cups and plates;
The desert was their own, they planned
To portion out the stars and dates:
The camels crossed the miles of sand.

Time was away and somewhere else.
The waiter did not come, the clock
Forgot them and the radio waltz
Came out like water from a rock:
Time was away and somewhere else.

Her fingers flicked away the ash
That bloomed again in tropic trees:
Not caring if the markets crash
When they had forests such as these,
Her fingers flicked away the ash.

God or whatever means the Good
Be praised that time can stop like this,
That what the heart has understood
Can verify in the body's peace
God or whatever means the Good.

Time was away and she was here
And life no longer what it was,
The bell was silent in the air
And all the room one glow because
Time was away and she was here.

224

One day I wrote her name vpon the strand,
   but came the waues and washed it away:
   agayne I wrote it with a second hand,
   but came the tyde, and made my paynes his pray.
Vayne man, sayd she, that doest in vaine assay,
   a mortall thing so to immortalize,
   for I my selue shall lyke to this decay,
   and eek my name bee wyped out lykewize.
Not so, (quod I) let baser things deuize
   to dy in dust, but you shall liue by fame:
   my verse your vertues rare shall eternize,
   and in the heuens wryte your glorious name.
Where whenas death shall all the world subdew,
   our loue shall liue, and later life renew.

Act Four
A DURABLE FIRE

In the mynde euer burnynge.
RALEGH 'As you came from the holy land'

All lands to him were Ithaca.
ROBERT GRAVES 'Ulysses'

Alter? When the hills do.
EMILY DICKINSON

Since it's like a bereavement once the labour's done
To find ourselves last workers in a dying trade,
Let flax be our matchmaker, our undertaker,
The provider of sheets for whatever the bed.
MICHAEL LONGLEY 'The Linen Industry'

Out upon it, I have lov'd
Three whole days together.
SUCKLING 'The Constant Lover'

225

In a Bath Teashop

'Let us not speak, for the love we bear one another –
   Let us hold hands and look.'
She, such a very ordinary little woman;
   He, such a thumping crook;
But both, for a moment, little lower than the angels
   In the teashop's ingle-nook.

226

    Alter? When the hills do.
    Falter? When the sun
    Question if his glory
    Be the perfect one.

    Surfeit? When the daffodil
    Doth of the dew:
    Even as herself, O friend!
    I will of you!

227

Go from me. Yet I feel that I shall stand
   Henceforward in thy shadow. Nevermore
   Alone upon the threshold of my door
Of individual life I shall command
The uses of my soul, nor lift my hand
   Serenely in the sunshine as before,
   Without the sense of that which I forbore –
Thy touch upon the palm. The widest land
Doom takes to part us, leaves thy heart in mine
   With pulses that beat double. What I do
And what I dream include thee, as the wine
   Must taste of its own grapes. And when I sue
God for myself, He hears that name of thine,
   And sees within my eyes the tears of two.

Happy

THE LEPER'S BRIDE

Why wail you, pretty plover? and what is it that you fear?
  Is he sick your mate like mine? have you lost him, is he fled?
And there – the heron rises from his watch beside the mere,
  And flies above the leper's hut, where lives the living-dead.

Come back, nor let me me know it! would he live and die alone?
  And has he not forgiven me yet, his over-jealous bride,
Who am, and was, and will be his, his own and only own,
  To share his living death with him, die with him side by side?

Is that the leper's hut on the solitary moor,
  Where noble Ulric dwells forlorn, and wears the leper's weed?
The door is open. He! is he standing at the door,
  My soldier of the Cross? it is he and he indeed!

My roses – will he take them *now* – mine, his – from off the tree
  We planted both together, happy in our marriage morn?
O God, I could blaspheme, for he fought Thy fight for Thee,
  And Thou hast made him leper to compass him with scorn –

Hast spared the flesh of thousands, the coward and the base,
  And set a crueller mark than Cain's on him, the good and brave!
He sees me, waves me from him. I will front him face to face.
  You need not wave me from you. I would leap into your grave.

*   *   *   *   *

My warrior of the Holy Cross and of the conquering sword,
  The roses that you cast aside – once more I bring you these.
No nearer? do you scorn me when you tell me, O my lord,
  You would not mar the beauty of your bride with your disease.

You say your body is so foul – then here I stand apart,
  Who yearn to lay my loving head upon your leprous breast.
The leper plague may scale my skin but never taint my heart;
  Your body is not foul to me, and body is foul at best.

I loved you first when young and fair, but now I love you most;
   The fairest flesh at last is filth on which the worm will feast;
This poor rib-grated dungeon of the holy human ghost,
   This house with all its hateful needs no cleaner than the beast,

This coarse diseaseful creature which in Eden was divine,
   This Satan-haunted ruin, this little city of sewers,
This wall of solid flesh that comes between your soul and mine,
   Will vanish and give place to the beauty that endures,

The beauty that endures on the Spiritual height,
   When we shall stand transfigured, like Christ on Hermon hill,
And moving each to music, soul in soul and light in light,
   Shall flash through one another in a moment as we will.

Foul! foul! the word was yours not mine, I worship that right hand
   Which felled the foes before you as the woodman fells the wood,
And swayed the sword that lightened back the sun of Holy land,
   And clove the Moslem crescent moon, and changed it into blood.

And once I worshipt all too well this creature of decay,
   For Age will chink the face, and Death will freeze the supplest limbs -
Yet you in your mid manhood – O the grief when yesterday
   They bore the Cross before you to the chant of funeral hymns.

'Libera me, Domine!' you sang the Psalm, and when
   The Priest pronounced you dead, and flung the mould upon your feet
A beauty came upon your face, not that of living men,
   But seen upon the silent brow when life has ceased to beat.

'Libera *nos*, Domine' – you knew not one was there
   Who saw you kneel beside your bier, and weeping scarce could see;
May I come a little nearer, I that heard, and changed the prayer
   And sang the married 'nos' for the solitary 'me'.

My beauty marred by you? by you! so be it. All is well
   If I lose it and myself in the higher beauty, yours.
My beauty lured that falcon from his eyry on the fell,
   Who never caught one gleam of the beauty which endures –

The Count who sought to snap the bond that linked us life to life,
    Who whispered me 'your Ulric loves' – a little nearer still –
He hissed, 'Let us revenge ourselves, your Ulric woos my wife' –
    A lie by which he thought he could subdue me to his will.

I knew that you were near me when I let him kiss my brow;
    Did he touch me on the lips? I was jealous, angered, vain,
And I meant to make *you* jealous. Are you jealous of me now?
    Your pardon, O my love, if I ever gave you pain.

You never once accused me, but I wept alone, and sighed
    In the winter of the Present for the summer of the Past;
That icy winter silence – how it froze you from your bride,
    Though I made one barren effort to break it at the last.

I brought you, you remember, these roses, when I knew
    You were parting for the war, and you took them though you
        frowned;
You frowned and yet you kissed them. All at once the trumpet blew,
    And you spurred your fiery horse, and you hurled them to the
        ground.

You parted for the Holy War without a word to me,
    And clear myself unasked – not I. My nature was too proud.
And him I saw but once again, and far away was he,
    When I was praying in a storm – the crash was long and loud –

That God would ever slant His bolt from falling on your head –
    Then I lifted up my eyes, he was coming down the fell –
I clapt my hands. The sudden fire from Heaven had dashed him dead,
    And sent him charred and blasted to the deathless fire of Hell.

See, I sinned but for a moment. I repented and repent,
    And trust myself forgiven by the God to whom I kneel.
A little nearer? Yes. I shall hardly be content
    Till I be leper like yourself, my love, from head to heel.

O foolish dreams, that you, that I, would slight our marriage oath:
    I held you at that moment even dearer than before;
Now God has made you leper in His loving care for both,
    That we might cling together, never doubt each other more.

The Priest, who joined you to the dead, has joined our hands of old;
  If man and wife be but one flesh, let mine be leprous too,
As dead from all the human race as if beneath the mould;
  If you be dead, then I am dead, who only live for you.

Would Earth though hid in cloud not be followed by the Moon?
  The leech forsake the dying bed for terror of his life?
The shadow leave the Substance in the brooding light of noon?
  Or if *I* had been the leper would you have left the wife?

Not take them? Still you wave me off – poor roses – must I go –
  I have worn them year by year – from the bush we both had set –
What? fling them to you? – well – that were hardly gracious. No!
  Your plague but passes by the touch. A little nearer yet!

There, there! he buried you, the Priest; the Priest is not to blame,
  He joins us once again, to his either office true:
I thank him. I am happy, happy. Kiss me. In the name
  Of the everlasting God, I will live and die with you.

229

Woman

'All things become thee, being thine,' I think sometimes
As I think of you. I think: 'How many faults
In thee have seemed a virtue!' While your taste is on my tongue
The years return, blessings innumerable
As the breaths that you have quickened, gild my flesh.
Lie there in majesty!
                    When, like Disraeli, I murmur
That you are more like a mistress than a wife,
More like an angel that a mistress; when, like Satan,
I hiss in your ear some vile suggestion,
Some delectable abomination,
You smile at me indulgently: 'Men, men!'

You smile at mankind, recognizing in it
The absurd occasion of your fall.
For men – as your soap operas, as your *Home Journals*,
As your hearts whisper – men are only children.
And you believe them. Truly, you are children.

Should I love you so dearly if you weren't?
If I weren't?
                    O morning star,
Each morning my dull heart goes out to you
And rises with the sun, but with the sun
Sets not, but all the long night nests within your eyes.

Men's share of grace, of all that can make bearable,
Lovable almost, the apparition, Man,
Has fallen to you. Erect, extraordinary
As a polar bear on roller skates, he passes
On into the Eternal . . .
                              From your pedestal, you watch
Admiringly, when you remember to.

Let us form, as Freud has said, 'a group of two.'
You are the best thing that this world can offer –
He said so. Or I remember that he said so;
If I am mistaken it's a Freudian error,
An error nothing but a man would make.
Women can't bear women. Cunningly engraved
On many an old wife's dead heart is 'Women,
Beware women!' And yet it was a man
Sick of too much sweetness – of a life
Rich with a mother, wife, three daughters, a wife's sister,
An abyss of analysands – who wrote: 'I cannot
Escape the notion (though I hesitate
To give it expression) that for women
The level of what is ethically normal
Is different from what it is in men.
Their superego' – he goes on without hesitation –
'Is never so inexorable, so impersonal,
So independent of its emotional
Origins as we require it in a man.'

Did not the angel say to Abraham
That he would spare the cities of the plain
If there were found in them ten unjust women?
– That is to say, merciful; that is to say,

Extravagant; that is to say, unjust as judges
Who look past judgment, always, to the eyes
(Long-lashed, a scapegoat's, yearning sheepishly)
Under the curly-yarned and finger-tickling locks
Of that dear-wooled, inconsequential head.

You save him and knit an afghan from his hair.
And in the cold tomb, save for you, and afghanless,
He leaves you to wage wars, build bridges, visit women
Who like to run their fingers through his hair.
He complains of you to them, describing you
As 'the great love of my life.' What pains it took
To win you, a mere woman! – 'worst of all,'
He ends, 'a woman who was not my type.'

But then, a woman never is a man's type.
Possessed by that prehistoric unforgettable
Other One, who never again is equaled
By anyone, he searches for his ideal,
The Good Whore who reminds him of his mother.
The realities are too much one or the other,
Too much like Mother or too bad . . . Too bad!
He resigns himself to them – as 'they are, after all,
The best things that are offered in that line';
And should he not spare Nineveh, that city
Wherein are more than sixscore thousand women
Who cannot tell their left hand from their right,
But smile up hopefully at the policeman?

Are you as mercenary as the surveys show?
What a way to put it! Let us write instead
That you are realists; or as a realist might say,
Naturalists. It's in man's nature – woman's nature
To want the best, and to be careless how it comes.
And what have we all to sell except ourselves?
Poor medlar, no sooner ripe than rotten!

You must be seized today, or stale tomorrow
Into a wife, a mother, a homemaker,
An Elector of the League of Women Voters.
Simply by your persistence, you betray
Yourselves and all that was yours, you momentary
And starry instances; are falling, falling
Into the sagging prison of your flesh,
Residuary legatees of earth, grandmothers
And legal guardians of the tribes of men.
If all Being showered down on you in gold
Would you not murmur, with averted breasts: 'Not now'?

When he looks upon your nakedness he is blinded.
Your breasts and belly are one incandescence
Like the belly of an idol: how can a man go in that fire
And come out living? 'The burnt child dreads the fire,'
He says later, warming his hands before the fire.
Last – last of all – he says that there are three things sure:
'That the Dog returns to his Vomit and the Sow returns to her Mire,
And the burnt Fool's bandaged finger goes wabbling back to the Fire.'

Part of himself is shocked at part of himself
As, beside the remnants of a horrible
Steak, a little champagne, he confesses
Candidly to you: 'In the beginning
There was a baby boy that loved its mother,
There was a baby girl that loved its mother.
The boy grew up and got to love a woman,
The girl grew up and had to love a man.
Because isn't that what's wrong with women? Men?
Isn't that the reason you're the way you are?
Why *are* you the way you are?'
                                    You say: 'Because.'

When you float with me through the Tunnel of Love
Or Chamber of Horrors – one of those concessions –
And a great hand, dripping, daggered, reaches out for you
And you scream, and it misses, and another hand,
Soiled, hairy, lustful, reaches out for you
And you faint, and it misses: when you come to,
You say, looking up weakly: 'Did you notice?
The second one had on a wedding ring.'

May the Devil fly away with the roof of the house
That you and I aren't happy in, you angel!
And yet, how quickly the bride's veils evaporate!
A girl hesitates a moment in mid-air
And settles to the ground a wife, a mother.
Each evening a tired spirit visits
Her full house; wiping his feet upon a mat
Marked *Women and Children First*, the husband looks
At this grown woman. She stands there in slacks
Among the real world's appliances,
Women, and children; kisses him hello
Just as, that morning, she kissed him goodbye,
And he sits down, till dinner, with the paper.
This home of theirs is haunted by a girl's
Ghost. At sunset a woodpecker knocks
At a tree by the window, asking their opinion
Of life. The husband answers, 'Life is life,'
And when his wife calls to him from the kitchen
He tells her who it was, and what he wanted.
Beating the whites of seven eggs, the beater
Asks her her own opinion; she says, 'Life
Is life.' 'See how it sounds to say it isn't,'
The beater tempts her. 'Life is not life,'
She says. It sounds the same. Putting her cake
Into the oven, she is satisfied
Or else dissatisfied: it sounds the same.
With knitted brows, with care's swift furrows nightly
Smoothed out with slow care, and come again with care
Each morning, she lives out her gracious life.

But you should gush out over being like a spring
The drinker sighs to lift his mouth from: a dark source
That brims over, with its shining, every cup
That is brought to it in shadow, filled there, broken there.
You look at us out of sunlight and of shade,
Dappled, inexorable, the last human power.
All earth is the labyrinth along whose ways
You walk mirrored: rosy-fingered, many-breasted
As Diana of the Ephesians, strewing garments
Before the world's eyes narrowed in desire.
Now, naked on my doorstep, in the sun
Gold-armed, white-breasted, pink-cheeked, and black-furred,

You call to me, 'Come'; and when I come say, 'Go,'
Smiling your soft contrary smile . . .

                               He who has these
Is secure from the other sorrows of the world.
While you are how am I alone? Your voice
Soothes me to sleep, and finds fault with my dreams,
Till I murmur in my sleep: 'Man is the animal
That finds fault.'

                 And you say: 'Who said that?'

But be, as you have been, my happiness;
Let me sleep beside you, each night, like a spoon;
When, starting from my dreams, I groan to you,
May your *I love you* send me back to sleep.
At morning bring me, grayer for its mirroring,
The heavens' sun perfected in your eyes.

230

Dover Beach

The sea is calm to-night.
The tide is full, the moon lies fair
Upon the straits; on the French coast the light
Gleams and is gone; the cliffs of England stand,
Glimmering and vast, out in the tranquil bay.
Come to the window, sweet is the night-air!
Only, from the long line of spray
Where the sea meets the moon-blanched land,
Listen! you hear the grating roar
Of pebbles which the waves draw back, and fling,
At their return, up the high strand,
Begin, and cease, and then again begin,
With tremulous cadence slow, and bring
The eternal note of sadness in.

Sophocles long ago
Heard it on the Ægæan, and it brought
Into his mind the turbid ebb and flow
Of human misery; we
Find also in the sound a thought,
Hearing it by this distant northern sea.

The Sea of Faith
Was once, too, at the full, and round earth's shore
Lay like the folds of a bright girdle furled.
But now I only hear
Its melancholy, long, withdrawing roar,
Retreating, to the breath
Of the night-wind, down the vast edges drear
And naked shingles of the world.

Ah, love, let us be true
To one another! for the world, which seems
To lie before us like a land of dreams,
So various, so beautiful, so new,
Hath really neither joy, nor love, nor light,
Nor certitude, nor peace, nor help for pain;
And we are here as on a darkling plain
Swept with confused alarms of struggle and flight,
Where ignorant armies clash by night.

231
Zeugma

Is it foolhardy to hope
that by some ingenious trope
we'll widen, and not hamper, our scope?

I do not think so,
for there is a knack we know
involving both passion and punctilio.

We are two words set free
from the common dictionary,
to act with a new, *ad hoc* complicity.

Our ony go-between, 'and',
carries its contraband
in a package the unpoetic may not understand.

232

House-Rules I: Reading

Among the white walls we read quietly.
The rugs beam up unnoticed.
We try not to read out the bits we like:

There you are swimming on your back in some dark lake
squinting with wet eyes at some friendly constellation
when this madman begins skimming out coloured stones.

The beautiful sofa of my cell
gets solitary, with you over there.
Life pours away, a whisky tape left on:

Here I am treading water out of sight of land
when up foams someone wearing nothing, in her hand
some bread and butter and the mermaids' local paper.

233

The Linen Industry

Pulling up flax after the blue flowers have fallen
And laying our handfuls in the peaty water
To rot those grasses to the bone, or building stooks
That recall the skirts of an invisible dancer,

We become a part of the linen industry
And follow its processes to the grubby town
Where fields are compacted into window-boxes
And there is little room among the big machines.

But even in our attic under the skylight
We make love on a bleach green, the whole meadow
Draped with material turning white in the sun
As though snow reluctant to melt were our attire.

What's passion but a battering of stubborn stalks,
Then a gentle combing out of fibres like hair
And a weaving of these into christening robes,
Into garments for a marriage or funeral?

[224]

Since it's like a bereavement once the labour's done
To find ourselves last workers in a dying trade,
Let flax be our matchmaker, our undertaker,
The provider of sheets for whatever the bed –

And be shy of your breasts in the presence of death,
Say that you look more beautiful in linen
Wearing white petticoats, the bow on your bodice
A butterfly attending the embroidered flowers.

234
Talking in Bed

Talking in bed ought to be easiest,
Lying together there goes back so far,
An emblem of two people being honest.

Yet more and more time passes silently.
Outside, the wind's incomplete unrest
Builds and disperses clouds about the sky,

And dark towns heap up on the horizon.
None of this cares for us. Nothing shows why
At this unique distance from isolation

It becomes still more difficult to find
Words at once true and kind,
Or not untrue and not unkind.

235
The Old Flame

My old flame, my wife!
Remember our lists of birds?
One morning last summer, I drove
by our house in Maine. It was still
on top of its hill –

Now a red ear of Indian maize
was splashed on the door.
Old Glory with thirteen stripes
hung on a pole. The clapboard
was old-red schoolhouse red.

Inside, a new landlord,
a new wife, a new broom!
Atlantic seaboard antique shop
pewter and plunder
shone in each room.

A new frontier!
No running next door
now to phone the sheriff
for his taxi to Bath
and the State Liquor Store!

No one saw your ghostly
imaginary lover
stare through the window,
and tighten
the scarf at his throat.

Health to the new people,
health to their flag, to their old
restored house on the hill!
Everything had been swept bare,
furnished, garnished and aired.

Everything's changed for the best –
how quivering and fierce we were,
there snowbound together,
simmering like wasps
in our tent of books!

Poor ghost, old love, speak
with your old voice
of flaming insight
that kept us awake all night.
In one bed and apart,

we heard the plow
groaning up hill –
a red light, then a blue,
as it tossed off the snow
to the side of the road.

236

In the Gallery

The wildly-colored girl with her round belly twisted
Further around, as one might twist a plum on its stem
In plucking, her face whacked apart into its aspects,
Steadies the pier-glass full of her reordered image,
Truth having made a mess of false beauty against a
Battlefield of screaming lozenges, all the carnage
Of decoration. Across the gallery the same
Painter allows another, linear, girl to go
Unviolated, guarded by the god of his sad
Heart, a fierce metamorphic beast who caresses her,
Thus warding off the violence that his shining, dark
Eyes would have otherwise commanded an obedient
Brush to execute, as on the girl across the room.

Between these battle-scenes in the wars of figure and
Form, she sits on a low bench and holds up the round glass
In the lid of her compact to her unviolent
Regard. Her tan hand emerges from the gathering
Of the clans of like tone – buff and beige and wheat and bran –
On the plain of what she wears. Beside her, with his hand
Extended to her tan knee as if to steady it,
He has eyes only for hers, she, for the monocled
Gaze of her mirror; yet in these sundry objects each
Espies the object of desire, but invisibly
Disguised as an image of itself. Those two will tear
In time their images, wreck the very subject of
Desire more wildly than whatever the painter wields.

Sex and the Over Forties

It's too good for them,
they look so unattractive undressed –
let them read paperbacks!

A few things to keep in readiness –
a flensing knife, a ceiling mirror,
a cassette of *The Broken Heart*.

More luncheons than lust,
more meetings on Northern Line stations,
more discussions of children's careers.

A postcard from years back –
I'm twenty-one, in Italy and in love!
Wagner wrote *Tristan* at forty-four.

Trying it with noises and in strange positions,
trying it with the young themselves,
trying to keep it up with the Joneses!

All words and no play,
all animals fleeing a forest fire,
all Apollo's grafters running.

Back to the dream in the garden,
back to the pictures in the drawer,
back to back, tonight and every night.

238

Circumstance

Two children in two neighbour villages
Playing mad pranks along the healthy leas;
Two strangers meeting at a festival;
Two lovers whispering by an orchard wall;
Two lives bound fast in one with golden ease;
Two graves grass-green beside a gray church-tower,
Washed with still rains and daisy blossomèd;
Two children in one hamlet born and bred;
So runs the round of life from hour to hour.

239

Song

Two doves upon the selfsame branch,
   Two lilies on a single stem,
Two butterflies upon one flower:–
   Oh happy they who look on them!

Who look upon them hand in hand
   Flushed in the rosy summer light;
Who look upon them hand in hand,
   And never give a thought to night.

240

John Anderson my jo, John,
   When we were first acquent;
Your locks were like the raven,
   Your bony brow was brent;
But now your brow is beld, John,
   Your locks are like the snaw;
But blessings on your frosty pow,
   John Anderson my Jo.

John Anderson my jo, John,
    We clamb the hill the gither;
And mony a canty day, John,
    We've had wi' ane anither:
Now we maun totter down, John,
    And hand in hand we'll go;
And sleep the gither at the foot,
    John Anderson my Jo.

241

In Nature There Is Neither Right
nor Left nor Wrong

Men are what they do, women are what they are.
These erect breasts, like marble coming up for air
Among the cataracts of my breathtaking hair,
Are goods in my bazaar, a door ajar
To the first paradise of whores and mothers.

Men buy their way back into me from the upright
Right-handed puzzle that men fit together
From their deeds, the pieces. Women shoot from
Or dive back into its interstices
As squirrels inhabit a geometry.

We women sell ourselves for sleep, for flesh,
To those wide-awake, successful spirits, men –
Who, lying each midnight with the sinister
Beings, their dark companions, women,
Suck childhood, beasthood, from a mother's breasts.

A fat bald rich man comes home at twilight
And lectures me about my parking tickets; gowned in gold
Lamé, I look at him and think: 'You're old,
I'm old.' Husband, I sleep with you every night
And like it; but each morning when I wake
I've dreamed of my first love, the subtle serpent.

242

The Stern Brow

You say my brow is stern and yet my smile
   (When I *do* smile) is sweet.
Seldom, ah seldom so! 'tis only while
   None see us when we meet.

It is your smile, Ianthe, and not mine,
   Altho' upon my lips;
Your's brought in thither; its pale rays decline
   Too soon in sad eclipse.

243

Love-Life

Her veil blows across my face
As we cling together in the porch.
Propped on the mantelpiece,
The photograph distils our ecstasy.
Each night we touch
The heart-shaped frame of our reliquary
And sigh for love.

Each morning we are young again –
Our cheeks brushed pink,
The highlights in our hair.
Our guests will be arriving soon.
We wait contentedly beyond the glass
For them to find us here,
Our smiles wrapped in lace.

244

Silver Wedding

In the middle of the night
He started up
At a cry from his sleeping Bride –
A bat from some ruin
In a heart he'd never searched,
Nay, hardly seen inside:

'Want me and take me
For the woman that I am
And not for her that died,
The lovely chit nineteen
I one time was,
And am no more' – she cried.

245

Love: Intimacy

They were so exceptionally well got-up for an ordinary Sunday
    afternoon stop-in at Deux Magots,
she in very chic deep black, he in a business suit, and they were so
    evidently just out of bed
but with very little to say to one another, much gazing off, elaborate
    lightings of her cigarettes,
she more proper than was to be believed, sipping with a flourished
    pinky at her Pimm's Cup,
that it occurred to me I was finally seeing one of those intriguing *Herald
    Tribune* classifieds –
a woman's name, a number – for 'escorts' or 'companions,' but then I
    had to change my mind:
she'd leaned toward him, deftly lifted a line of his thinning hair, and idly,
    with a mild pat,
had laid it back – not commiserating, really, just keeping record of the
    progress of the loss.

Versions of Love

'My love for you has faded' – thus the Bad
Quarto, the earliest text, whose midget page
Derived from the imperfect memories
Of red-nosed, small-part actors
Or the atrocious shorthand of the age.

However, the far superior Folio had
'My love for you was fated' – thus implying
Illicit passion, a tragic final act.
And this was printed from the poet's own
Foul papers, it was reckoned;
Supported by the reading of the Second
Quarto, which had those sombre words exact.

Such evidence was shaken when collation
Showed that the Folio copied slavishly
The literals of that supposedly
Independent Quarto. Thus one had to go
Back to the first text of all.

'My love for you has faded' – quite impossible.
Scholars produced at last the emendation:
'My love for you fast endured.'
Our author's ancient hand that must have been
Ambiguous and intellectual
Foxed the compositors of a certainty.
And so the critical editions gave
Love the sound status that she ought to have
In poetry so revered.

But this conjecture cannot quite destroy
The question of what the poet really wrote
In the glum middle reaches of his life:
Too sage, too bald, too fearful of fiasco
To hope beyond his wife,
Yet aching almost as promptly as a boy.

In the morning, in the morning,
  In the happy field of hay,
Oh they looked at one another
  By the light of day.

In the blue and silver morning
  On the haycock as they lay,
Oh they looked at one another
  And they looked away.

248

It chanced his lips did meet her forehead cool.
She had no blush, but slanted down her eye.
Shamed nature, then, confesses love can die:
And most she punishes the tender fool
Who will believe what honours her the most!
Dead! is it dead? She has a pulse, and flow
Of tears, the price of blood-drops, as I know,
For whom the midnight sobs around Love's ghost,
Since then I heard her, and so will sob on.
The love is here; it has but changed its aim.
O bitter barren woman! what's the name?
The name, the name, the new name thou hast won?
Behold me striking the world's coward stroke!
That will I not do, though the sting is dire.
– Beneath the surface this, while by the fire
They sat, she laughing at a quiet joke.

249

The sweetest heresy received
That man and woman know,
Each other's convert –
Though the faith accommodate but two.

The churches are so frequent,
The ritual so small,
The Grace so unavoidable,
To fail – is infidel.

250

You smiled, you spoke, and I believed,
By every word and smile deceived.
Another man would hope no more;
Nor hope I what I hoped before:
But let not this last wish be vain;
Deceive, deceive me once again!

251

Oh, when I was in love with you,
    Then I was clean and brave,
And miles around the wonder grew
    How well did I behave.

And now the fancy passes by,
    And nothing will remain,
And miles around they'll say that I
    Am quite myself again.

252

Fidelity

Fidelity and love are two different things, like a flower and a gem.
And love, like a flower, will fade, will change into something else
or it would not be flowery.

O flowers they fade because they are moving swiftly; a little torrent of
    life
leaps up to the summit of the stem, gleams, turns over round the bend
of the parabola of curved flight,
sinks, and is gone, like a comet curving into the invisible.

O flowers they are all the time travelling
like comets, and they come into our ken
for a day, for two days, and withdraw, slowly vanish again.

And we, we must take them on the wing, and let them go.
Embalmed flowers are not flowers, immortelles are not flowers;
flowers are just a motion, a swift motion, a coloured gesture;
that is their loveliness. And that is love.

But a gem is different. It lasts so much longer than we do
so much much much longer
that it seems to last forever.
Yet we know it is flowing away
as flowers are, and we are, only slower.
The wonderful slow flowing of the sapphire!

All flows, and every flow is related to every other flow.
Flowers and sapphires and us, diversely streaming.
In the old days, when sapphires were breathed upon and brought forth
during the wild orgasms of chaos
time was much slower, when the rocks came forth.
It took æons to make a sapphire, æons for it to pass away.

And a flower it takes a summer.

And man and woman are like the earth, that brings forth flowers
in summer, and love, but underneath is rock.
Older than flowers, older than ferns, older than foraminiferæ
older than plasm altogether is the soul of a man underneath.

And when, throughout all the wild orgasms of love
slowly a gem forms, in the ancient, once-more-molten rocks
of two human hearts, two ancient rocks, a man's heart and a woman's,
that is the crystal of peace, the slow hard jewel of trust,
the sapphire of fidelity.
The gem of mutual peace emerging from the wild chaos of love.

The sloe was lost in flower,
  The April elm was dim;
That was the lover's hour,
  The hour for lies and him.

If thorns are all the bower,
  If north winds freeze the fir,
Why, 'tis another's hour,
  The hour for truth and her.

That thou hast her it is not all my griefe,
And yet it may be said I lou'd her deerely,
That she hath thee is of my wayling cheefe,
A losse in loue that touches me more neerely.
Louing offendors thus I will excuse yee,
Thou doost loue her, because thou knowst I loue her,
And for my sake euen so doth she abuse me,
Suffring my friend for my sake to approoue her,
If I loose thee, my losse is my loues gaine,
And loosing her, my friend hath found that losse,
Both finde each other, and I loose both twaine,
And both for my sake lay on me this crosse,
  But here's the ioy, my friend and I are one,
  Sweete flattery, then she loues but me alone.

The Perfidious

Go on! go on! and love away!
Mine was, another's is, the day.
Go on, go on, thou false one! now
Upon his shoulder rest thy brow,
And look into his eyes until
Thy own, to find them colder, fill.

256

When I was one-and-twenty
  I heard a wise man say,
'Give crowns and pounds and guineas
  But not your heart away;
Give pearls away and rubies
  But keep your fancy free.'
But I was one-and-twenty,
  No use to talk to me.

When I was one-and-twenty
  I heard him say again,
'The heart out of the bosom
  Was never given in vain;
'Tis paid with sighs a plenty
  And sold for endless rue.'
And I am two-and-twenty,
  And oh, 'tis true, 'tis true.

257

O dear, what can the matter be?
Dear, dear, what can the matter be?
O dear, what can the matter be?
Johnny's so long at the fair.

He promised he'd buy me a fairing should please me,
And then for a kiss, oh! he vowed he would tease me,
He promised he'd bring me a bunch of blue ribbons
To tie up my bonny brown hair.

And it's O dear, what can the matter be?
Dear, dear, what can the matter be?
O dear, what can the matter be?
Johnny's so long at the fair.

He promised to buy me a pair of sleeve buttons,
A pair of new garters that cost him but two pence,
He promised he'd bring me a bunch of blue ribbons
To tie up my bonny brown hair.

And it's O dear, what can the matter be?
Dear, dear, what can the matter be?
O dear, what can the matter be?
Johnny's so long at the fair.

He promised he'd bring me a basket of posies,
A garland of lilies, a garland of roses,
A little straw hat, to set off the blue ribbons
That tie up my bonny brown hair.

258

1

Why should a foolish Marriage Vow
    Which long ago was made,
Oblige us to each other now
    When Passion is decay'd?
We lov'd, and we lov'd, as long as we cou'd,
    Till our love was lov'd out in us both:
But our Marriage is dead, when the Pleasure is fled:
    'Twas Pleasure first made it an Oath.

2

If I have Pleasures for a Friend,
    And farther love in store,
What wrong has he whose joys did end,
    And who cou'd give no more?

'Tis a madness that he
Should be jealous of me,
Or that I shou'd bar him of another:
For all we can gain,
Is to give our selves pain,
When neither can hinder the other.

The Echo-Elf Answers

How much shall I love her?
For life, or not long?
   'Not long.'

Alas! When forget her?
In years, or by June?
   'By June.'

And whom woo I after?
No one, or a throng?
   'A throng.'

Of these shall I wed one
Long hence, or quite soon?
   'Quite soon.'

And which will my bride be?
The right or the wrong?
   'The wrong.'

And my remedy – what kind?
Wealth-wove, or earth-hewn?
   'Earth-hewn.'

260

The Indifferent

I can love both faire and browne,
Her whom abundance melts, and her whom want betraies,
Her who loves lonenesse best, and her who maskes and plaies,
Her whom the country form'd, and whom the town,
Her who beleeves, and her who tries,
Her who still weepes with spungie eyes,
And her who is dry corke, and never cries;
I can love her, and her, and you and you,
I can love any, so she be not true.

Will no other vice content you?
Wil it not serve your turn to do, as did your mothers?
Or have you all old vices spent, and now would finde out others?
Or doth a feare, that men are true, torment you?
Oh we are not, be not you so,
Let mee, and doe you, twenty know.
Rob mee, but binde me not, and let me goe.
Must I, who came to travaile thorow you,
Grow your fixt subject, because you are true?

Venus heard me sigh this song,
And by Loves sweetest Part, Variety, she swore,
She heard not this till now; and that it should be so no more.
She went, examin'd, and return'd ere long,
And said, alas, Some two or three
Poore Heretiques in love there bee,
Which thinke to stablish dangerous constancie.
But I have told them, since you will be true,
You shall be true to them, who'are false to you.

261

Down, Wanton, Down!

Down, wanton, down! Have you no shame
That at the whisper of Love's name,
Or Beauty's, presto! up you raise
Your angry head and stand at gaze?

Poor bombard-captain, sworn to reach
The ravelin and effect a breach –
Indifferent what you storm or why,
So be that in the breach you die!

Love may be blind, but Love at least
Knows what is man and what mere beast;
Or Beauty wayward, but requires
More delicacy from her squires.

Tell me, my witless, whose one boast
Could be your staunchness at the post,
When were you made a man of parts
To think fine and profess the arts?

Will many-gifted Beauty come
Bowing to your bald rule of thumb,
Or Love swear loyalty to your crown?
Be gone, have done! Down, wanton, down!

262

A Satire on an Inconstant Lover

You are as faithless as a Carthaginian,
To love at once Kate, Nell, Doll, Martha, Jenny, Ann.

263

To the Tune –
'But I fancy Lovely Nancy,' &c.

Surely now I'm out of danger,
And no more need fear my heart;
Who loves thus to be a ranger,
Ne'er will fix in any part;
All the graces
Of fair faces
I have seen, and yet am free:
I like many, but not any
Shall subdue my libertee.

Anne was once the word which movèd
Most my heart, I'll it avow;
Twelve at least so call'd, I've lovèd,
But I care not for them now:
Yet if ever
I endeavour
For a mistress, that's her name;
These are fancies,
But with Nancies
Luckiest still hath been my flame.

With three Betties I was taken;
Yet no more, than whilst in sight:
One of them is now forsaken,
And her sister has her right.
T'other's pretty,
But (what pity!)
In a castle she is penn'd:
The third plenty
Has for twenty,
But she's courted by my friend.

Lucies there are two; for beauty,
Virtue, wit, beyond compare:
Th' one's too high for love, in duty
I respect, but no more dare:
As for t'other,
Though a mother
(As I take't) to half a score;
Had she tarried
To be married,
She'd have had one suitor more.

I know two, and each a Mary,
One's the greatest of this land:
Th' Oxford-vintner made me wary
Least I should a-gazing stand.
Though I like her,
Most unlike her
Is the second; and I swear,
Had her portion
Some proportion
With my wants, I'd marry there.

Katherne has a lip that's ruddy,
Swelling so, it seems to pout;
How to kiss her I did study,
But could never bring't about.
Beauteous Frances
Loves romances,
But (alas!) she's now a wife;
She makes verses,
And rehearses
With great grace Primaleon's life.

[243]

Doll has purest breasts much whiter
Than their milk, but naked still;
That's the reason why I slight her,
For I'd seen them to my fill.
Jane is slender,
But God send her
Less opinion of her race!
Nell's so spotted
That sh' has blotted
Almost out, her little face.

Peg is blithe; but O she tattles;
Nothing's so demure as Ruth.
Susan's head is full of rattles,
Rachel preacheth well, in truth.
Were not Tolly
Melancholy,
She hath parts I most could prize:
Amorous Sophy
Rears no trophy
On my heart, with her grey eyes.

Thus I still find somewhat wanting,
Always full of ifs, or ands;
Where there's beauty, money's scanting;
Something still my choice withstands.
'Tis my fortune,
I'll importune
With no my prayers my destiny:
If I'm scornèd,
I'm not hornèd;
That's some joy in misery.

264

Stella's Birthday

WRITTEN IN THE YEAR 1718

Stella this day is thirty-four,
(We shan't dispute a year or more:)
However Stella, be not troubled,
Although thy size and years are doubled,
Since first I saw thee at sixteen,
The brightest virgin on the green.
So little is thy form declined;
Made up so largely in thy mind.

   Oh, would it please the gods to *split*
Thy beauty, size, and years, and wit,
No age could furnish out a pair
Of nymphs so graceful, wise and fair:
With half the lustre of your eyes,
With half your wit, your years, and size:
And then before it grew too late,
How should I beg of gentle fate,
(That either nymph might have her swain,)
To split my worship too in twain.

265

The Lovers' Litany

Eyes of grey – a sodden quay,
Driving rain and falling tears,
As the steamer puts to sea
In a parting storm of cheers.
   Sing, for Faith and Hope are high –
   None so true as you and I –
   Sing the Lovers' Litany:–
   'Love like ours can never die!'

Eyes of black – a throbbing keel,
Milky foam to left and right;
Whispered converse near the wheel
In the brilliant tropic night.
    Cross that rules the Southern Sky!
    Stars that sweep, and turn, and fly
    Hear the Lovers' Litany:–
    'Love like ours can never die!'

Eyes of brown – a dusty plain
Split and parched with heat of June.
Flying hoof and tightened rein,
Hearts that beat the ancient tune.
    Side by side the horses fly,
    Frame we now the old reply
    Of the Lovers' Litany:–
    'Love like ours can never die!'

Eyes of blue – the Simla Hills
Silvered with the moonlight hoar;
Pleading of the waltz that thrills,
Dies and echoes round Benmore.
    'Mabel,' 'Officers,' 'Good-bye,'
    Glamour, wine, and witchery –
    On my soul's sincerity,
    'Love like ours can never die!'

Maidens, of your charity,
Pity my most luckless state.
Four times Cupid's debtor I –
Bankrupt in quadruplicate.
    Yet, despite my evil case,
    An a maiden showed me grace,
    Four-and-forty times would I
    Sing the Lovers' Litany:–
    'Love like ours can never die!'

266

from *Don Juan*

I love the sex, and sometimes would reverse
    The tyrant's wish, 'that mankind only had
One neck, which he with one fell stroke might pierce:'
    My wish is quite as wide, but not so bad,
And much more tender on the whole than fierce;
    It being (not *now*, but only while a lad)
That womankind had but one rosy mouth,
To kiss them all at once from North to South.

267

Ulysses

To the much-tossed Ulysses, never done
    With woman whether gowned as wife or whore,
Penelope and Circe seemed as one:
She like a whore made his lewd fancies run,
    And wifely she a hero to him bore.

Their counter-changings terrified his way:
    They were the clashing rocks, Symplegades,
Scylla and Charybdis too were they;
Now they were storms frosting the sea with spray
    And now the lotus island's drunken ease.

They multiplied into the Sirens' throng,
    Forewarned by fear of whom he stood bound fast
Hand and foot helpless to the vessel's mast,
Yet would not stop his ears: daring their song
    He groaned and sweated till that shore was past.

One, two and many: flesh had made him blind,
    Flesh had one pleasure only in the act,
Flesh set one purpose only in the mind –
Triumph of flesh and afterwards to find
    Still those same terrors wherewith flesh was racked.

His wiles were witty and his fame far known,
Every king's daughter sought him for her own,
    Yet he was nothing to be won or lost.
    All lands to him were Ithaca: love-tossed
He loathed the fraud, yet would not bed alone.

268

Pickin em Up and Layin em Down

There's a long-legged girl
in San Francisco
by the Golden Gate.
She said she'd give me all I wanted
but I just couldn't wait.

I started to
Pickin em up
                and layin em down,
Pickin em up
                and layin em down,
Pickin em up
                and layin em down,
gettin to the next town
Baby.

There's a pretty brown
in Birmingham
Boys, she little and cute
but when she like to tied me down
I had to grab my suit and started to
Pickin em up
                and layin em down,
Pickin em up
                and layin em down,
Pickin em up
                and layin em down,
gettin to the next town
Baby.

I met that lovely Detroit lady
and thought my time had come
But just before I said 'I do'
I said 'I got to run' and started to
Pickin em up
          and layin em down,
Pickin em up
          and layin em down,
Pickin em up
          and layin em down,
gettin to the next town
Baby.

There ain't no words for what I feel
about a pretty face
But if I stay I just might miss
a prettier one some place
I start to
Pickin em up
          and layin em down,
Pickin em up
          and layin em down,
Pickin em up
          and layin em down,
gettin to the next town
Baby.

269

Change

Although thy hand and faith, and good workes too,
Have seal'd thy love which nothing should undoe,
Yea though thou fall backe, that apostasie
Confirme thy love; yet much, much I feare thee.
Women are like the Arts, forc'd unto none,
Open to'all searchers, unpriz'd, if unknowne.
If I have caught a bird, and let him flie,
Another fouler using these meanes, as I,

May catch the same bird; and, as these things bee,
Women are made for men, not him, nor mee.
Foxes and goats; all beasts change when they please,
Shall women, more hot, wily, wild than these,
Be bound to one man, and did Nature then
Idly make them apter to'endure than men?
They'are our clogges, not their owne; if a man bee
Chain'd to a galley, yet the galley'is free;
Who hath a plow-land, casts all his seed corne there,
And yet allowes his ground more corne should beare;
Though Danuby into the sea must flow,
The sea receives the Rhene, Volga, and Po.
By nature, which gave it, this liberty
Thou lov'st, but Oh! canst thou love it and mee?
Likenesse glues love: and if that thou so doe,
To make us like and love, must I change too?
More than thy hate, I hate'it, rather let mee
Allow her change, than change as oft as shee,
And soe not teach, but force my'opinion
To love not any one, nor every one.
To live in one land, is captivitie,
To runne all countries, a wild roguery;
Waters stincke soone, if in one place they bide,
And in the vast sea are more putrifi'd:
But when they kisse one banke, and leaving this
Never looke backe, but the next banke doe kisse,
Then are they purest; Change'is the nursery
Of musicke, joy, life, and eternity.

270

Exhausted now her sighs, and dry her tears,
For twenty youths these more than twenty years,
Anne, turning nun, swears God alone shall have her . . .
God ought to bow profoundly for the favour.

'And if I did, what then?
Are you aggrieved therefore?
The sea hath fish for every man,
And what would you have more?'

Thus did my mistress once
Amaze my mind with doubt;
And popped a question for the nonce,
To beat my brains about.

Whereto I thus replied:
'Each fisherman can wish
That all the seas at every tide
Were his alone to fish;

And so did I, in vain;
But since it may not be,
Let such fish there as find the gain,
And leave the loss for me.

And with such luck and loss
I will content myself,
Till tides of turning time may toss
Such fishers on the shelf.

And when they stick on sands,
That every man may see,
Then will I laugh and clap my hands,
As they do now at me.'

Comin thro' the rye, poor body,
    Comin thro' the rye,
She draigl't a' her petticoatie
    Comin thro' the rye.
        Oh Jenny's a' weet, poor body,
            Jenny's seldom dry;
        She draigl't a' her petticoatie
            Comin thro' the rye.

Gin a body meet a body
    Comin thro' the rye,
Gin a body kiss a body
    Need a body cry.
        Oh Jenny's a' weet, &c.

Gin a body meet a body
    Comin thro' the glen;
Gin a body kiss a body
    Need the warld ken!
        Oh Jenny's a' weet, &c.

273

Lies About Love

We are all liars, because
the truth of yesterday becomes a lie tomorrow,
whereas letters are fixed,
and we live by the letter of truth.
The love I feel for my friend, this year,
is different from the love I felt last year.
If it were not so, it would be a lie.
Yet we reiterate love! love! love!
as if it were coin with a fixed value
instead of a flower that dies, and opens a different bud.

274

The constant Lover

Out upon it, I have lov'd
    Three whole days together;
And am like to love three more,
    If it hold fair weather.

Time shall moult away his wings
    Ere he shall discover
In the whole wide world agen
    Such a constant Lover.

But a pox upon't, no praise
　　There is due at all to me:
Love with me had made no stay,
　　Had it any been but she.

Had it any been but she
　　And that very very Face,
There had been at least ere this
　　A dozen dozen in her place.

275

Girl

From the crowded platform
Of this end-of-line resort
You wave goodbye to me.

There are tears in your eyes
As you scan the new arrivals
For your next lover.

276

Love and Jealousy

When gods had framed the sweet of women's face,
　　And locked men's looks within their golden hair,
That Phoebus blushed to see their matchless grace,
　　And heavenly gods on earth did make repair;
To quip fair Venus' overweening pride,
Love's happy thoughts to jealousy were tied.

Then grew a wrinkle on fair Venus' brow;
　　The amber sweet of love was turned to gall;
Gloomy was heaven; bright Phoebus did avow
　　He could be coy, and would not love at all,
Swearing, no greater mischief could be wrought
Than love united to a jealous thought.

277

Against Iealousie

Wretched and foolish Jealousie,
How cam'st thou thus to enter me?
    I n(e)'re was of thy kind;
    Nor have I yet the narrow mind
        To vent that poore desire,
That others should not warme them at my fire,
      I wish the Sun should shine
On all mens Fruit, and flowers, as well as mine.

But under the Disguise of love,
Thou sai'st, thou only cam'st to prove
    What my Affections were.
    Think'st thou that love is help'd by feare?
      Goe, get thee quickly forth,
Loves sicknesse, and his noted want of worth,
      Seeke doubting Men to please,
I ne're will owe my health to a disease.

278

Jealosie

Fond woman, which would'st have thy husband die,
And yet complain'st of his great jealousie;
If swolne with poyson, hee lay in'his last bed,
His body with a sere-barke covered,
Drawing his breath, as thick and short, as can
The nimblest crocheting Musitian,
Ready with loathsome vomiting to spue
His Soule out of one hell, into a new,
Made deafe with his poore kindreds howling cries,
Begging with few feign'd teares, great legacies,
Thou would'st not weepe, but jolly,'and frolicke bee,
As a slave, which to morrow should be free;
Yet weep'st thou, when thou seest him hungerly
Swallow his owne death, hearts-bane jealousie.
O give him many thanks, he'is courteous,
That in suspecting kindly warneth us.

Wee must not, as wee us'd, flout openly,
In scoffing ridles, his deformitie;
Nor at his boord together being satt,
With words, nor touch, scarce lookes adulterate.
Nor when he swolne, and pamper'd with great fare
Sits downe, and snorts, cag'd in his basket chaire,
Must wee usurpe his owne bed any more,
Nor kisse and play in his house, as before.
Now I see many dangers; for that is
His realme, his castle, and his diocesse.
But if, as envious men, which would revile
Their Prince, or coyne his gold, themselves exile
Into another countrie,'and doe it there,
Wee play'in another house, what should we feare?
There we will scorne his houshold policies,
His seely plots, and pensionary spies,
As the inhabitants of Thames right side
Do Londons Major; or Germans, the Popes pride.

279

The Queen of Hearts

How comes it, Flora, that, whenever we
Play cards together, you invariably,
    However the pack parts,
    Still hold the Queen of Hearts?

I've scanned you with a scrutinizing gaze,
Resolved to fathom these your secret ways:
    But, sift them as I will,
    Your ways are secret still.

I cut and shuffle; shuffle, cut, again;
But all my cutting, shuffling, proves in vain:
    Vain hope, vain forethought too;
    That Queen still falls to you.

I dropped her once, prepense; but, ere the deal
Was dealt, your instinct seemed her loss to feel:
    'There should be one card more,'
    You said, and searched the floor.

I cheated once; I made a private notch
In Heart-Queen's back, and kept a lynx-eyed watch;
    Yet such another back
    Deceived me in the pack:

The Queen of Clubs assumed by arts unknown
An imitative dint that seemed my own;
    This notch, not of my doing,
    Misled me to my ruin.

280

When I in Praise

When I in praise of babies speak,
    She coldly smiles like winter's snow,
And looks on me with no soft eye:
    Yet I have seen her kiss them so,
Her wealth of rapture made them cry.

Sometimes it seems her blood's too cold
    For Love to even wet his toes,
Much less to paddle all about;
    But when she's kissed till her eyes close,
That god is warmer in than out.

I laugh, when she for other men
    Confesses love; but when she says
She hated one man she could kill,
    My heart is all one jealous blaze,
For, pity me, she hates him still!

281

Hey ho, what shall I say?
Sir John hath carried my wife away.
    They were gone ere I wist,
    She will come when she list.
Hey trolly lolly,
    Come again, ho!

Bill 'Awkins

'''As anybody seen Bill 'Awkins?'
        'Now 'ow in the devil would I know?'
'''E's taken my girl out walkin',
        An' I've got to tell 'im so –
                Gawd – bless – 'im!
        I've got to tell 'im so.'

'D'yer know what 'e's like, Bill 'Awkins?'
        'Now what in the devil would I care?'
'''E's the livin', breathin' image of an organ-grinder's monkey,
        With a pound of grease in 'is 'air –
                Gawd – bless – 'im!
        An' a pound o' grease in 'is 'air.'

'An' s'pose you met Bill 'Awkins,
        Now what in the devil 'ud ye do?'
'I'd open 'is cheek to 'is chin-strap buckle,
        An' bung up 'is both eyes, too –
                Gawd – bless – 'im!
        An' bung up 'is both eyes, too!'

'Look 'ere, where' e comes, Bill 'Awkins!
        Now, what in the devil will you say?'
'It isn't fit an' proper to be fightin' on a Sunday,
        So I'll pass 'im the time o' day –
                Gawd – bless – 'im!
        I'll pass 'im the time o' day!'

283

To Carrey Clavel

You turn your back, you turn your back,
    And never your face to me,
Alone you take your homeward track
    And scorn my company.

What will you do when Charley's seen
    Dewbeating down this way?
– You'll turn your back as now, you mean?
    Nay, Carrey Clavel, nay!

You'll see none's looking; put your lip
    Up like a tulip, so;
And he will coll you, bend, and sip:
    Yes, Carrey, yes; I know!

284

For my Lover,
returning to his Wife

She is all there.
She was melted carefully down for you
and cast up from your childhood,
cast up from your one hundred favorite aggies.

She has always been there, my darling.
She is, in fact, exquisite.
Fireworks in the dull middle of February
and as real as a cast-iron pot.

Let's face it, I have been momentary.
A luxury. A bright red sloop in the harbor.
My hair rising like smoke from the car window.
Littleneck clams out of season.

She is more than that. She is your have to have,
has grown you your practical your tropical growth.
This is not an experiment. She is all harmony.
She sees to oars and oarlocks for the dinghy,

[258]

has placed wild flowers at the window at breakfast,
sat by the potter's wheel at midday,
set forth three children under the moon,
three cherubs drawn by Michelangelo,

done this with her legs spread out
in the terrible months in the chapel.
If you glance up, the children are there
like delicate balloons resting on the ceiling.

She has also carried each one down the hall
after supper, their heads privately bent,
two legs protesting, person to person,
her face flushed with a song and their little sleep.

I give you back your heart.
I give you permission –

for the fuse inside her, throbbing
angrily in the dirt, for the bitch in her
and the burying of her wound –
for the burying of her small red wound alive –

for the pale flickering flare under her ribs,
for the drunken sailor who waits in her left pulse,
for the mother's knee, for the stockings,
for the garter belt, for the call –

the curious call
when you will burrow in arms and breasts
and tug at the orange ribbon in her hair
and answer the call, the curious call.

She is so naked and singular.
She is the sum of yourself and your dream.
Climb her like a monument, step after step.
She is solid.

As for me, I am a watercolor.
I wash off.

285

The Roadmap

If I saw you liked that dull unhappy boy
and let you be, and did not react
to see you driving off together
to the country on Sundays
                              it was
to make your position indefensible
and, that established,
must not my own lack of blame
survive, copious?
(How can you answer back? You were in the wrong.)

I teased a schoolmaster when I was twelve
until his accumulated rage
was out of proportion to the offence.
Thus, I reasoned, there could be no offence.
My emotions drew up a roadmap.

Now my mind catches up and looks back.

And wreckages of trust litter the route
each an offence against me.
I gaze back
              in hardened innocence.

286

Dear, though the night is gone,
The dream still haunts to-day
That brought us to a room,
Cavernous, lofty as
A railway terminus,
And crowded in that gloom
Were beds, and we in one
In a far corner lay.

Our whisper woke no clocks,
We kissed and I was glad
At everything you did,
Indifferent to those
Who sat with hostile eyes
In pairs on every bed,
Arms round each other's necks,
Inert and vaguely sad.

O but what worm of guilt
Or what malignant doubt
Am I the victim of;
That you then, unabashed,
Did what I never wished,
Confessed another love;
And I, submissive, felt
Unwanted and went out?

287

The Drained Cup

'T' snow is witherin' off'n th' gress –
    Lad, should I tell thee summat?
T' snow is witherin' off'n th' gress
An' mist is suckin' at th' spots o' snow,
An' ower a' the thaw an' mess
There's a moon, full blow.
    Lad, but I'm tellin' thee summat!

Tha's bin snowed up i' this cottage wi' me –
    'Ark, tha'rt for hearin' summat!
Tha's bin snowed up i' this cottage wi' me
While t' clocks 'as a' run down an' stopped,
An' t' short days goin' unknown ter thee
Unbeknown has dropped.
    Yi, but I'm tellin' thee summat.

How many days dost think has gone
    Now, lad, I'm axin' thee summat.
How many days dost think has gone?
How many times has t' candle-light shone
On thy face as tha got more white an' wan?
    – Seven days, my lad, or none!
        Aren't ter hearin' summat?

Tha come ter say good-bye ter me,
    Tha wert frit o' summat.
Tha come ter ha' finished an' done wi' me
An' off to a gel as wor younger than me,
An' fresh an' more nicer for marryin' wi' –
    Yi, but tha'rt frit o' summat.

Ah wunna kiss thee, tha trembles so!
    Tha'rt daunted, or summat.
Tha arena very flig ter go.
Dost want me ter want thee again? Nay though,
There's hardly owt left o' thee; get up an' go!
    Or dear o' me, say summat.

Tha wanted ter leave me that bad, tha knows!
    Doesn't ter know it?
But tha wanted me more ter want thee, so's
Tha could let thy very soul out. A man
Like thee can't rest till his last spunk goes
Out of 'im into a woman as can
    Draw it out of 'im. Did ter know it?

Tha thought tha wanted a little wench,
    Ay, lad, I'll tell thee thy mind.
Tha thought tha wanted a little wench
As 'ud make thee a wife an' look up ter thee.
As 'ud wince when that touched 'er close, an' blench
An' lie frightened ter death under thee.
    She worn't hard ter find.

Tha thought tha wanted ter be rid o' me.
    'Appen tha did, an' a'.
Tha thought tha wanted ter marry an' see
If ter couldna be master an' th' woman's boss.
Tha'd need a woman different from me,
An' tha knowed it; ay, yet tha comes across
    Ter say good-bye! an' a'.

I tell thee tha won't be satisfied,
    Tha might as well listen, tha knows.
I tell thee tha won't be satisfied
Till a woman has drawn the last last drop
O' thy spunk, an' tha'rt empty an' mortified.
Empty an' empty from bottom to top.
    It's true, tha knows.

Tha'rt one o' th' men as has got to drain
    – An' I've loved thee for it,
Their blood in a woman, to the very last vein.
Tha *must*, though tha tries ter get away.
Tha wants it, and everything else is in vain.
    An' a woman like me loves thee for it.

Maun tha cling to the wa' as tha stan's?
    Ay, an' tha maun.
An' tha looks at me, an' tha understan's.
Yi, tha can go. Tha hates me now.
But tha'lt come again. Because when a man's
Not finished, he hasn't, no matter how.
    Go then, sin' tha maun.

Tha come ter say good-bye ter me.
    Now go then, now then go.
It's ta'en thee seven days ter say it ter me.
Now go an' marry that wench an' see
How long it'll be afore tha'lt be
Weary an' sick o' the likes o' she,
    An' hankerin' for me. But go!

Never seek to tell thy love,
Love that never told can be;
For the gentle wind does move
Silently, invisibly.

I told my love, I told my love.
I told her all my heart;
Trembling, cold, in ghastly fears,
Ah! she doth depart.

Soon as she was gone from me,
A traveller came by,
Silently, invisibly:
He took her with a sigh.

289

Non Sum Qualis Eram Bonae
Sub Regno Cynarae

Last night, ah, yesternight, betwixt her lips and mine
There fell thy shadow, Cynara! thy breath was shed
Upon my soul between the kisses and the wine;
And I was desolate and sick of an old passion,
    Yea, I was desolate and bow'd my head:
I have been faithful to thee, Cynara! in my fashion.

All night upon mine heart I felt her warm heart beat,
Night-long within mine arms in love and sleep she lay;
Surely the kisses of her bought red mouth were sweet;
But I was desolate and sick of an old passion,
    When I awoke and found the dawn was gray:
I have been faithful to thee, Cynara! in my fashion.

I have forgot much, Cynara! gone with the wind,
Flung roses, roses, riotously with the throng,
Dancing, to put thy pale lost lilies out of mind;
But I was desolate and sick of an old passion,
    Yea, all the time, because the dance was long:
I have been faithful to thee, Cynara! in my fashion.

I cried for madder music and for stronger wine,
But when the feast is finish'd and the lamps expire,
Then falls thy shadow, Cynara! the night is thine;
And I am desolate and sick of an old passion,
    Yea, hungry for the lips of my desire:
I have been faithful to thee, Cynara! in my fashion.

290

Clio's

Am I to be blamed for the state of it now? – Surely not –
Her poor wee fractured soul that I loved for its lightness and left?
Now she rings up pathetically, not to make claims of me,
Only to be in her wild way solicitous:
'Do you know of a restaurant called *Clio's* – or something like that –
At number *forty-three* in its road or street, – and the owner
Is beautiful, rich and Italian – you see, I dreamt of it,
And I can't relax without telling you never to go there,
Divining, somehow, that for you the place is *danger* –'

(But I dine at Clio's every night, poor lamb.)

291

Mr Waterman

'Now, we're quite private in here. You can tell me your troubles. The pond, I think you said . . .'
    'We never really liked that pond in the garden. At times it was choked with a sort of weed, which, if you pulled one thread, gleefully unravelled until you had an empty basin before you and the whole of the pond in a soaking heap at your side. Then at other times it was as clear as gin, and lay in the grass staring upwards. If you came anywhere near, the gaze shifted sideways, and it was you that was being stared at, not the empty sky. If you were so bold as to come right up to the edge, swaggering and talking loudly to show you were not afraid, it presented you with so perfect a reflection that you stayed there spellbound and nearly missed dinner getting to know yourself. It had hypnotic powers.'
    'Very well. Then what happened?'
    'Near the pond was a small bell hung on a bracket, which the milkman used to ring as he went out to tell us upstairs in the bedroom that we could

go down and make the early-morning tea. This bell was near a little avenue of rose-trees. One morning, very early indeed, it tinged loudly and when I looked out I saw that the empty bottles we had put out the night before were full of bright green pondwater. I had to go down and empty them before the milkman arrived. This was only the beginning. One evening I was astounded to find a brace of starfish coupling on the ornamental stone step of the pool, and, looking up, my cry to my wife to come and look was stifled by the sight of a light peppering of barnacles on the stems of the rose-trees. The vermin had evidently crept there, taking advantage of the thin film of moisture on the ground after the recent very wet weather. I dipped a finger into the pond and tasted it: it was brackish.'

'But it got worse.'

'It got worse: one night of howling wind and tempestuous rain I heard muffled voices outside shouting in rural tones: "Belay there, you lubbers!" "Box the foresail capstan!" "A line! A line! Give me a line there, for Davy Jones' sake!" and a great creaking of timbers. In the morning, there was the garden-seat, which was too big to float, dragged tilting into the pond, half in and half out.'

'But you could put up with all this. How did the change come about?'

'It was getting playful, obviously, and inventive, if ill-informed, and might have got dangerous. I decided to treat it with the consideration and dignity which it would probably later have insisted on, and I invited it in as a lodger, bedding it up in the old bathroom. At first I thought I would have to run canvas troughs up the stairs so it could get to its room without soaking the carpet, and I removed the flap from the letter-box so it would be free to come and go, but it soon learnt to keep its form quite well, and get about in macintosh and goloshes, opening doors with gloved fingers.'

'Until a week ago . . .'

'A week ago it started sitting with us in the lounge (and the electric fire had to be turned off, as the windows kept on steaming up). It had accidentally included a goldfish in its body, and when the goggling dolt swam up the neck into the crystal-clear head, it dipped its hand in and fumbled about with many ripples and grimaces, plucked it out, and offered the fish to my wife, with a polite nod. She was just about to go into the kitchen and cook the supper, but I explained quickly that goldfish were bitter to eat, and he put it back. However, I was going to give him a big plate of ice-cubes, which he would have popped into his head and enjoyed sucking, although his real tipple is distilled water, while we watched television, but he didn't seem to want anything. I suppose he thinks he's big enough already.'

'Free board and lodging, eh?'

'I don't know what rent to charge him. I thought I might ask him to join the river for a spell and bring us back some of the money that abounds there: purses lost overboard from pleasure-steamers, rotting away in the mud, and so forth. But he has grown very intolerant of dirt, and might find it difficult to get clean again. Even worse, he might not be able to free himself from his rough dirty cousins, and come roaring back as an impossible green seething giant, tall as the river upended, buckling into the sky, and swamp us and the whole village as well. I shudder to think what would happen if he got as far as the sea, his spiritual home: the country would be in danger. I am at my wits' end, for he is idle, and lounges about all day.'

'Well, that's harmless enough . . .'

'If he's not lounging, he toys with his shape, restlessly. Stripping off his waterproof, he is a charming dolls'-house of glass, with doors and windows opening and shutting; a tree that thrusts up and fills the room; a terrifying shark-shape that darts about between the legs of the furniture, or lurks in the shadows of the room, gleaming in the light of the television-tube; a fountain that blooms without spilling a drop; or, and this image constantly recurs, a very small man with a very large head and streaming eyes, who gazes mournfully up at my wife (she takes no notice), and collapses suddenly into his tears wth a sob and a gulp. Domestic, pastoral-phallic, maritime-ghastly, stately-gracious or grotesque-pathetic: he rings the changes on a gamut of moods, showing off, while I have to sit aside slumped in my armchair unable to compete, reflecting what feats he may be able to accomplish in due course with his body, what titillating shapes impose, what exaggerated parts deploy, under his macintosh. I dread the time (for it will come) when I shall arrive home unexpectedly early, and hear a sudden scuffle-away in the wastepipes, and find my wife ('just out of the shower, dear') with that moist look in her eyes, drying her hair: and then to hear him swaggering in from the garden drains, talking loudly about his day's excursion, as if nothing at all had been going on. For he learns greater charm each day, this Mr Waterman, and can be as stubborn as winter and gentle as the warm rains of spring.'

I should say that you have a real problem there, but it's too early for a solution yet, until I know you better. Go away, take a week off from the office, spend your time with your wife, relax, eat plenty of nourishing meals, plenty of sex and sleep. Then come and see me again. Good afternoon.

'The next patient, nurse. Ah, Mr Waterman. Sit down, please. Does the gas fire trouble you? No? I can turn it off if you wish. Well now, we're quite private in here. You can tell me your troubles. A married, air-breathing woman, I think you said . . .'

'Is my team ploughing,
    That I was used to drive
And hear the harness jingle
    When I was man alive?'

Ay, the horses trample,
    The harness jingles now;
No change though you lie under
    The land you used to plough.

'Is football playing
    Along the river shore,
With lads to chase the leather,
    Now I stand up no more?'

Ay, the ball is flying,
    The lads play heart and soul;
The goal stands up, the keeper
    Stands up to keep the goal.

'Is my girl happy,
    That I thought hard to leave,
And has she tired of weeping
    As she lies down at eve?'

Ay, she lies down lightly,
    She lies not down to weep:
Your girl is well contented.
    Be still, my lad, and sleep.

'Is my friend hearty,
    Now I am thin and pine,
And has he found to sleep in
    A better bed than mine?'

Yes, lad, I lie easy,
    I lie as lads would choose;
I cheer a dead man's sweetheart,
    Never ask me whose.

Act Five

DEAR GHOST

Sometimes these cogitations still amaze
The troubled midnight and the noon's repose.
ELIOT 'La Figlia Che Piange'

Back to thy solitude again!
ARNOLD 'Isolation: To Marguerite'

We miss our cue.
WILLIAM EMPSON 'Villanelle'

Simpleton! will you never learn
That girls and time will not return.
LANDOR 'Defiance'

Dear ghost, in the past did you ever find
The thought 'What profit,' move me much?
Yet abides the fact, indeed, the same, –
You are past love, praise, indifference, blame.
HARDY 'Your Last Drive'

Meeting

If we shall live, we live:
   If we shall die, we die:
If we live we shall meet again:
    But to-night, good-bye.
One word, let but one be heard –
     What, not one word?

If we sleep we shall wake again
    And see to-morrow's light:
If we wake, we shall meet again:
     But to-night, good-night.
     Good-night, my lost and found –
      Still not a sound?

     If we live, we must part:
If we die, we part in pain:
    If we die, we shall part
    Only to meet again.
By those tears on either cheek,
    To-morrow you will speak.

    To meet, worth living for:
    Worth dying for, to meet.
    To meet, worth parting for:
    Bitter forgot in sweet.
    To meet, worth parting before,
    Never to part more.

Shake hands, we shall never be friends, all's over;
    I only vex you the more I try.
All's wrong that ever I've done or said,
And nought to help it in this dull head:
    Shake hands, here's luck, good-bye.

But if you come to a road where danger
    Or guilt or anguish or shame's to share,
Be good to the lad that loves you true
And the soul that was born to die for you,
    And whistle and I'll be there.

295

Twilight Night

I

We met hand to hand,
    We clasped hands close and fast,
As close as oak and ivy stand:
    But it is past;
Come day, come night, day comes at last.

We loosed hand from hand,
    We parted face from face:
Each went his way to his own land
    At his own pace,
Each went to fill his separate place.

If we should meet one day,
    If both should not forget,
We shall clasp hands the accustomed way,
    As when we met,
So long ago, as I remember yet.

Where my heart is (wherever that may be)
   Might I but follow!
If you fly thither over heath and lea,
O honey-seeking bee,
   O careless swallow,
Bid some for whom I watch keep watch for me.

Alas that we must dwell, my heart and I,
   So far asunder!
Hours wax to days, and days and days creep by;
I watch with wistful eye,
   I wait and wonder:
When will that day draw nigh – that hour draw nigh?

Not yesterday, and not I think to-day;
   Perhaps to-morrow.
Day after day 'To-morrow' thus I say:
I watched so yesterday
   In hope and sorrow,
Again to-day I watch the accustomed way.

296

Good-bye for a Long Time

A furnished room beyond the stinging of
The sea, reached by a gravel road in which
Puddles of rain stare up with clouded eyes:

The photographs of other lives than ours;
The scattered evidence of your so brief
Possession; daffodils fading in a vase.

Our kisses here as they have always been,
Half sensual, half sacred, bringing like
A scent our years together, crowds of ghosts.

And then among the thousand thoughts of parting
The kisses grow perfunctory; the years
Are waved away by your retreating arm.

And now I am alone. I am once more
The far-off boy without a memory,
Wandering with an empty deadened self.

Suddenly under my feet there is the small
Body of a bird, startling against the gravel.
I see its tight shut eye, a trace of moisture.

And, ruffling its gentle breast the wind, its beak
Sharpened by death: and I am yours again,
Hurt beyond hurting, never to forget.

297

from *Diana*

Dear to my soul! then leave me not forsaken!
Fly not! my heart within thy bosom sleepeth:
Even from myself and sense I have betaken
Me unto thee, for whom my spirit weepeth;
And on the shore of that salt teary sea,
Couched in a bed of unseen seeming pleasure
Where, in imaginary thoughts, thy fair self lay;
But being waked, robbed of my life's best treasure,
I call the heavens, air, earth, and seas to hear
My love, my truth, and black disdained estate,
Beating the rocks with bellowings of despair,
Which still with plaints my words reverberate:
   Sighing, 'Alas, what shall become of me?'
   Whilst Echo cries, 'What shall become of me?'

298

Love Letter

The movies and the magazines are all of them liars
Pretending that love has anything to do with pleasure,
With the bland Horatian life of culture and wines
      And conversational friendship.

For love has a puritanical loathing of art and
Food, and even of sensible average people
Who are glad to tell him the time: for spiders and men
      Love is a destroyer of cities.

Now, when my work is over, I sit at the window,
The senses huddled like cattle observing nothing,
Or run to the lavatory; in the net of the ribs
      The heart flails like a salmon.

O but I was mad to come here, even for money:
To have put myself at the mercy of the postman and the daydream,
That incorrigible nightmare in which you lie weeping or ill,
      Or drowned in the arms of another;

To have left you now, when I know what this warm May weather
Does to the city: how it brings out the plump little girls and
Truculent sailors into the parks and sets
      The bowels of boys on fire.

When, after all, what reason have you to love me,
Who have neither the prettiness and moisture of youth, the appeal of the
      baby,
The fencing wit of the old successful life,
      Nor brutality's fascination?

Some say there's a treasure in all; but, in some, to find it
Takes an anthropologist's patience: grown-up in a prison,
The heart shrinks back from the visitor's hand like a child
      That only knows how to be punished.

Have you really the wish to endure the boredom of healing
What without you will never get well? O never leave me.
Never. Only the closest attention of your mouth
      Can make me worthy of loving.

As you came from the holy land
    Of Walsinghame
Mett you not with my true loue
    By the way as you came?

How shall I know your trew loue
    That haue mett many one
As I went to the holy lande
    That haue come, that haue gone?

She is neyther whyte nor browne
    Butt as the heauens fayre
There is none hathe a forme so diuine
    In the earth or the ayre.

Such an one did I meet, good Sir,
    Suche an Angelyke face,
Who lyke a queene, lyke a nymph, did appere
    By her gate, by her grace.

She hath lefte me here all alone,
    All allone as vnknowne,
Who somtymes did me lead with her selfe,
    And me loude as her owne.

Whats the cause that she leaues you alone
    And a new waye doth take;
Who loued you once as her owne
    And her ioye did you make?

I haue loude her all my youth,
    Butt now ould, as you see,
Loue lykes not the fallyng frute
    From the wythered tree.

Know that loue is a careless chylld
    And forgets promyse paste,
He is blynd, he is deaff when he lyste
    And in faythe neuer faste.

His desyre is a dureless contente
    And a trustless ioye
He is wonn with a world of despayre
    And is lost with a toye.

Of women kynde suche indeed is the loue
    Or the word Loue abused
Vnder which many chyldysh desyres
    And conceytes are excusde.

Butt true Loue is a durable fyre
    In the mynde euer burnynge;
Neuer sycke, neuer ould, neuer dead,
    From itt selfe neuer turnynge.

300

They fle from me that sometyme did me seke
    With naked fote stalking in my chambre.
I have sene theim gentill tame and meke
    That nowe are wyld and do not remembre
    That sometyme they put theimself in daunger
To take bred at my hand; and nowe they raunge
Besely seking with a continuell chaunge.

Thancked be fortune, it hath ben othrewise
    Twenty tymes better; but ons in speciall,
In thyn arraye after a pleasaunt gyse,
    When her lose gowne from her shoulders did fall,
    And she me caught in her armes long and small;
Therewithall swetely did me kysse,
And softely saide, *dere hert, howe like you this?*

It was no dreme: I lay brode waking.
    But all is torned thorough my gentilnes
Into a straunge fasshion of forsaking;
    And I have leve to goo of her goodenes,
    And she also to vse new fangilnes.
But syns that I so kyndely ame serued,
I would fain knowe what she hath deserued.

[277]

On His Mistris

By our first strange and fatall interview,
By all desires which thereof did ensue,
By our long starving hopes, by that remorse
Which my words masculine perswasive force
Begot in thee, and by the memory
Of hurts, which spies and rivals threatned me,
I calmly beg: But by thy fathers wrath,
By all paines, which want and divorcement hath,
I conjure thee, and all the oathes which I
And thou have sworne to seale joynt constancy,
Here I unsweare, and overswear them thus,
Thou shalt not love by wayes so dangerous.
Temper, ô faire Love, loves impetuous rage,
Be my true Mistris still, not my faign'd Page;
I'll goe, and, by thy kinde leave, leave behinde
Thee, onely worthy to nurse in my minde,
Thirst to come backe; ô if thou die before,
My soule from other lands to thee shall soare.
Thy (else Almighty) beautie cannot move
Rage from the Seas, nor thy love teach them love,
Nor tame wilde Boreas harshnesse; Thou hast reade
How roughly hee in peeces shivered
Faire Orithea, whom he swore he lov'd.
Fall ill or good, tis madnesse to have prov'd
Dangers unurg'd; Feed on this flattery,
That absent Lovers one in th'other be.
Dissemble nothing, not a boy, nor change
Thy bodies habite, nor mindes; bee not strange
To thy selfe onely; All will spie in thy face
A blushing womanly discovering grace;
Richly cloath'd Apes, are call'd Apes, and as soon
Ecclips'd as bright we call the Moone the Moone.
Men of France, changeable Camelions,
Spittles of diseases, shops of fashions,
Loves fuellers, and the rightest company
Of Players, which upon the worlds stage be,
Will quickly know thee, and no lesse, alas!
Th'indifferent Italian, as we passe

His warme land, well content to thinke thee Page,
Will hunt thee with such lust, and hideous rage,
As *Lots* faire guests were vext. But none of these
Nor spungy hydroptique Dutch shall thee displease,
If thou stay here. O stay here, for, for thee
England is onely a worthy Gallerie,
To walke in expectation, till from thence
Our greatest King call thee to his presence.
When I am gone, dreame me some happinesse,
Nor let thy lookes our long hid love confesse,
Nor praise, nor dispraise me, nor blesse nor curse
Openly loves force, nor in bed fright thy Nurse
With midnights startings, crying out, oh, oh
Nurse, ô my love is slaine, I saw him goe
O'r the white Alpes alone; I saw him I,
Assail'd, fight, taken, stabb'd, bleed, fall, and die.
Augure me better chance, except dread *Jove*
Thinke it enough for me to'have had thy love.

302

Farewell thou art too deare for my possessing,
And like enough thou knowst thy estimate,
The Charter of thy worth giues thee releasing:
My bonds in thee are all determinate.
For how do I hold thee but by thy granting,
And for that ritches where is my deseruing?
The cause of this faire guift in me is wanting,
And so my pattent back againe is sweruing.
Thy selfe thou gau'st, thy owne worth then not knowing,
Or mee to whom thou gau'st it, else mistaking,
So thy great guift vpon misprision growing,
Comes home againe, on better iudgement making.
  Thus haue I had thee as a dreame doth flatter,
  In sleepe a King, but waking no such matter.

303
Divided

Two spheres on meeting may so softly collide
They stay, as if still kissing, side by side.
Lovers may part for ever – the cause so small
Not even a lynx could see a gap at all.

304
A Valediction: forbidding Mourning

As virtuous men passe mildly away,
   And whisper to their soules, to goe,
Whilst some of their sad friends doe say,
   The breath goes now, and some say, no:

So let us melt, and make no noise,
   No teare-floods, nor sigh-tempests move,
T'were prophanation of our joyes
   To tell the layetie our love.

Moving of th'earth brings harmes and feares,
   Men reckon what it did and meant,
But trepidation of the spheares,
   Though greater farre, is innocent.

Dull sublunary lovers love
   (Whose soule is sense) cannot admit
Absence, because it doth remove
   Those things which elemented it.

But we by a love, so much refin'd,
   That our selves know not what it is,
Inter-assured of the mind,
   Care lesse, eyes, lips, and hands to misse.

Our two soules therefore, which are one,
   Though I must goe, endure not yet
A breach, but an expansion,
   Like gold to ayery thinnesse beate.

If they be two, they are two so
    As stiffe twin compasses are two,
Thy soule the fixt foot, makes no show
    To move, but doth, if the'other doe.

And though it in the center sit,
    Yet when the other far doth rome,
It leanes, and hearkens after it,
    And growes erect, as that comes home.

Such wilt thou be top mee, who must
    Like th'other foot, obliquely runne;
Thy firmnes drawes my circle just,
    And makes me end, where I begunne.

305

Parting with Lucasia, A Song

Well, we will do that rigid thing
    Which makes spectators think we part;
Though Absence hath for none a sting
    But those who keep each other's heart.

And when our sense is dispossest,
    Our labouring souls will heave and pant,
And gasp for one another's breast,
    Since their conveyances they want.

Nay, we have felt the tedious smart
    Of absent Friendship, and do know
That when we die we can but part;
    And who knows what we shall do now?

Yet I must go: we will submit,
    And so our own disposers be;
For while we nobly suffer it,
    We triumph o'er Necessity.

By this we shall be truly great,
    If having other things o'ercome,
To make our victory complete
    We can be conquerors at home.

Nay then to meet we may conclude,
    And all obstructions overthrow,
Since we our passion have subdu'd,
    Which is the strongest thing I know.

306
from *Don Juan*

'They tell me 'tis decided you depart:
    'Tis wise – 'tis well, but not the less a pain;
I have no further claim on your young heart,
    Mine is the victim, and would be again:
To love too much has been the only art
    I used; – I write in haste, and if a stain
Be on this sheet, 'tis not what it appears;
My eyeballs burn and throb, but have no tears.

'I loved, I love you, for this love have lost
    State, station, heaven, mankind's, my own esteem,
And yet cannot regret what it hath cost,
    So dear is still the memory of that dream;
Yet, if I name my guilt, 'tis not to boast,
    None can deem harshlier of me than I deem:
I trace this scrawl because I cannot rest –
I've nothing to reproach or to request.

'Man's love is of man's life a thing apart,
    'Tis woman's whole existence; man may range
The court, camp, church, the vessel, and the mart;
    Sword, gown, gain, glory, offer in exchange
Pride, fame, ambition, to fill up his heart,
    And few there are whom these cannot estrange;
Men have all these resources, we but one,
To love again, and be again undone.

'You will proceed in pleasure, and in pride,
   Beloved and loving many; all is o'er
For me on earth, except some years to hide
   My shame and sorrow deep in my heart's core:
These I could bear, but cannot cast aside
   The passion which still rages as before, –
And so farewell – forgive me, love me – No,
That word is idle now – but let it go.

'My breast has been all weakness, is so yet;
   But still I think I can collect my mind;
My blood still rushes where my spirit's set,
   As roll the waves before the settled wind;
My heart is feminine, nor can forget –
   To all, except one image, madly blind;
So shakes the needle, and so stands the pole,
As vibrates my fond heart to my fix'd soul.

'I have no more to say, but linger still,
   And dare not set my seal upon this sheet,
And yet I may as well the task fulfil.
   My misery can scarce be more complete:
I had not lived till now, could sorrow kill;
   Death shuns the wretch who fain the blow would meet,
And I must even survive this last adieu,
And bear with life to love and pray for you!'

307

La Figlia che Piange

O quam te memorem virgo . . .

Stand on the highest pavement of the stair –
Lean on a garden urn –
Weave, weave the sunlight in your hair –
Clasp your flowers to you with a pained surprise –
Fling them to the ground and turn
With a fugitive resentment in your eyes:
But weave, weave the sunlight in your hair.

So I would have had him leave,
So I would have had her stand and grieve,
So he would have left
As the soul leaves the body torn and bruised,
As the mind deserts the body it has used.
I should find
Some way incomparably light and deft,
Some way we both should understand,
Simple and faithless as a smile and shake of the hand.

She turned away, but with the autumn weather
Compelled my imagination many days,
Many days and many hours:
Her hair over her arms and her arms full of flowers.

And I wonder how they should have been together!
I should have lost a gesture and a pose.
Sometimes these cogitations still amaze
The troubled midnight and the noon's repose.

308

Before Sunset

Love's twilight wanes in heaven above,
    On earth ere twilight reigns:
Ere fear may feel the chill thereof,
    Love's twilight wanes.

Ere yet the insatiate heart complains
    'Too much, and scarce enough,'
The lip so late athirst refrains.

Soft on the neck of either dove
    Love's hands let slip the reins:
And while we look for light of love
    Love's twilight wanes.

When we two parted
  In silence and tears,
Half broken-hearted
  To sever for years,
Pale grew thy cheek and cold,
  Colder thy kiss;
Truly that hour foretold
  Sorrow to this.

The dew of the morning
  Sunk chill on my brow –
It felt like the warning
  Of what I feel now.
Thy vows are all broken,
  And light is thy fame:
I hear thy name spoken,
  And share in its shame.

They name thee before me,
  A knell to mine ear;
A shudder comes o'er me –
  Why wert thou so dear?
They know not I knew thee,
  Who knew thee too well:–
Long, long shall I rue thee,
  Too deeply to tell.

In secret we met –
  In silence I grieve,
That thy heart could forget,
  Thy spirit deceive.
If I should meet thee
  After long years,
How should I greet thee?
  With silence and tears.

310

The Expiration

So, so, breake off this last lamenting kisse,
    Which sucks two soules, and vapors Both away,
Turne thou ghost that way, and let mee turne this,
    And let our selves benight our happiest day,
We ask'd none leave to love; nor will we owe
    Any, so cheape a death, as saying, Goe;

Goe; and if that word have not quite kil'd thee,
    Ease mee with death, by bidding mee goe too.
Oh, if it have, let my word worke on mee,
    And a just office on a murderer doe.
Except it be too late, to kill me so,
    Being double dead, going, and bidding, goe.

311

The Surrender

My once dear Love! hapless that I no more
Must call thee so; the rich affection's store
That fed our hopes, lies now exhaust and spent,
Like sums of treasure unto bankrupts lent.

We, that did nothing study but the way
To love each other, with which thoughts the day
Rose with delight to us, and with them, set,
Must learn the hateful art, how to forget.

We, that did nothing wish that Heav'n could give,
Beyond ourselves, nor did desire to live
Beyond that wish, all these now cancel must,
As if not writ in faith, but words and dust.

Yet witness those clear vows which lovers make,
Witness the chaste desires that never brake
Into unruly heats; witness that breast
Which in thy bosom anchor'd his whole rest,
'Tis no default in us; I dare acquite
Thy maiden faith, thy purpose fair and white,
As thy pure self. Cross planets did envy
Us to each other, and Heaven did untie
Faster than vows could bind. O that the stars,
When lovers meet, should stand oppos'd in wars!

Since then some higher Destinies command,
Let us not strive nor labour to withstand
What is past help. The longest date of grief
Can never yield a hope of our relief;
And though we waste ourselves in moist laments,
Tears may drown us, but not our discontents.

Fold back our arms, take home our fruitless loves,
That must new fortunes try, like turtle-doves
Dislodged from their haunts. We must in tears
Unwind a love knit up in many years.
In this last kiss I here surrender thee
Back to thyself, so thou again art free.
Thou in another, sad as that, resend
The truest heart that lover ere did lend.

Now turn from each. So fare our sever'd hearts,
As the divorc'd soul from her body parts.

312

Before Parting

A month or twain to live on honeycomb
Is pleasant; but one tires of scented time,
Cold sweet recurrence of accepted rhyme,
And that strong purple under juice and foam
Where the wine's heart has burst;
Nor feel the latter kisses like the first.

Once yet, this poor one time; I will not pray
Even to change the bitterness of it,
The bitter taste ensuing on the sweet,
To make your tears fall where your soft hair lay
All blurred and heavy in some perfumed wise
Over my face and eyes.

And yet who knows what end the scythèd wheat
Makes of its foolish poppies' mouths of red?
These were not sown, these are not harvested,
They grow a month and are cast under feet
And none has care thereof,
As none has care of a divided love.

I know each shadow of your lips by rote,
Each change of love in eyelids and eyebrows;
The fashion of fair temples tremulous
With tender blood, and colour of your throat;
I know not how love is gone out of this,
Seeing that all was his.

Love's likeness there endures upon all these:
But out of these one shall not gather love.
Day hath not strength nor the night shade enough
To make love whole and fill his lips with ease,
As some bee-builded cell
Feels at filled lips the heavy honey swell.

I know not how this last month leaves your hair
Less full of purple colour and hid spice,
And that luxurious trouble of closed eyes
Is mixed with meaner shadow and waste care;
And love, kissed out by pleasure, seems not yet
Worth patience to regret.

313

from *Idea*

Since there's no help, come let us kiss and part –
Nay, I have done, you get no more of me;
And I am glad, yea, glad with all my heart,
That thus so cleanly I myself can free.
Shake hands for ever, cancel all our vows,
And when we meet at any time again,
Be it not seen in either of our brows
That we one jot of former love retain.
Now at the last gasp of love's latest breath,
When, his pulse failing, passion speechless lies,
When faith is kneeling by his bed of death,
And innocence is closing up his eyes, –
   Now, if thou wouldst, when all have given him over,
   From death to life thou might'st him yet recover!

314

Ianthe! you are call'd to cross the sea!
   A path forbidden *me!*
Remember, while the Sun his blessing sheds
   Upon the mountain-heads,
How often we have watcht him laying down
   His brow, and dropt our own
Against each other's, and how faint and short
   And sliding the support!
What will succede it now? Mine is unblest,
   Ianthe! nor will rest
But on the very thought that swells with pain.
   O bid me hope again!
O give me back what Earth, what (without you)
   Not Heaven itself can do –
One of the golden days that we have past,
   And let it be my last!
Or else the gift would be, however sweet,
   Fragile and incomplete.

Les Vaches

The skies have sunk and hid the upper snow,
Home, Rose, and home, Provence and La Palie,
The rainy clouds are filing fast below,
And wet will be the path, and wet shall we.
Home, Rose, and home, Provence and La Palie.

Ah dear, and where is he, a year agone
Who stepped beside and cheered us on and on?
My sweetheart wanders far away from me,
In foreign land or o'er a foreign sea.
Home, Rose, and home, Provence and La Palie.

The lightning zigzags shot across the sky,
(Home, Rose, and home, Provence and La Palie,)
And through the vale the rains go sweeping by,
Ah me, and when in shelter shall we be?
Home, Rose, and home, Provence and La Palie.

Cold, dreary cold, the stormy winds feel they
O'er foreign lands and foreign seas that stray.
(Home, Rose, and home, Provence and La Palie.)
And doth he e'er, I wonder, bring to mind
The pleasant huts and herds he left behind?
And doth he sometimes in his slumbering see
The feeding kine, and doth he think of me,
My sweetheart wandering wheresoe'er it be?
Home, Rose and home, Provence and La Palie.

The thunder bellows far from snow to snow,
(Home, Rose, and home, Provence and La Palie)
And loud and louder roars the flood below.
Heigh ho! but soon in shelter shall we be.
Home, Rose, and home, Provence and La Palie.

Or shall he find before his term be sped,
Some comelier maid that he shall wish to wed?
(Home, Rose, and home, Provence and La Palie,)
For weary is work, and weary day by day
To have your comfort miles on miles away.
Home, Rose, and home, Provence and La Palie.
Or may it be 'tis I shall find my mate,
And he returning see himself too late?
For work we must, and what we see, we see,
And God he knows, and what must be, must be,
When sweethearts wander far away from me.
Home, Rose, and home, Provence and La Palie.

The sky behind is brightening up anew,
(Home, Rose, and home, Provence and La Palie),
The rain is ending, and our journey too;
Heigh ho! aha! for here at home are we:–
In, Rose, and in, Provence and La Palie.

316

Isolation. To Marguerite

We were apart; yet, day by day,
I bade my heart more constant be.
I bade it keep the world away,
And grow a home for only thee;
Nor feared but thy love likewise grew,
Like mine, each day, more tried, more true.

The fault was grave! I might have known,
What far too soon, alas! I learned –
The heart can bind itself alone,
And faith may oft be unreturned.
Self-swayed our feelings ebb and swell –
Thou lov'st no more; – Farewell! Farewell!

Farewell! – and thou, thou lonely heart,
Which never yet without remorse
Even for a moment didst depart
From thy remote and spheréd course
To haunt thy place where passions reign –
Back to thy solitude again!

Back! with the conscious thrill of shame
Which Luna felt, that summer-night,
Flash through her pure immortal frame,
When she forsook the starry height
To hang over Endymion's sleep
Upon the pine-grown Latmian steep.

Yet she, chaste queen, had never proved
How vain a thing is mortal love,
Wandering in Heaven, far removed.
But thou hast long had place to prove
This truth – to prove, and make thine own:
'Thou hast been, shalt be, art, alone.'

Or, if not quite alone, yet they
Which touch thee are unmating things –
Ocean and clouds and night and day;
Lorn autumns and triumphant springs;
And life, and others' joy and pain,
And love, if love, of happier men.

Of happier men – for they, at least,
Have *dreamed* two human hearts might blend
In one, and were through faith released
From isolation without end
Prolonged; nor knew, although not less
Alone than thou, their loneliness.

317
To Marguerite – Continued

Yes! in the sea of life enisled,
With echoing straits between us thrown,
Dotting the shoreless watery wild,
We mortal millions live *alone*.
The islands feel the enclasping flow,
And then their endless bounds they know.

But when the moon their hollows lights,
And they are swept by balms of spring,
And in their glens, on starry nights,
The nightingales divinely sing;
And lovely notes, from shore to shore,
Across the sounds and channels pour –

Oh! then a longing like despair
Is to their farthest caverns sent;
For surely once, they feel, we were
Parts of a single continent!
Now round us spreads the watery plain –
Oh might our marges meet again!

Who ordered, that their longing's fire
Should be, as soon as kindled, cooled?
Who renders vain their deep desire? –
A God, a God their severance ruled!
And bade betwixt their shores to be
The unplumbed, salt, estranging sea.

318

On the Departure Platform

We kissed at the barrier; and passing through
She left me, and moment by moment got
Smaller and smaller, until to my view
        She was but a spot;

A wee white spot of muslin fluff
That down the diminishing platform bore
Through hustling crowds of gentle and rough
        To the carriage door.

Under the lamplight's fitful glowers,
Behind dark groups from far and near,
Whose interests were apart from ours,
        She would disappear,

Then show again, till I ceased to see
That flexible form, that nebulous white;
And she who was more than my life to me
    Had vanished quite . . .

We have penned new plans since that fair fond day,
And in season she will appear again –
Perhaps in the same soft white array –
    But never as then!

– 'And why, young man, must eternally fly
A joy you'll repeat, if you love her well?'
– O friend, nought happens twice thus; why,
    I cannot tell!

319

To Lucasta,
Going to the Warres

Tell me not (Sweet) I am unkinde,
    That from the Nunnerie
Of thy chaste breast, and quiet minde,
    To Warre and Armes I flie.

True; a new Mistresse now I chase,
    The first Foe in the Field;
And with a stronger Faith imbrace
    A Sword, a Horse, a Shield.

Yet this Inconstancy is such,
    As you too shall adore;
I could not love thee (Deare) so much,
    Lov'd I not Honour more.

To Lucasta,
Going beyond the Seas

If to be absent were to be
        Away from thee;
     Or that when I am gone,
     You or I were alone;
Then my *Lucasta* might I crave
Pity from blustring winde, or swallowing wave.

But I'le not sigh one blast or gale
        To swell my saile,
     Or pay a teare to swage
     The foaming blew-Gods rage;
For whether he will let me passe
Or no, I'm still as happy as I was.

Though Seas and Land betwixt us both,
        Our Faith and Troth,
     Like separated soules,
     All time and space controules:
Above the highest sphere wee meet
Unseene, unknowne, and greet as Angels greet.

Sweet William's Farewell to
Black-Ey'd Susan

A BALLAD

All in the *Downs* the fleet was moor'd,
    The streamers waving in the wind,
When black-ey'd *Susan* came aboard.
    Oh! where shall I my true love find!
Tell me, ye jovial sailors, tell me true,
If my sweet *William* sails among the crew.

William, who high upon the yard,
    Rock'd with the billow to and fro,
Soon as her well-known voice he heard,
    He sigh'd, and cast his eyes below:
The cord slides swiftly through his glowing hands,
And, (quick as lightning,) on the deck he stands.

    So the sweet lark, high-pois'd in air,
        Shuts close his pinions to his breast,
    (If, chance, his mate's shrill call he hear)
        And drops at once into her nest.
The noblest Captain in the *British* fleet,
Might envy *William*'s lip those kisses sweet.

    O *Susan, Susan*, lovely dear,
        My vows shall ever true remain;
    Let me kiss off that falling tear,
        We only part to meet again.
Change, as ye list, ye winds; my heart shall be
The faithful compass that still points to thee.

    Believe not what the landmen say,
        Who tempt with doubts thy constant mind:
    They'll tell thee, sailors, when away,
        In ev'ry port a mistress find.
Yes, yes, believe them when they tell thee so,
For thou art present wheresoe'er I go.

    If to far *India*'s coast we sail,
        Thy eyes are seen in di'monds bright,
    Thy breath is *Africk*'s spicy gale,
        Thy skin is ivory, so white.
Thus ev'ry beauteous object that I view,
Wakes in my soul some charm of lovely *Sue*.

    Though battel call me from thy arms,
        Let not my pretty *Susan* mourn;
    Though cannons roar, yet safe from harms,
        William shall to his Dear return.
Love turns aside the balls that round me fly,
Lest precious tears should drop from *Susan*'s eye.

The boatswain gave the dreadful word,
   The sails their swelling bosom spread,
No longer must she stay aboard:
   They kiss'd, she sigh'd, he hung his head.
Her less'ning boat, unwilling rows to land:
Adieu, she cries! and waves her lilly hand.

322
To Avisa

Nay then, farewell, if this be so:
If you be of the purer stamp,
'Gainst wind and tide I cannot row,
I have no oil to feed that lamp:
   Be not too rash, deny not flat,
   For you refuse you know not what.

But rather take a farther day
For farther trial of my faith,
And rather make some wise delay
To see, and take some farther breath:
   He may too rashly be denied
   Whose faithful heart was never tried.

And though I be by jury cast,
Yet let me live a while in hope:
And though I be condemned at last,
Yet let my fancy have some scope:
   And though the body fly away,
   Yet let me with the shadow play.

323
Fare Thee Well

'Alas! they had been friends in youth:
But whispering tongues can poison truth;
And constancy lives in realms above;
And life is thorny; and youth is vain;
And to be wroth with one we love,
Doth work like madness in the brain;
    . . . .

But never either found another
To free the hollow heart from paining –
They stood aloof, the scars remaining,
Like cliffs which had been rent asunder;
A dreary sea now flows between.
But neither heat, nor frost, nor thunder,
Shall wholly do away, I ween,
The marks of that which once hath been.'
                    COLERIDGE's *Christabel*

Fare thee well! and if for ever,
    Still for ever, fare thee well:
Even though unforgiving, never
    'Gainst thee shall my heart rebel.

Would that breast were bared before thee
    Where thy head so oft hath lain.
While that placid sleep came o'er thee
    Which thou ne'er canst know again:

Would that breast, by thee glanced over,
    Every inmost thought could show!
Then thou wouldst at last discover
    'Twas not well to spurn it so.

Though the world for this commend thee –
    Though it smile upon the blow,
Even its praises must offend thee,
    Founded on another's woe:

Though my many faults defaced me,
    Could no other arm be found,
Than the one which once embraced me,
    To inflict a cureless wound?

[298]

Yet, oh yet, thyself deceive not;
    Love may sink by slow decay,
But by sudden wrench, believe not
    Hearts can thus be torn away:

Still thine own its life retaineth,
    Still must mine, though bleeding, beat;
And the undying thought which paineth
    Is – that we no more may meet.

These are words of deeper sorrow
    Than the wail above the dead;
Both shall live, but every morrow
    Wake us from a widow'd bed.

And when thou wouldst solace gather,
    When our child's first accents flow,
Wilt thou teach her to say 'Father!'
    Though his care she must forego?

When her little hands shall press thee,
    When her lip to thine is press'd,
Think of him whose prayer shall bless thee,
    Think of him thy love had bless'd!

Should her lineaments resemble
    Those thou never more may'st see,
Then thy heart will softly tremble
    With a pulse yet true to me.

All my faults perchance thou knowest,
    All my madness none can know;
All my hopes, where'er thou goest,
    Wither, yet with *thee* they go.

Every feeling hath been shaken:
    Pride, which not a world could bow,
Bows to thee – by thee forsaken,
    Even my soul forsakes me now:

But 'tis done – all words are idle –
    Words from me are vainer still;
But the thoughts we cannot bridle
    Force their way without the will.

Fare thee well! thus disunited,
    Torn from every nearer tie,
Sear'd in heart, and lone, and blighted,
    More than this I scarce can die.

324
To Mrs M. A. upon Absence

'Tis now since I began to die
    Four months, yet still I gasping live;
Wrapp'd up in sorrow do I lie,
    Hoping, yet doubting a reprieve.
Adam from Paradise expell'd
Just such a wretched being held.

'Tis not thy love I fear to lose,
    That will in spite of absence hold;
But 'tis the benefit and use
    Is lost, as in imprison'd gold:
Which though the sum be ne'er so great,
Enriches nothing but conceit.

What angry star then governs me
    That I must feel a double smart,
Prisoner to fate as well as thee;
    Kept from thy face, link'd to thy heart?
Because my love all love excels,
Must my grief have no parallels?

Sapless and dead as Winter here
    I now remain, and all I see
Copies of my wild state appear,
    But I am their epitome.
Love me no more, for I am grown
Too dead and dull for thee to own.

325

They that haue powre to hurt, and will doe none,
That doe not do the thing, they most do showe,
Who mouing others, are themselues as stone,
Vnmooued, could, and to temptation slow:
They rightly do inherrit heauens graces,
And husband natures ritches from expence,
They are the Lords and owners of their faces,
Others, but stewards of their excellence:
The sommers flowre is to the sommer sweet,
Though to it selfe, it onely liue and die,
But if that flowre with base infection meete,
The basest weed out-braues his dignity:
    For sweetest things turne sowrest by their deedes,
    Lillies that fester, smell far worse then weeds.

326

He would not stay for me; and who can wonder?
    He would not stay for me to stand and gaze.
I shook his hand and tore my heart in sunder
    And went with half my life about my ways.

327
In a Year

Never any more,
    While I live
Need I hope to see his face
    As before.
Once his love grown chill,
    Mine may strive:
Bitterly we re-embrace,
    Single still.

Was it something said,
    Something done,
Vexed him? was it touch of hand,
    Turn of head?
Strange! that very way
    Love begun:
I as little understand
    Love's decay.

When I sewed or drew,
    I recall
How he looked as if I sung,
    – Sweetly too.
If I spoke a word,
    First of all
Up his cheek the colour sprung,
    Then he heard.

Sitting by my side,
    At my feet,
So he breathed but air I breathed,
    Satisfied!
I, too, at love's brim
    Touched the sweet:
I would die if death bequeathed
    Sweet to him.

'Speak, I love thee best!'
    He exclaimed:
'Let thy love my own foretell!'
    I confessed:
'Clasp my heart on thine,
    'Now unblamed,
'Since upon thy soul as well
    'Hangeth mine!'

Was it wrong to own,
    Being truth?
Why should all the giving prove
    His alone?
I had wealth and ease,
    Beauty, youth:
Since my lover gave me love,
    I gave these.

That was all I meant,
    – To be just,
And the passion I had raised,
    To content.
Since he chose to change
    Gold for dust,
If I gave him what he praised
    Was it strange?

Would he loved me yet,
    On and on,
While I found some way undreamed
    – Paid my debt!
Gave more life and more,
    Till, all gone,
    He should smile 'She never seemed
    'Mine before.

'What, she felt the while,
    'Must I think?
'Love's so different with us men!'
    He should smile:
'Dying for my sake –
    'White and pink!
'Can't we touch these bubbles then
    'But they break?'

Dear, the pang is brief,
    Do thy part,
Have thy pleasure! How perplexed
    Grows belief!
Well, this cold clay clod
    Was man's heart:
Crumble it, and what comes next?
    Is it God?

328
The Last Leaf

'The leaves throng thick above: –
Well, I'll come back, dear Love,
    When they all are down!'

She watched that August tree,
(None now scorned summer as she),
    Till it broidered it brown.

And then October came blowing,
And the leaves showed signs they were going,
    And she saw up through them.

O how she counted them then!
– November left her but ten,
    And started to strew them.

'Ah, when they all are gone,
And the skeleton-time comes on,
    Whom shall I see!'

– When the fifteenth spread its sky
That month, her upturned eye
    Could count but three.

And at the close of the week
A flush flapped over her cheek:
    The last one fell.

But – he did not come. And, at length,
Her hope of him lost all strength,
    And it was as a knell. . . .

When he did come again,
Years later, a husband then,
    Heavy somewhat,

With a smile she reminded him:
And he cried: 'Ah, that vow of our whim! –
    Which I forgot.

'As one does! – And was that the tree?
So it was! – Dear me, dear me:
    Yes: I forgot.'

329

Hoping against Hope

If he would come to-day, to-day, to-day,
    Oh what a day to-day would be!
But now he's away, miles and miles away
    From me across the sea.

O little bird, flying, flying, flying
    To your nest in the warm west,
Tell him as you pass that I am dying,
    As you pass home to your nest.

    I have a sister, I have a brother,
    A faithful hound, a tame white dove;
But I had another, once I had another,
    And I miss him, my love, my love!

In this weary world it is so cold, so cold,
    While I sit here all alone;
I would not like to wait and to grow old,
    But just to be dead and gone.

Make me fair when I lie dead on my bed,
    Fair where I am lying:
Perhaps he may come and look upon me dead –
    He for whom I am dying.

Dig my grave for two, with a stone to show it,
    And on the stone write my name:
If he never comes, I shall never know it,
    But sleep on all the same.

330

Because I liked you better
    Than suits a man to say,
It irked you, and I promised
    To throw the thought away.

To put the world between us
    We parted, stiff and dry;
'Good-bye', said you, 'forget me.'
    'I will, no fear', said I.

If here, where clover whitens
    The dead man's knoll, you pass,
And no tall flower to meet you
    Starts in the trefoiled grass,

Halt by the headstone naming
    The heart no longer stirred,
And say the lad that loved you
    Was one that kept his word.

Tan ta ra: cries Mars on bloody rampier.
Fa la la: cries Venus in a chamber.
     Toodle loodle loo!
     Cries Pan, that cuckoo,
     With bells at his shoe,
     And a fiddle too.
Ay me, but I, alas, lie weeping,
For Death hath slain my sweeting,
Which hath my heart in keeping.

332

Break, break, break,
  On thy cold gray stones, O Sea!
And I would that my tongue could utter
  The thoughts that arise in me.

O well for the fisherman's boy,
  That he shouts with his sister at play!
O well for the sailor lad,
  That he sings in his boat on the bay!

And the stately ships go on
  To their haven under the hill;
But O for the touch of a vanished hand,
  And the sound of a voice that is still!

Break, break, break,
  At the foot of thy crags, O Sea!
But the tender grace of a day that is dead
  Will never come back to me.

333
The Ghost

'Who knocks?' 'I, who was beautiful,
   Beyond all dreams to restore,
I, from the roots of the dark thorn am hither.
   And knock on the door.'

'Who speaks?' 'I – once was my speech
   Sweet as the bird's on the air,
When echo lurks by the waters to heed;
   'Tis I speak thee fair.'

'Dark is the hour!' 'Ay, and cold.'
   'Lone is my house.' 'Ah, but mine?'
'Sight, touch, lips, eyes yearned in vain.'
   'Long dead these to thine . . .'

Silence. Still faint on the porch
   Brake the flames of the stars.
In gloom groped a hope-wearied hand
   Over keys, bolts, and bars.

A face peered. All the grey night
   In chaos of vacancy shone;
Nought but vast sorrow was there –
   The sweet cheat gone.

334
Buried

Thou sleepest where the lilies fade,
   Thou dwellest where the lilies fade not:
Sweet, when thine earthly part decayed
   Thy heavenly part decayed not.

Thou dwellest where the roses blow,
   The crimson roses bud and blossom:
While on thine eyes is heaped the snow –
   The snow upon thy bosom.

The half-moon westers low, my love,
    And the wind brings up the rain;
And wide apart lie we, my love,
    And seas between the twain.

I know not if it rains, my love,
    In the land where you do lie;
And oh, so sound you sleep, my love,
    You know no more than I.

336
No Road

Since we agreed to let the road between us
Fall to disuse,
And bricked our gates up, planted trees to screen us,
And turned all time's eroding agents loose,
Silence, and space, and strangers – our neglect
Has not had much effect.

Leaves drift unswept, perhaps; grass creeps unmown;
No other change.
So clear it stands, so little overgrown,
Walking that way tonight would nto seem strange,
And still would be allowed. A little longer,
And time will be the stronger,

Drafting a world where no such road will run
From you to me;
To watch that world come up like a cold sun,
Rewarding others, is my liberty.
Not to prevent it is my will's fulfilment.
Willing it, my ailment.

337

TO WHOM
IT MAY
CONCERN

Cast up
with my
spirited
friend, I
assisted him
off with his
cap. Citizen
Smirnoff, I said,
Tell me about yourself.
He opened his heart to me,
outpouring silence distilled
all those years on the shelf
into philosophy, into poetry,
concluding: You have fulfilled
my destiny. Comrade, I said,
will you fulfil mine? Gladly.
He lets me give him a light,
smokes in silence as I write:
Love, come up and see me here.
Love, my label says DRINK ME.
Love, 1935 was a vintage year.
Snuffing his candle I return
his cap, and watch him start
unsteadily out of the room,
with a message over his heart
for whom it may concern.

338

Alone

The abode of the nightingale is bare,
Flowered frost congeals in the gelid air,
The fox howls from his frozen lair:
    Alas, my loved one is gone,
    I am alone;
    It is winter.

Once the pink cast a winy smell,
The wild bee hung in the hyacinth bell,
Light in effulgence of beauty fell:
> Alas, my loved one is gone,
> I am alone;
> It is winter.

My candle a silent fire doth shed,
Starry Orion hunts o'erhead;
Come moth, come shadow, the world is dead:
> Alas, my loved one is gone,
> I am alone;
> It is winter.

339
Villanelle

It is the pain, it is the pain, endures.
Your chemic beauty burned my muscles through.
Poise of my hands reminded me of yours.

What later purge from this deep toxin cures?
What kindness now could the old salve renew?
It is the pain, it is the pain, endures.

The infection slept (custom or change inures)
And when pain's secondary phase was due
Poise of my hands reminded me of yours.

How safe I felt, whom memory assures,
Rich that your grace safely by heart I knew.
It is the pain, it is the pain, endures.

My stare drank deep beauty that still allures.
My heart pumps yet the poison draught of you.
Poise of my hands reminded me of yours.

You are still kind whom the same shape immures.
Kind and beyond adieu. We miss our cue.
It is the pain, it is the pain, endures.
Poise of my hands reminded me of yours.

Mariana

With blackest moss the flower-plots
   Were thickly crusted, one and all:
The rusted nails fell from the knots
   That held the pear to the gable-wall.
The broken sheds looked sad and strange:
   Unlifted was the clinking latch;
   Weeded and worn the ancient thatch
Upon the lonely moated grange.
     She only said, 'My life is dreary,
       He cometh not,' she said;
     She said, 'I am aweary, aweary,
       I would that I were dead!'

Her tears fell with the dews at even;
   Her tears fell ere the dews were dried;
She could not look on the sweet heaven,
   Either at morn or eventide.
After the flitting of the bats,
   When thickest dark did trance the sky,
   She drew her casement-curtain by,
And glanced athwart the glooming flats.
     She only said, 'The night is dreary,
       He cometh not,' she said;
     She said, 'I am aweary, aweary,
       I would that I were dead!'

Upon the middle of the night,
   Waking she heard the night-fowl crow:
The cock sung out an hour ere light:
   From the dark fen the oxen's low
Came to her: without hope of change,
   In sleep she seemed to walk forlorn,
   Till cold winds woke the grey-eyed morn
About the lonely moated grange.
     She only said, 'The day is dreary,
       He cometh not,' she said;
     She said, 'I am aweary, aweary,
       I would that I were dead!'

About a stone-cast from the wall
   A sluice with blackened waters slept,
And o'er it many, round and small,
   The clustered marish-mosses crept.
Hard by a poplar shook alway,
   All silver-green with gnarlèd bark:
   For leagues no other tree did mark
The level waste, the rounding gray.
      She only said, 'My life is dreary,
         He cometh not,' she said;
      She said, 'I am aweary, aweary,
         I would that I were dead!'

And ever when the moon was low,
   And the shrill winds were up and away,
In the white curtain, to and fro,
   She saw the gusty shadow sway.
But when the moon was very low,
   And wild winds bound within their cell,
   The shadow of the poplar fell
Upon her bed, across her brow.
      She only said, 'The night is dreary,
         He cometh not,' she said;
      She said, 'I am aweary, aweary,
         I would that I were dead!'

All day within the dreamy house,
   The doors upon their hinges creaked;
The blue fly sung in the pane; the mouse
   Behind the mouldering wainscot shrieked,
Or from the crevice peered about.
   Old faces glimmered through the doors,
   Old footsteps trod the upper floors,
Old voices called her from without.
      She only said, 'My life is dreary,
         He cometh not,' she said;
      She said, 'I am aweary, aweary,
         I would that I were dead!'

The sparrow's chirrup on the roof,
   The slow clock ticking, and the sound
Which to the wooing wind aloof
   The poplar made, did all confound
Her sense; but most she loathed the hour
   When the thick-moted sunbeam lay
   Athwart the chambers, and the day
Was sloping toward his western bower.
   Then, said she, 'I am very dreary,
     He will not come,' she said;
   She wept, 'I am aweary, aweary,
     Oh God, that I were dead!'

341
Winter Remembered

Two evils, monstrous either one apart,
Possessed me, and were long and loath at going:
A cry of Absence, Absence, in the heart,
And in the wood the furious winter blowing.

Think not, when fire was bright upon my bricks,
And past the tight boards hardly a wind could enter,
I glowed like them, the simple burning sticks,
Far from my cause, my proper heat and center.

Better to walk forth in the frozen air
And wash my wound in the snows; that would be healing;
Because my heart would throb less painful there,
Being caked with cold, and past the smart of feeling.

And where I walked, the murderous winter blast
Would have this body bowed, these eyeballs streaming,
And though I think this heart's blood froze not fast
It ran too small to spare one drop for dreaming.

Dear love, these fingers that had known your touch,
And tied our separate forces first together,
Were ten poor idiot fingers not worth much,
Ten frozen parsnips hanging in the weather.

The Going

Why did you give no hint that night
That quickly after the morrow's dawn,
And calmly, as if indifferent quite,
You would close your term here, up and be gone
      Where I could not follow
      With wing of swallow
To gain one glimpse of you ever anon!

      Never to bid good-bye,
      Or lip me the softest call,
Or utter a wish for a word, while I
Saw morning harden upon the wall,
      Unmoved, unknowing
      That your great going
Had place that moment, and altered all.

Why do you make me leave the house
And think for a breath it is you I see
At the end of the alley of bending boughs
Where so often at dusk you used to be;
      Till in darkening dankness
      The yawning blankness
Of the perspective sickens me!

      You were she who abode
      By those red-veined rocks far West.
You were the swan-necked one who rode
Along the beetling Beeny Crest,
      And, reining nigh me,
      Would muse and eye me,
While Life unrolled us its very best.

Why, then, latterly did we not speak,
Did we not think of those days long dead,
And ere your vanishing strive to seek
That time's renewal? We might have said,
      'In this bright spring weather
      We'll visit together
Those places that once we visited.'

Well, well! All's past amend,
    Unchangeable. It must go.
I seem but a dead man held on end
To sink down soon . . . O you could not know
    That such swift fleeing
    No soul foreseeing –
Not even I – would undo me so!

343
Non Piangere, Liù

A card comes to tell you
you should report
to have your eyes tested.

But your eyes melted in the fire
and the only tears, which soon dried,
fell in the chapel.

Other things still come –
invoices, subscription renewals,
shiny plastic cards promising credit –
not much for a life spent
in the service of reality.

You need answer none of them.
Nor my asking you for one drop
of succour in my own hell.

Do not cry, I tell myself,
the whole thing is a comedy
and comedies end happily.

The fire will come out of the sun
and I shall look in the heart of it.

344
An End

Love, strong as Death, is dead.
Come, let us make his bed
Among the dying flowers:
A green turf at his head;
And a stone at his feet,
Whereon we may sit
In the quiet evening hours.

He was born in the spring,
And died before the harvesting:
On the last warm summer day
He left us; he would not stay
For autumn twilight cold and grey.
Sit we by his grave, and sing
He is gone away.

To few chords and sad and low
Sing we so:
Be our eyes fixed on the grass
Shadow-veiled as the years pass,
While we think of all that was
In the long ago.

345

When the lamp is shattered
The light in the dust lies dead –
When the cloud is scattered
The rainbow's glory is shed.
When the lute is broken,
Sweet tones are remembered not;
When the lips have spoken,
Loved accents are soon forgot.

As music and splendour
Survive not the lamp and the lute,
    The heart's echoes render
No song when the spirit is mute:—
    No song but sad dirges,
Like the wind through a ruined cell,
    Or the mournful surges
That ring the dead seaman's knell.

When hearts have once mingled
Love first leaves the well-built nest;
    The weak one is singled
To endure what it once possessed.
    O Love! who bewailest
The frailty of all things here,
    Why choose you the frailest
For your cradle, your home, and your bier?

Its passions will rock thee
As the storms rock the ravens on high;
    Bright reason will mock thee,
Like the sun from a wintry sky.
    From thy nest every rafter
Will rot, and thine eagle home
    Leave thee naked to laughter,
When leaves fall and cold winds come.

346
Down by the Salley Gardens

Down by the salley gardens my love and I did meet;
She passed the salley gardens with little snow-white feet.
She bid me take love easy, as the leaves grow on the tree;
But I, being young and foolish, with her would not agree.

In a field by the river my love and I did stand,
And on my leaning shoulder she laid her snow-white hand.
She bid me take life easy, as the grass grows on the weirs;
But I was young and foolish, and now am full of tears.

So, we'll go no more a roving
   So late into the night.
Though the heart be still as loving,
   And the moon be still as bright.

For the sword outwears its sheath,
   And the soul wears out the breast,
And the heart must pause to breathe,
   And love itself have rest.

Though the night was made for loving,
   And the day returns too soon,
Yet we'll go no more a roving
   By the light of the moon.

348

Lost Love

His eyes are quickened so with grief,
He can watch a grass or leaf
Every instant grow; he can
Clearly through a flint wall see,
Or watch the startled spirit flee
From the throat of a dead man.
   Across two counties he can hear
And catch your words before you speak.
The woodlouse or the maggot's weak
Clamour rings in his sad ear,
And noise so slight it would surpass
Credence – drinking sound of grass,
Worm talk, clashing jaws of moth
Chumbling holes in cloth;
The groan of ants who undertake
Gigantic loads for honour's sake
(Their sinews creak, their breath comes thin);
Whir of spiders when they spin,
And minute whispering, mumbling, sighs
Of idle grubs and flies.

This man is quickened so with grief,
He wanders god-like or like thief
Inside and out, below, above,
Without relief seeking lost love.

349
The Blossoming of the Solitary Date-Tree

A LAMENT

I

Beneath the blaze of a tropical sun the mountain peaks are the Thrones of Frost, through the absence of objects to reflect the rays. 'What no one with us shares, seems scarce our own.' The presence of a ONE,

The best belov'd, who loveth me the best,

is for the heart, what the supporting air from within is for the hollow globe with its suspended car. Deprive it of this, and all without, that would have buoyed it aloft even to the seat of the gods, becomes a burthen and crushes it into flatness.

2

The finer the sense for the beautiful and the lovely, and the fairer and lovelier the object presented to the sense; the more exquisite the individual's capacity of joy, and the more ample his means and opportunities of enjoyment, the more heavily will he feel the ache of solitariness, the more unsubstantial becomes the feast spread around him. What matters it, whether in fact the viands and the ministering graces are shadowy or real, to him who has not hand to grasp nor arms to embrace them?

3

Imagination; honourable aims;
Free commune with the choir that cannot die;
Science and song; delight in little things,
The buoyant child surviving in the man;
Fields, forests, ancient mountains, ocean, sky,

With all their voices – O dare I accuse
My earthly lot as guilty of my spleen,
Or call my destiny niggard! O no! no!
It is her largeness, and her overflow,
Which being incomplete, disquieteth me so!

4

For never touch of gladness stirs my heart,
But tim'rously beginning to rejoice
Like a blind Arab, that from sleep doth start
In lonesome tent, I listen for thy voice.
Belovéd! 'tis not thine; thou art not there!
Then melts the bubble into idle air,
And wishing without hope I restlessly despair.

5

The mother with anticipated glee
Smiles o'er the child, that, standing by her chair
And flatt'ning its round cheek upon her knee,
Looks up, and doth its rosy lips prepare
To mock the coming sounds. At that sweet sight
She hears her own voice with a new delight;
And if the babe perchance should lisp the notes aright,

6

Then is she tenfold gladder than before!
But should disease or chance the darling take,
What then avail those songs, which sweet of yore
Were only sweet for their sweet echo's sake?
Dear maid! no prattler at a mother's knee
Was e'er so dearly prized as I prize thee:
Why was I made for Love and Love denied to me?

350

The rainy Pleiads wester,
    Orion plunges prone,
The stroke of midnight ceases
    And I lie down alone.

The rainy Pleiads wester
    And seek beyond the sea
The head that I shall dream of
    That will not dream of me.

351

from *Maud*

O that 'twere possible
After long grief and pain
To find the arms of my true love
Round me once again!

When I was wont to meet her
In the silent woody places
By the home that gave me birth,
We stood tranced in long embraces
Mixt with kisses sweeter sweeter
Than anything on earth.

A shadow flits before me,
Not thou, but like to thee:
Ah Christ, that it were possible
For one short hour to see
The souls we loved, that they might tell us
What and where they be.

It leads me forth at evening,
It lightly winds and steals
In a cold white robe before me,
When all my spirit reels
As the shouts, the leagues of lights,
And the roaring of the wheels.

Half the night I waste in sighs,
Half in dreams I sorrow after
The delight of early skies;
In a wakeful doze I sorrow
For the hand, the lips, the eyes,
For the meeting of the morrow,
The delight of happy laughter,
The delight of low replies.

'Tis a morning pure and sweet,
And a dewy splendour falls
On the little flower that clings
To the turrets and the walls;
'Tis a morning pure and sweet,
And the light and shadow fleet;
She is walking in the meadow,
And the woodland echo rings;
In a moment we shall meet;
She is singing in the meadow
And the rivulet at her feet
Ripples on in light and shadow
To the ballad that she sings.

Do I hear her sing as of old,
My bird with the shining head,
My own dove with the tender eye?
But there rings on a sudden a passionate cry,
There is some one dying or dead,
And a sullen thunder is rolled;
For a tumult shakes the city,
And I wake, my dream is fled;
In the shuddering dawn, behold,
Without knowledge, without pity,
By the curtains of my bed
That abiding phantom cold.

Get thee hence, nor come again,
Mix not memory with doubt,
Pass, thou deathlike type of pain,
Pass and cease to move about!
'Tis the blot upon the brain
That *will* show itself without.

Then I rise, the eavedrops fall,
And the yellow vapours choke
The great city sounding wide;
The day comes, a dull red ball
Wrapt in drifts of lurid smoke
On the misty river-tide.

Through the hubbub of the market
I steal, a wasted frame,
It crosses here, it crosses there,
Through all that crowd confused and loud,
The shadow still the same;
And on my heavy eyelids
My anguish hangs like shame.

Alas for her that met me,
That heard me softly call,
Came glimmering through the laurels
At the quiet evenfall,
In the garden by the turrets
Of the old manorial hall.

Would the happy spirit descend,
From the realms of light and song,
In the chamber or the street,
As she looks among the blest,
Should I fear to greet my friend
Or to say 'Forgive the wrong,'
Or to ask her, 'Take me, sweet,
To the regions of thy rest'?

But the broad light glares and beats,
And the shadow flits and fleets
And will not let me be;
And I loathe the squares and streets,
And the faces that one meets,
Hearts with no love for me:
Always I long to creep
Into some still cavern deep,
There to weep, and weep, and weep
My whole soul out to thee.

352

Ffarewell Love and all thy lawes for ever:
   Thy bayted hookes shall tangill me no more;
   Senec and Plato call me from thy lore,
   To perfaict welth my wit for to endever.
In blynde error when I did perseuer,
   Thy sherpe repulse that pricketh ay so sore
   Hath taught me to sett in tryfels no store
   And scape fourth, syns libertie is lever.
Therefore farewell: goo trouble yonger hertes
   And in me clayme no more authoritie;
   With idill youth goo vse thy propertie
And theron spend thy many brittil dertes;
   For hetherto though I have lost all my tyme
   Me lusteth no lenger rotten boughes to clymbe.

353

Loves Feast

I pray thee spare me, gentle Boy,
Presse me no more for that slight toy,
That foolish trifle of an heart;
I swear it will not do its part,
Though thou dost thine, employ'st thy power and art.

For through long custom it has known
The little secrets, and is grown
Sullen and wise, will have its will,
And like old Hawks pursues that still
That makes least sport, flies onely where't can kill.

Some youth that has not made his story,
Will think perchance the pain's the glory,
And mannerly sit out Loves Feast;
I shall be carving of the best,
Rudely call for the last course 'fore the rest.

And oh! when once that course is past,
How short a time the Feast doth last!
Men rise away, and scarce say grace,
Or civilly once thank the face
That did invite, but seek another place.

354

Palinodia

Nec meus hic sermo est, sed quem praecepit –
HORACE

There was a time, when I could feel
    All passion's hopes and fears;
And tell what tongues can ne'er reveal
    By smiles, and sighs, and tears.
The days are gone! no more – no more
    The cruel Fates allow;
And, though I'm hardly twenty-four, –
    I'm not a lover now.
        Lady, the mist is on my sight,
          The chill is on my brow:
        My day is night, my bloom is blight;
          I'm not a lover now!

I never talk about the clouds,
    I laugh at girls and boys,
I'm growing rather fond of crowds,
    And very fond of noise;
I never wander forth alone
    Upon the mountain's brow;
I weighed, last winter, sixteen stone; –
    I'm not a lover now!

I never wish to raise a veil,
    I never raise a sigh;
I never tell a tender tale,
    I never tell a lie:
I cannot kneel, as once I did;
    I've quite forgot my bow;
I never do as I am bid; –
    I'm not a lover now!

I make strange blunders every day,
    If I would be gallant;
Take smiles for wrinkles, black for grey,
    And nieces for their aunt:
I fly from folly, though it flows
    From lips of loveliest glow:
I don't object to length of nose; –
    I'm not a lover now!

I find my Ovid very dry,
    My Petrarch quite a pill,
Cut Fancy for Philosophy,
    Tom Moore for Mr Mill.
And belles may read, and beaux may write, –
    I care not who or how;
I burnt my Album, Sunday night; –
    I'm not a lover now!

I don't encourage idle dreams
    Of poison or of ropes:
I cannot dine on airy schemes;
    I cannot sup on hopes:
New milk, I own, is very fine,
    Just foaming from the cow;
But yet, I want my pint of wine; –
    I'm not a lover now!

When Laura sings young hearts away,
    I'm deafer than the deep;
When Leonora goes to play,
    I sometimes go to sleep;
When Mary draws her white gloves out,
    I never dance, I vow, –
'Too hot to kick one's heels about!'
    I'm not a lover now!

I'm busy, now, with state affairs;
    I prate of Pitt and Fox;
I ask the price of rail-road shares,
    I watch the turns of stocks.
And this is life! no verdure blooms
    Upon the withered bough:
I save a fortune in perfumes; –
    I'm not a lover now!

I may be yet, what others are,
    A boudoir's babbling fool,
The flattered star of Bench or Bar,
    A party's chief, or tool: –
Come shower or sunshine, hope or fear,
    The palace or the plough, –
My heart and lute are broken here;
    I'm not a lover now!
        Lady, the mist is on my sight,
            The chill is on my brow
        My day is night, my bloom is bright;
            I'm not a lover now!

He Abjures Love

At last I put off love,
    For twice ten years
The daysman of my thought.
    And hope, and doing;
Being ashamed thereof,
    And faint of fears
And desolations, wrought
    In his pursuing,

Since first in youthtime those
    Disquietings
That heart-enslavement brings
    To hale and hoary,
Became my housefellows.
    And, fool and blind,
I turned from kith and kind
    To give him glory.

I was as children be
    Who have no care;
I did not shrink or sigh,
    I did not sicken;
But lo, Love beckoned me
    And I was bare,
And poor, and starved, and dry,
    And fever-stricken.

Too many times ablaze
    With fatuous fires,
Enkindled by his wiles
    To new embraces,
Did I, by wilful ways
    And baseless ires,
Return the anxious smiles
    Of friendly faces.

No more will now rate I
    The common rare,
The midnight drizzle dew,
    The gray hour golden,
The wind a yearning cry,
    The faulty fair,
Things dreamt, of comelier hue
    Than things beholden! . . .

– I speak as one who plumbs
    Life's dim profound,
One who at length can sound
    Clear views and certain.
But – after love what comes?
    A scene that lours,
A few sad vacant hours,
    And then, the Curtain.

356
Desire

Ah, in the past, towards rare individuals
I have felt the pull of desire:
Oh come, come nearer, come into touch!
Come physically nearer, be flesh to my flesh –

But say little, oh say little,
and afterwards, leave me alone.
Keep your aloneness, leave me my aloneness. –
I used to say this, in the past – but now no more.
It has always been a failure.
They have always insisted on love
and on talking about it
and on the me-and-thee and what we meant to each other.

So now I have no desire any more
Except to be left, in the last resort, alone, quite alone.

Against Coupling

I write in praise of the solitary act:
of not feeling a trespassing tongue
forced into one's mouth, one's breath
smothered, nipples crushed against the
ribcage, and that metallic tingling
in the chin set off by a certain odd nerve:

unpleasure. Just to avoid those eyes would help –
such eyes as a young girl draws life from,
listening to the vegetal
rustle within her, as his gaze
stirs polypal fronds in the obscure
sea-bed of her body, and her own eyes blur.

There is much to be said for abandoning
this no longer novel exercise –
for not 'participating in
a total experience' – when
one feels like the lady in Leeds who
had seen *The Sound of Music* eighty-six times;

or more, perhaps, like the school drama mistress
producing *A Midsummer Night's Dream*
for the seventh year running, with
yet another cast from 5B.
Pyramus and Thisbe are dead, but
the hole in the wall can still be troublesome.

I advise you, then, to embrace it without
encumbrance. No need to set the scene,
dress up (or undress), make speeches.
Five minutes of solitude are
enough – in the bath, or to fill
that gap between the Sunday papers and lunch.

First Things First

Woken, I lay in the arms of my own warmth and listened
To a storm enjoying its storminess in the winter dark
Till my ear, as it can when half-asleep or half-sober,
Set to work to unscramble that interjectory uproar,
Construing its airy vowels and watery consonants
Into a love-speech indicative of a Proper Name.

Scarcely the tongue I should have chosen, yet, as well
As harshness and clumsiness would allow, it spoke in your praise,
Kenning you a god-child of the Moon and the West Wind
With power to tame both real and imaginary monsters,
Likening your poise of being to an upland county,
Here green on purpose, there pure blue for luck.

Loud though it was, alone as it certainly found me,
It reconstructed a day of peculiar silence
When a sneeze could be heard a mile off, and had me walking
On a headland of lava beside you, the occasion as ageless
As the stare of any rose, your presence exactly
So once, so valuable, so there, so now.

This, moreover, at an hour when only too often
A smirking devil annoys me in beautiful English,
Predicting a world where every sacred location
Is a sand-buried site all cultured Texans do,
Misinformed and thoroughly fleeced by their guides,
And gentle hearts are extinct like Hegelian Bishops.

Grateful, I slept till a morning that would not say
How much it believed of what I said the storm had said
But quietly drew my attention to what had been done
– So many cubic metres the more in my cistern
Against a leonine summer –, putting first things first:
Thousands have lived without love, not one without water.

359
Basta!

When a man can love no more
and feel no more
and desire has failed
and the heart is numb

then all he can do
is to say: It is so!
I've got to put up with it
and wait.
This is a pause, how long a pause I know not,
in my very being.

360
Defiance

Catch her and hold her if you can . . .
See, she defies you with her fan,
Shuts, opens, and then holds it spred
In threat'ning guize above your head.
Ah! why did you not start before
She reacht the porch and closed the door?
Simpleton! will you never learn
That girls and time will not return;
Of each you should have made the most.
Once gone, they are for ever lost.
In vain your knuckles knock your brow,
In vain will you remember how
Like a slim brook the gamesome maid
Sparkled, and ran into the shade.

361

Former Beauties

These market-dames, mid-aged, with lips thin-drawn.
    And tissues sere,
Are they the ones we loved in years agone,
    And courted here?

Are these the muslined pink young things to whom
    We vowed and swore
In nooks on summer Sundays by the Froom,
    Or Budmouth shore?

Do they remember those gay tunes we trod
    Clasped on the green;
Aye; trod till moonlight set on the beaten sod
    A satin sheen?

They must forget, forget! They cannot know
    What once they were,
Or memory would transfigure them, and show
    Them always fair.

362

Broken Dreams

The women sleep.
We look for them in their dreams.

When we bump into a piece of the scenery,
It falls, waking them.

They open eyes full of broken love.
Love that we have broken.

363
Reproof of Thanks

Nay, thank me not again for those
Camelias, that untimely rose;
But if, whence you might please the more,
And win the few unwon before,
I sought the flowers you loved to wear,
O'erjoy'd to see them in your hair,
Upon my grave, I pray you, set
One primrose or one violet.
. . . Stay . . . I can wait a little yet.

364
A Song

I thought no more was needed
Youth to prolong
Than dumb-bell and foil
To keep the body young.
O who could have foretold
That the heart grows old?

Though I have many words,
What woman's satisfied,
I am no longer faint
Because at her side?
O who could have foretold
That the heart grows old?

I have not lost desire
But the heart that I had;
I thought 'twould burn my body
Laid on the death-bed,
For who could have foretold
That the heart grows old?

Love ran with me, then walk'd, then sate,
Then said *'Come, come! it grows too late:'*
And then he would have gone . . . but . . . no . . .
You caught his eye; he could not go.

366

Music, when soft voices die,
Vibrates in the memory –
Odours, when sweet violets sicken,
Live within the sense they quicken.
Rose leaves, when the rose is dead,
Are heaped for the belovèd's bed;
And so thy thoughts, when thou art gone,
Love itself shall slumber on.

367

The place where soon I think to lie,
In its old creviced wall hard-by
   Rears many a weed.
Whoever leads you there, will you
Drop slily in a grain or two
   Of wall-flower seed?

I shall not see it, and (too sure)
I shall not ever know that your
   Dear hand was there;
But the rich odor some fine day
Shall (what I can not do) repay
   That little care.

368
Preserving

Making the marmalade this year, I carve
Some peel to form the initial of your name.

Perhaps you'll come across it when I'm gone,
For even in mourning mornings will go on.

So such surprise as ancient love contrives
Will change to the kind of shock that stunned our prime.

369
Confessions

What is he buzzing in my ears?
  'Now that I come to die,
'Do I view the world as a vale of tears?'
  Ah, reverend sir, not I!

What I viewed there once, what I view again
  Where the physic bottles stand
On the table's edge, – is a suburb lane,
  With a wall to my bedside hand.

That lane sloped, much as the bottles do,
  From a house you could descry
O'er the garden-wall: is the curtain blue
  Or green to a healthy eye?

To mine, it serves for the old June weather
  Blue above lane and wall;
And that farthest bottle labelled 'Ether'
  Is the house o'ertopping all.

At a terrace, somewhere near the stopper,
  There watched for me, one June,
A girl: I know, sir, it's improper,
  My poor mind's out of tune.

Only, there was a way . . . you crept
   Close by the side, to dodge
Eyes in the house, two eyes except:
   They styled their house 'The Lodge.'

What right had a lounger up their lane?
   But, by creeping very close,
With the good wall's help, – their eyes might strain
   And stretch themselves to Oes,

Yet never catch her and me together,
   As she left the attic, there,
By the rim of the bottle labelled 'Ether,'
   And stole from stair to stair,

And stood by the rose-wreathed gate. Alas,
   We loved, sir – used to meet:
How sad and bad and mad it was –
   But then, how it was sweet!

370
Since

On a mid-December day,
frying sausages
for myself, I abruptly
felt under fingers
thirty years younger the rim
of a steering-wheel,
on my cheek the parching wind
of an August noon,
as passenger beside me
You as then you were.

Slap across a veg-growing
alluvial plain
we raced in clouds of white dust,
and geese fled screaming
as we missed them by inches,
making a bee-line
for mountains gradually
enlarging eastward,
joyfully certain nightfall
would occasion joy.

It did. In a flagged kitchen
we were served broiled trout
and a rank cheese: for a while
we talked by the fire,
then, carrying candles, climbed
steep stairs. Love was made
then and there: so halcyoned,
soon we fell asleep
to the sound of a river
swabbling through a gorge.

Since then, other enchantments
have blazed and faded,
enemies changed their address,
and War made ugly
an uncountable number
of unknown neighbors,
precious as us to themselves:
but round your image
there is no fog, and the Earth
can still astonish.

Of what, then, should I complain,
pottering about
a neat suburban kitchen?
Solitude? Rubbish!
It's social enough with real
faces and landscapes
for whose friendly countenance
I at least can learn
to live with obesity
and a little fame.

The Widower

For a season there must be pain –
For a little, little space
I shall lose the sight of her face,
Take back the old life again
While She is at rest in her place.

For a season this pain must endure,
For a little, little while
I shall sigh more often than smile
Till Time shall work me a cure,
And the pitiful days beguile.

For that season we must be apart,
For a little length of years,
Till my life's last hour nears,
And, above the beat of my heart,
I hear Her voice in my ears.

But I shall not understand –
Being set on some later love,
Shall not know her for whom I strove,
Till she reach me forth her hand,
Saying, 'Who but I have the right?'
And out of a troubled night
Shall draw me safe to the land.

372
R. Alcona to J. Brenzaida

Cold in the earth, and the deep snow piled above thee!
Far, far removed, cold in the dreary grave!
Have I forgot, my Only Love, to love thee,
Severed at last by Time's all-wearing wave?

Now, when alone, do my thoughts no longer hover
Over the mountains on Angora's shore;
Resting their wings where heath and fern-leaves cover
That noble heart for ever, ever more?

Cold in the earth, and fifteen wild Decembers
From those brown hills have melted into spring –
Faithful indeed is the spirit that remembers
After such years of change and suffering!

Sweet Love of youth, forgive if I forget thee
While the World's tide is bearing me along:
Sterner desires and darker hopes beset me,
Hopes which obscure but cannot do thee wrong.

No other Sun has lightened up my heaven;
No other Star has ever shone for me:
All my life's bliss from thy dear life was given –
All my life's bliss is in the grave with thee.

But when the days of golden dreams had perished
And even Despair was powerless to destroy,
Then did I learn how existence could be cherished,
Strengthened and fed without the aid of joy;

Then did I check the tears of useless passion,
Weaned my young soul from yearning after thine;
Sternly denied its burning wish to hasten
Down to that tomb already more than mine!

And even yet, I dare not let it languish,
Dare not indulge in Memory's rapturous pain;
Once drinking deep of that divinest anguish,
How could I seek the empty world again?

After a Journey

Hereto I come to view a voiceless ghost;
    Whither, O whither will its whim now draw me?
Up the cliff, down, till I'm lonely, lost,
    And the unseen waters' ejaculations awe me.
Where you will next be there's no knowing,
    Facing round about me everywhere,
        With your nut-coloured hair,
And gray eyes, and rose-flush coming and going.

Yes: I have re-entered your olden haunts at last;
    Through the years, through the dead scenes I have tracked you;
What have you now found to say of our past –
    Scanned across the dark space wherein I have lacked you?
Summer gave us sweets, but autumn wrought division?
    Things were not lastly as firstly well
        With us twain, you tell?
But all's closed now, despite Time's derision.

I see what you are doing: you are leading me on
    To the spots we knew when we haunted here together,
The waterfall, above which the mist-bow shone
    At the then fair hour in the then fair weather,
And the cave just under, with a voice still so hollow
    That it seems to call out to me from forty years ago,
        When you were all aglow,
And not the thin ghost that I now fraily follow!

Ignorant of what there is flitting here to see,
    The waked birds preen and the seals flop lazily;
Soon you will have, Dear, to vanish from me,
    For the stars close their shutters and the dawn whitens hazily.
Trust me, I mind not, though Life lours,
    The bringing me here; nay, bring me here again!
        I am just the same as when
Our days were a joy, and our paths through flowers.

The Voice

Woman much missed, how you call to me, call to me,
Saying that now you are not as you were
When you had changed from the one who was all to me,
But as at first, when our day was fair.

Can it be you that I hear? Let me view you, then,
Standing as when I drew near to the town
Where you would wait for me: yes, as I knew you then,
Even to the original air-blue gown!

Or is it only the breeze, in its listlessness
Travelling across the wet mead to me here,
You being ever dissolved to wan wistlessness,
Heard no more again far or near?

  Thus I; faltering forward,
  Leaves around me falling,
Wind oozing thin through the thorn from norward.
  And the woman calling.

List of Numbered Poems

Act One HOLES IN THE HEART

1 Emily Dickinson, 'Love is anterior to life'
2 Gavin Ewart, 'A Dialogue between the Head and Heart'
3 A. H. Clough, 'Juxtaposition, in fine; and what is juxtaposition?' (*Amours de Voyage*, III.vi and vii)
4 Lord Byron, 'Oh, Love! no habitant of earth thou art' (*Childe Harold's Pilgrimage*, sts. 121–3)
5 D. H. Lawrence, 'Search for Love'
6 George Peele, 'What thing is love?' (from *The Hunting of Cupid*)
7 Thomas Hood, 'Love'
8 Sir Philip Sidney, 'In truth, o Love, with what a boyish kind' (*Astrophil and Stella*, no. 11)
9 John Keats, 'And what is love? It is a doll dressed up'
10 Anon, 'Love is Weal, Love is Wo'
11 Samuel Daniel, 'Love'
12 Anon, 'Four arms, two necks, one wreathing' (in Weelkes's *Airs or Fantastic Spirits*, 1608)
13 Gavin Ewart, 'The Lover Writes a One-word Poem'
14 W. S. Landor, 'Proud word you never spoke, but you will speak'
15 John Lyly, 'Syrinx'
16 W. S. Landor, 'Does it become a girl so wise'
17 W. B. Yeats, 'Brown Penny'
18 Thomas Vautor, 'Mother, I will have a husband' (from *Songs of divers Airs and Natures*, 1619)
19 Ben Jonson, 'The Dreame'
20 John Donne, 'Aire and Angels'
21 W. B. Yeats, 'Before the World was Made'
22 W. H. Auden, 'The Prophets'
23 Emily Dickinson, 'He fumbles at your spirit'
24 Anon, 'There is a lady sweet and kind' (in Ford, *Music of Sundry Kinds*, 1607)
25 Ben Jonson, 'Her Triumph' ('A Celebration of Charis in ten Lyrick Peeces', 4)
26 Edmund Spenser, 'It fell vpon a holly eue' (from 'August' in *The Shepheardes Calender*)
27 Richard Lovelace, 'In mine one Monument I lye'
28 Edmund Waller, 'An Apology for having Loved Before'
29 William Drummond, 'Madrigal'
30 William Drummond, 'Of Phyllis'

73 Anon, 'Love me little, love me long'
74 John Cleveland, 'To Julia to expedite her Promise'
75 William Shakespeare, 'It was a Louer, and his lasse' (from *As You Like It*)
76 Ira Gershwin, 'Embraceable You' (from *Girl Crazy*)
77 Andrew Marvell, 'To his Coy Mistress'
78 Emily Dickinson, 'If you were coming in the fall'
79 William Shakespeare, 'O Mistris mine where are you roming?' (from *Twelfth Night*)
80 Ben Jonson, 'Come my CELIA, let us proue' (from *Volpone*)
81 William Hammond, 'Delay, upon Advice to defer Love's Consummation'
82 John Gay, 'Were I laid on Greenland's Coast' (*The Beggar's Opera*, Air xvi)

Act Two FOOL – ONLY TOUCH HER!

83 Queen Elizabeth I, 'Importune me no more'
84 Sir Francis Kynaston, 'To Cynthia'
85 Henry King, 'Sonnet. The Double Rock'
86 Andrew Marvell, 'The Mower's Song'
87 Thomas Campion, 'Thrice toss these oaken ashes in the air'
88 Anon, 'Lord, when I think' (in Weelkes, *Airs or Fantastic Spirits*, 1608)
89 Sir Walter Ralegh, 'Hir face, Hir tong, Hir wit'
90 William Herbert, Earl of Pembroke, 'Disdain me still, that I may ever love'
91 John Keats, 'La Belle Dame Sans Merci'
92 Thomas Stanley, 'The Deposition'
93 Cole Porter, 'Night and Day' (from *Gay Divorcee*)
94 W. B. Yeats, 'Politics'
95 John Keats, 'You say you love, but with a voice'
96 A. C. Swinburne, 'A Leave-taking'
97 John Clare, 'Song'
98 Percy Shelley, 'The Indian Serenade'
99 Emily Dickinson, 'Wild nights! Wild nights!'
100 John Keats, 'Bright star! Would I were steadfast as thou art'
101 Andrew Marvell, 'The Mower to the Glo-Worms'
102 Thomas Campion, 'Kind are her answers'
103 Cole Porter, 'Nobody's Chasing Me' (from *Out of this World*)
104 A. C. Swinburne, 'A Match'
105 Emily Dickinson, 'The way I read a letter's this'
106 William Hammond, 'On the Infrequency of Celia's Letters'
107 A. C. Swinburne, 'Love and Sleep'
108 Medbh McGuckian, 'The Time Before You'
109 John Davies of Hereford, 'So shoots a star as doth my mistress glide'
110 W. H. Davies, 'A Dream'
111 Robert Browning, 'Eurydice to Orpheus, a picture by Leighton'
112 John Milton, 'Methought I saw my late espoused Saint'
113 Robert Weever, 'Of youth he singeth'
114 Anon, 'And is it night? are they thine eyes that shine?' (in Jones, *A Musical Dreame*, 1609)
115 John Donne, 'The Dreame'

Acknowledgements

The editor and publishers gratefully acknowledge permission from the following to reprint poems or extracts from works in copyright:

Oxford University Press for a poem by Fleur Adcock from her *Selected Poems* (1983); Random House, Inc., New York, for a poem by Maya Angelou from *Oh Pray My Wings Are Gonna Fit Me Well*, copyright © 1975 by Maya Angelou; Faber and Faber Ltd. for poems by W. H. Auden from *Collected Poems*; the Estate of W. H. Auden for 'Love Letter' by W. H. Auden from *Hika* (Kenyon College, Gambier, Ohio), copyright © 1990 by The Estate of W. H. Auden; John Murray (Publishers) Ltd. for poems by John Betjeman from his *Collected Poems*; New Directions Publishing Corporation, New York, for a poem by Gregory Corso from *The Happy Birthday of Death*, copyright © 1960 by New Directions Publishing Corporation; the Literary Trustees of Walter de la Mare and The Society of Authors as their representatives for poems from *The Complete Poems of Walter de la Mare, 1969*; Faber and Faber Ltd. for a poem by T. S. Eliot from *Collected Poems 1909–1962*; Carcanet Press Ltd. for a poem by Alistair Elliot from *My Country*; Chatto & Windus Ltd. and the Estate of William Empson for poems by William Empson from *Collected Poems*; Random Century Ltd. for poems by Gavin Ewart from *The Collected Ewart*; Martin Secker & Warburg for poems by Roy Fuller from *Collected Poems* and *Consolations*; Warner Chappell Music Ltd. for songs by George and Ira Gershwin; A. P. Watt Ltd. on behalf of The Trustees of the Robert Graves Copyright Trust for poems by Robert Graves from *Collected Poems 1975*; Faber and Faber Ltd. for a poem by Thom Gunn from *Jack Straw's Castle*; Faber and Faber Ltd. for poems by Seamus Heaney from *Station Island* and *Field Work*; Macmillan and Mrs Hodgson for a poem by Ralph Hodgson from *The Skylark*; Faber and Faber Ltd. for a poem by Michael Hofmann from *Nights in the Iron Hotel*; Martin Secker & Warburg for a poem by John Hollander from *Powers of Thirteen*. Also reprinted by permission of Atheneum Publishers, an imprint of Macmillan Publishing Company, New York, copyright © 1983 by John Hollander; Chatto & Windus Ltd. for a poem by Mick Imlah from *Birthmarks*; Macmillan Publishers, Inc., New York, for poems by Randall Jarrell from *The Lost World*. 'Woman', copyright © Randall Jarrell 1964, 1965, 'In Nature There is Neither Right Nor Left Nor Wrong', copyright ©

Index of Poets

Reference is made to the numbers of the poems

Index of Titles and First Lines

[363]

[371]